A DICTIONARY OF
PHILOSOPHICAL LOGIC

Dedicated to my mother,
Carol C. Cook,
who made sure that I got to learn all this stuff,
and to
George Schumm, Stewart Shapiro, and Neil Tennant,
who taught me much of it.

A DICTIONARY OF PHILOSOPHICAL LOGIC

Roy T. Cook

Edinburgh University Press

© Roy T. Cook, 2009

Edinburgh University Press Ltd
22 George Square, Edinburgh

Typeset in Ehrhardt
by Norman Tilley Graphics Ltd, Northampton,
printed and bound in Great Britain by
CPI Group (UK) Ltd, Croydon CR0 4YY

A CIP record for this book is available from the
British Library

ISBN 978 0 7486 2559 8 (hardback)

The right of Roy T. Cook
to be identified as author of this work
has been asserted in accordance with
the Copyright, Designs and Patents Act 1988.

Contents

Acknowledgements

I would like to thank the staff at Edinburgh University Press for making this volume possible, and for showing admirable patience in the face of the numerous extensions to the deadline that I requested. In addition, thanks are due to the University of Minnesota for providing me with research funds in order to hire a graduate student to assist with the final stages of preparing this manuscript, and to Joshua Kortbein for being that graduate student. A special debt is owed to the philosophy department staff at the University of Minnesota – Pamela Groscost, Judy Grandbois, and Anita Wallace – for doing all the important things involved in running a university department so that academics like myself have the time and energy to undertake tasks such as this. Finally, thank you Alice, for everything.

Introduction

The mathematical study of logic, and philosophical thought about logic, are two of the oldest and most important human undertakings. As a result, great advances have been made. The downside of this, of course, is that one needs to master a great deal of material, both technical and philosophical, before one is in a position to properly appreciate these advances.

This dictionary is meant to aid the reader in gaining such a mastery. It is not a textbook, and need not be read as one. Instead, it is intended as a reference, supplementing traditional study in the field – a place where the student of logic, of whatever level, can look up concepts and results that might be unfamiliar or have been forgotten.

The entries in the dictionary are extensively cross-referenced. Within each entry, the reader will notice that some terms are in bold face. These are terms that have their own entries elsewhere in the dictionary. Thus, if the reader, upon reading an entry, desires more information, these keywords provide a natural starting point. In addition, many entries are followed by a list of additional cross-references.

In writing the dictionary a number of choices had to be made. First was the selection of entries. In this dictionary I have tried to provide coverage, both broad and deep, of the major viewpoints, trends, and technical tools within philosophical logic. In doing so, however, I found it necessary to include quite a bit more. As a result, the reader will find many entries that do not seem to fall squarely under the heading "philosophical logic" or even "mathematical logic." In particular, a number of entries concern set theory, philosophy of mathematics, mereology, philosophy of language, and other fields connected to, but not identical with, current research in philosophical logic. The inclusion of these additional entries seemed natural, however, since a work intending to cover all aspects of philosophical logic should also cover those areas where the concerns of philosophical logic blur into the concerns of other subdisciplines of philosophy.

In choosing the entries, another issue arose: what to do about expressions that are used in more than one way in the literature. Three distinct sorts of cases arose along these lines.

The first is when the same exact sequence of letters is used in the literature to refer to two clearly distinct notions. An example is "Law of Non-Contradiction," which refers to both a theorem in classical propositional logic and a semantic principle occurring in the metatheory of classical logic. In this sort of case I created two entries, distinguished by subscripted numerals. So the dictionary contains, in the example at hand, entries for Law of Non-Contradiction$_1$ and Law of Non-Contradiction$_2$. The reader should remember that these subscripts are nothing more than a device for disambiguation.

The second case of this sort is when a term is used in two ways in the literature, but instead of there being two separate notions that unfortunately have the same name, there just seems to be terminological confusion. An example of this is "Turing computable," which is used in the literature to refer to both functions computable by Turing machines and to functions that are computable in the intuitive sense – i.e. those that are effectively computable. In this case, and others like it, I chose to provide the definition that seemed like the correct usage. So, in the present example, a Turing computable function is one that is computable by a Turing machine. Needless to say, such cases depend on my intuitions regarding what "correct usage" amounts to. I am optimistic that in most cases, however, my intuitions will square with my readers'.

Finally, there were cases where the confusion seemed so widespread that I could not form an opinion regarding what "correct usage" amounted to. An example is the pair of concepts "strong negation" and "weak negation" – each of these has, in numerous places, been used to refer to exclusion negation and to choice negation. In such cases I contented myself with merely noting the confusion.

Related to the question of what entries to include is the question of how to approach writing those entries. In particular, a decision needed to be made regarding how much formal notation to include. The unavoidable answer I arrived at is: quite a lot. While it would be nice to be able to explain all of the concepts and views in this volume purely in everyday, colloquial, natural language, the task proved impossible. As a result, many entries contain formulas in the notation of various formal languages. Nevertheless, in writing the entries I strove to provide informal glosses of these formulas whenever possible. In places where this was not possible, however, and readers are faced with a formula they do not understand, I can guarantee that an explanation of the various symbols contained in the formula is to be found elsewhere in this volume.

Regarding alphabetization, I have treated expressions beginning with, or containing, Greek or Hebrew letters as if these letters were their Latin equivalents. Thus, the Hebrew א occurs in the "A" section of the book, while "κ-categorical" occurs in the "K" section. Also, numbers have been entered according to their spelling. Thus, "S4" is alphabetized as if it were "Sfour," and so occurs after "set theory" and before "sharpening."

In many cases there were concepts or views which have more than one name in the literature. In such cases I have attempted to place the definition under the name which is most common, cross-referencing other names to this entry. In a very few cases, however, where I felt there were good reasons for diverging from this practice, I placed the definition under the heading which I felt ought to be the common one. An example of such an instance is the entry for "Open Pair," which is more commonly called the "No–No paradox." In this case I think that the former terminology is far superior, so that is where I located the actual definition.

There are two things that the reader might expect from a work such as this that are missing. The first of these are bibliographical entries on famous or influential logicians. In preparing the manuscript I originally planned to include such entries, but found that length constraints forced these entries to be too short – in every case the corresponding entries on internet resources such as *The Stanford Encyclopedia of Philosophy*, the *Internet Encyclopedia of Philosophy*, or even Wikipedia ended up being far more informative. Thus, I discarded these entries in favor of including more entries on philosophical logic itself. The reader will find a list of important logicians in an appendix at the end of the volume, however.

Second, the reader might wonder why each entry does not have a suggestion for further reading. Again, space considerations played a major role here. With well over one thousand entries, such references would have taken up precious space that could be devoted to additional philosophical content. Instead, I have included an extensive bibliography, with references organized by major topics within philosophical logic.

A

A see **Abelian Logic**

א The first letter of the Hebrew alphabet, א denotes the **infinite cardinal numbers**. Subscripted **ordinal numbers** are used to distinguish and order the אs (and thus the infinite cardinal numbers themselves). $\aleph_0$ is the first infinite cardinal number – that is, the cardinal number of any **countably infinite set**; $\aleph_1$ is the second infinite cardinal number; $\aleph_2$ is the third infinite cardinal number … $\aleph_\omega$ is the ωth infinite cardinal number; $\aleph_{\omega+1}$ is the $\omega + 1^{th}$ infinite cardinal number … and so on.

See also: **ℶ, c, Cantor's Theorem, Continuum Hypothesis, Cumulative Hierarchy, Generalized Continuum Hypothesis**

ABACUS COMPUTABLE see **Register Computable**

ABACUS MACHINE see **Register Machine**

ABDUCTION An abduction (or **inference to the best explanation**, or **retroduction**) is an **inductive argument** whose **premise** (or premises) constitute the available evidence, and whose **conclusion** is a hypothesis regarding what best explains the evidence. Abduction often takes the same general form as the **fallacious deductive argument affirming the consequent**:

$$\frac{\begin{array}{l} A \to B \\ B \end{array}}{A}$$

where B is the evidence at hand, and A is the hypothesis regarding what brought about B.

See also: **Cogent Inductive Argument, Fallacy, Informal Fallacy, Strong Inductive Argument**

ABELIAN LOGIC   Abelian logic (or **A**) is a **relevance logic**. Abelian logic is obtained by rejecting **contraction** and liberalizing the following **theorem** of **classical propositional logic**:

$$((A \to \perp) \to \perp) \to A$$

to:

$$((A \to B) \to B) \to A$$

The latter principle is the **axiom of relativity**.

Abelian logic is one of a very few **non-standard logics** which **extends** classical propositional logic. Abelian logic is not a **sub-logic** of classical logic; it contains **theorems** which are not theorems of classical logic and which result in **triviality** if added to classical logic.

See also: **Commutativity**

ABSOLUTE CONSISTENCY see **Post Consistency**

ABSOLUTE INCONSISTENCY see **Post Consistency**

ABSOLUTE INFINITE   The absolute infinite is an **infinity** greater than the infinite **cardinal number** associated with any **set**. Thus, the **proper class** of all sets is an instance of the absolute infinite.

See also: **Indefinite Extensibility, Iterative Conception of Set, Limitation-of-Size Conception of Set, Universal Set**

ABSORBSION   Given two **binary functions** f and g, absorbsion holds between f and g if and only if, for all a and b:

$$f(a, g(a, b)) = g(a, f(a, b)) = a$$

Within **Boolean algebra**, absorbsion holds between the **meet** and **join operators** – that is:

$$A \cap (A \cup B) = A$$
$$A \cup (A \cap B) = A$$

In **classical propositional logic**, absorbsion holds between the **truth functions** associated with **conjunction** and **disjunction** – that is:

$$A \wedge (A \vee B)$$

and:

$$A \lor (A \land B)$$

are **logically equivalent** to:

A

The principle of **contraction**:

$$(A \rightarrow (A \rightarrow B)) \rightarrow (A \rightarrow B)$$

is also sometimes referred to as absorbsion.

See also: **Distributivity, Rule of Replacement**

ABSTRACT OBJECT   An abstract object is any object that is not **part** of the physical or material world, or alternatively any object that is not causally efficacious. Typical examples of abstract objects include mathematical objects such as **numbers** and **sets**, as well as objects connected with **logic** such as **propositions, languages,** and **concepts**. An object that is not abstract is a **concrete object**.

See also: **Abstraction, Mathematical Abstractionism, Nominalism, Platonism**

ABSTRACTION₁ The process by which we come to understand universal representations of particular objects (that is, universals) by attending only to those things the objects have in common.

See also: **Abstract Object, Abstraction Principle, Concept**

ABSTRACTION₂   Abstraction is the process of obtaining knowledge of **abstract objects** through the stipulation of **abstraction principles**.

See also: **Abstraction Operator, Bad Company Objection, Basic Law V, Caesar Problem, Hume's Principle, Mathematical Abstractionism**

ABSTRACTION OPERATOR   The **function implicitly defined** by an **abstraction principle** is an abstraction operator. For example, the abstraction operator **defined** by **Hume's Principle** is the function that maps **concepts** to their associated **cardinal number**, and the abstraction operator (intended to be) defined by the **inconsistent Basic Law V** is the function that maps each concept to the set (or **extension**) containing, as **members**, exactly the instances of the concept in question.

See also: **Bad Company Objection, Caesar Problem, Mathematical Abstractionism, Singular Term**

ABSTRACTION PRINCIPLE An abstraction principle is any **formula** of the form:

$$(\forall\alpha)(\forall\beta)(\text{Abst}(\alpha) = \text{Abst}(\beta) \leftrightarrow \text{Equ}(\alpha, \beta))$$

where Abst is an **abstraction operator** mapping the type of entities ranged over by α and β (typically objects, **concepts, functions,** or **sequences** of these) to objects, and "Equ" is an **equivalence relation** on the type of entities ranged over by α and β.

According to **mathematical abstractionism**, abstraction principles are **implicit definitions** of the objects that fall in the **range** of the abstraction operator "Abst," and we gain knowledge of these objects merely through the stipulation of appropriate abstraction principles.

The most important abstraction principles are **Hume's Principle** and **Basic Law V.**

See also: **Bad Company Objection, Caesar Problem**

ABSTRACTIONISM see **Mathematical Abstractionism**

ABSURDITY RULE see **Ex Falso Quodlibet**

ACCESSIBILITY RELATION Within **formal semantics** for **modal logic,** an accessibility relation is a **relation** on the **set** of **possible worlds** in a **model** that indicates which worlds are accessible from which other worlds. The **validity** of different **modal axioms** is associated with different conditions on the accessibility relation. For example, the axiom **T**:

$$\Box\, A \rightarrow A$$

is valid if and only if the accessibility relation is **reflexive.**

See also: **Actual World, Kripke Semantics, Kripke Structure, Ternary Semantics**

ACKERMANN FUNCTION The Ackermann function (or **Ackermann-Péter function**) is a **binary recursive function defined** as:

$$A(m, n) = \quad n + 1 \qquad\qquad\quad \text{if } m = 0.$$

$$A(m - 1, 1) \qquad\qquad \text{if } m > 0 \text{ and } n = 0.$$

$$A(m - 1, A(m, n - 1)) \quad \text{if } m > 0 \text{ and } n > 0.$$

The Ackermann function is a central example in **recursive function theory**, since it is recursive, but not **primitive recursive**. It is also an example of a function that grows rapidly – that is, the function outputs very large numbers for relatively small inputs.

See also: **Arithmetic**

ACKERMANN–PÉTER FUNCTION see **Ackermann Function**

ACTION TABLE   An action table (or **transition function**) is the table of instructions governing the operation of a **Turing machine**.

See also: **Automaton, Deterministic Turing Machine, Non-Deterministic Turing Machine, Recursive Function Theory, Register Machine**

ACTUAL INFINITY see **Complete Infinity**

ACTUAL WORLD   The actual world is the **possible world** we actually inhabit. It has been suggested that "actual" as used within **modal logic** (and thus the term "actual world") is an **indexical**. Thus, the actual world, for any reasoner in any possible world, is not the world we inhabit, but the one that they do.

See also: **Barcan Formula, Converse Barcan Formula, Counterpart Theory, Impossible World, Mere Possibilia, Trans-World Identity**

ACTUALISM see **Modal Actualism**

ACZEL SET THEORY see **Non-Well-Founded Set Theory**

ADDITION   Addition (or **disjunction introduction**, or **or introduction**) is the **rule of inference** that allows one to **infer** a **disjunction** from either of the **disjuncts**. In symbols:

$$\frac{A}{A \lor B}$$

or:

$$\frac{B}{A \vee B}$$

See also: **Classical Dilemma, Constructive Dilemma, Destructive Dilemma, Disjunctive Syllogism, Introduction Rule, Vel**

AD HOMINEM Ad hominem (Latin, literally "to the man") is an **informal fallacy** which occurs when the reasoner, in attempting to demonstrate the inadequacy of another person's **argument**, attacks the character of the person presenting the argument instead of legitimately discrediting the **evidence** provided.

See also: **Straw Man, Tu Quoque**

ADICITY The adicity (or **arity**, or **degree**) of a **function** or **relation** is the number of inputs (or **arguments**) that it takes. Thus, a **unary function** is a function of adicity 1, and the adicity of a **binary relation** is 2.

See also: **Binary Function, N-ary Function, N-ary Relation, Ternary Function, Ternary Relation, Unary Relation**

AD IGNORANTIUM Latin for "to the point of ignorance," the phrase "ad ignorantium" is used to indicate an **informal fallacy** which occurs when the reasoner attempts to support a **conclusion** merely by pointing out that we have no **evidence** for the **negation** of the conclusion.

AD INFINITUM Latin for "to infinity," the phrase "ad infinitum" is used to indicate that a process is to be continued indefinitely, or that a particular **function** or operation is to be applied **infinitely** many times.

See also: **Complete Infinity, Cumulative Hierarchy, Hierarchy, Iteration, Iterative Conception of Set, Potential Infinity**

ADJUNCTION see **Conjunction Introduction**

ADMISSIBLE RULE A **rule of inference** is an admissible rule, relative to a particular **formal system**, if and only if its addition to the system does not allow one to **prove** any **theorems** or **demonstrate** the **validity** of any **arguments** that were not already provable using the original rules of the system.

An admissible rule is also a **derivable rule** if a **schema** can be provided which **demonstrates** how to obtain the **conclusion** of the derivable rule from the **premises** of the rule. Not every admissible rule is derivable, however.

See also: **Cut, Cut Elimination, Derivation, Sequent Calculus**

ADMISSIBLE SHARPENING see **Sharpening**

AFFINE LOGICS   Affine logics are **substructural logics** within which the **structural rule contraction**:

$$\frac{\Delta, A, A \Rightarrow \Phi}{\Delta, A \Rightarrow \Phi}$$

fails.

See also: **Abelian Logic, Sequent Calculus**

AFFIRMATIVE PROPOSITION   The **quality** of a **categorical proposition** is affirmative – that is, the categorical proposition is an affirmative proposition (or **positive proposition**) – if and only if it asserts that (some or all) **members** of the **class denoted** by the **subject term** are also **members** of the class denoted by the **predicate term**. **A-propositions** and **I-propositions** are affirmative, while **E-propositions** and **O-propositions** are not. Categorical propositions that are not affirmative are **negative**.

See also: **Particular Proposition, Quantity, Square of Opposition, Universal Proposition**

AFFIRMING THE ANTECEDENT see **Modus Ponens**

AFFIRMING THE CONSEQUENT   Affirming the consequent is the **formal fallacy** that occurs when one moves from a **conditional**, and the **consequent** of that conditional, to the **antecedent** of that conditional. In symbols:

$$\frac{P \to Q}{\underline{Q}}{P}$$

See also: **Abduction, Conditional Proof, Denying the Antecedent, Material Conditional, Modus Ponens, Modus Tollens**

ALETHIC MODAL LOGIC Alethic modal logic is the branch of **modal logic** that deals with the modal **operators** "it is **necessary** that Φ" and "it is **possible** that Φ," typically symbolized as "□ Φ" and " ◇ Φ" or "L Φ" and "M Φ," respectively. Any modal logic dealing with modal operators other than these, such as **deontic modal logic, doxastic modal logic, epistemic modal logic,** and **temporal modal logic,** are **non-alethic modal logics** or **analethic modal logics.**

See also: **Contingency, Impossibility, Kripke Semantics, Kripke Structure, Normal Modal Logic, Possibility**

ALGEBRA An algebra is a **set** of objects and one or more **functions** or **relations** on that set. Within **logic,** important algebras include the **natural numbers,** the **real numbers, Boolean algebras, lattices,** and orderings of various types. One fruitful way to view a **formal system** is as an algebra where the set in question contains all **well-formed formulas** and the operations are the functions defined by the **formation rules** (e.g. **conjunction** is associated with the **binary** function that takes two **formulas** as inputs and gives their conjunction as output).

See also: **Algebraic Logic, Induction on Well-formed Formulas, Partial Ordering**

ALGEBRAIC LOGIC The branch of **mathematical logic** that studies the algebraic structures – that is, **algebras** – associated with particular **formal systems.** Algebraic logic is especially useful when studying **many-valued logics,** since one can compare the algebras generated by these systems to the **Boolean algebras** generated by **classical logics.**

See also: **Lattice, Partial Ordering**

ALGORITHM see **Effective Procedure**

ALTERNATE DENIAL see **Sheffer Stroke**

ALTERNATIVE LOGIC see **Non-Standard Logic**

AMBIGUITY An expression displays ambiguity if it has more than one legitimate meaning or interpretation in a given context.

See also: **Amphiboly, Equivocation, Informal Fallacy, Punctuation**

AMPHIBOLY   A type of **ambiguity**, amphiboly occurs when a complex expression has more than one legitimate interpretation, and the ambiguity in question is not due to any single word having more than one meaning. In cases of amphiboly, the multiple interpretations are due instead to a structural, **logical**, or grammatical defect in the construction of the expression.

See also: **Equivocation, Informal Fallacy, Punctuation**

ANALETHIC LOGIC   Analethic logic is a **three-valued logic** where the third **truth value** is the **truth value gap** "neither **true** nor **false**" (typically denoted "N"), and the **designated values** are "true" and "neither true nor false." **Compound sentences** are assigned truth values based on the **truth tables** for the **strong Kleene connectives**. Analethic logic has the same **proof-theoretic** behavior of the **logic of paradox**, without requiring the acceptance of a **truth value glut**.

See also: **Contradiction, Designated Value, Dialetheism, Dialethic Logic, Ex Falso Quodlibet, Paraconsistent Logic**

ANALETHIC MODAL LOGIC see **Alethic Modal Logic**

ANALYSIS   Analysis is either the **first-order theory** of the **real numbers** or the **second-order theory** of the **natural numbers** (that is, **second-order arithmetic**). There is no **ambiguity** here, since the two theories are equivalent in **proof-theoretic** strength.

See also: **Intuitionistic Mathematics, Non-standard Analysis**

ANALYTIC   A **statement** is analytic if and only if it is **true** in virtue of the meanings of the expressions contained in it. If a statement is not analytic, then it is **synthetic**.

ANAPHORA   Anaphora occurs when the **referent** of an expression depends on the referent of another expression occurring in the same **statement** or in another appropriately connected statement. For example, in:

Bobby was tired. He said he was suffering from lack of sleep.

"He" occurs anaphorically. Often (but not always) anaphoric terms are pronouns such as "it," "she," "there," etc.

See also: **Demonstrative, Indexical**

ANCESTRAL   The ancestral of a **relation** R is the relation R* that holds between x and y if and only if there is a chain of objects z_1, z_2, ... z_n such that Rxz_1, Rz_1z_2, ... Rz_ny. Within **second-order logic** the ancestral is **defined** as follows. First, a **concept** F is **hereditary** relative to a relation R if and only if:

$$\text{Hered}(F, R) \quad = \quad (\forall x)(\forall y)(\,Rxy \rightarrow (Fx \rightarrow Fy))$$

Loosely, F is hereditary relative to R if and only if everything R-related to an F is an F. We can now define the ancestral of R:

$$R^*(x, y) \quad = \quad (\forall F)(((\forall z)(Rxz \rightarrow Fz) \wedge \text{Her}(F, R)) \rightarrow Fy)$$

See also: **Frege's Theorem, Transitive Closure**

AND see **Conjunction**

AND ELIMINATION see **Conjunction Elimination**

AND INTRODUCTION see **Conjunction Introduction**

ANTECEDENT   The antecedent of a **conditional** is the **subformula** of the conditional occurring between the "if" and the "then," or, if the conditional is not in strict "If ... then ..." form, then the antecedent is the subformula occurring between "if" and "then" in the "if ... then ..." statement **logically equivalent** to the original conditional.

See also: **Affirming the Consequent, Consequent, Denying the Antecedent, Modus Ponens, Modus Tollens**

ANTI-EXTENSION   The anti-extension of a **predicate** is the **set** of objects that fail to **satisfy** the predicate. Thus, the anti-extension of "is red" is the set of things that fail to be red. More generally, the anti-extension of an n-ary **relation** is the set of **n-tuples** that fail to satisfy the relation.

Typically, the anti-extension of a predicate is the **complement** of the **extension** of the predicate. Some **non-standard logics**, however, such as **supervaluational semantics**, allow there to be objects that are in neither the extension nor the anti-extension of a predicate.

See also: **Disjoint, Exclusive, Exhaustive, Partition, Sharpening**

ANTI-FOUNDATION AXIOM   The anti-foundation axiom is the **axiom** that replaces the **axiom of foundation** within **non-well-founded set theory**, and which allows for **sets** with **non-well-founded membership relations**. The axiom states that, given any directed graph, there is a **function** f from the universe of sets **V** onto the nodes of that graph such that, for any two sets A and B, A is a member of B if and only if there is an edge in the graph leading from the node f(A) to the node f(B). For example, the graph:

represents the non-well-founded set Ω where Ω = {Ω}.

See also: **Iterative Conception of Set, Non-Well-Founded Set Theory**

ANTILOGISM   An antilogism (or **inconsistent triad**) is any triple of **statements** such that the **truth** of any two of them guarantees the **falsity** of the third. Antilogisms were used as a tool for testing the **validity** of **categorical syllogisms**, since a categorical syllogism will be valid if and only if the triple containing the two **premises** and the **contradictory** of the **conclusion** is an antilogism.

See also: **Term Logic, Venn Diagram**

ANTINOMY   An antinomy occurs when two laws, or two **conclusions** of apparently acceptable **arguments**, are incompatible with each other. The term "antinomy" is also sometimes used more loosely as a synonym for "**paradox**."

See also: **Insolubilia, Sophism, Sophisma**

ANTIREALISM see **Logical Antirealism**

ANTISYMMETRY   A **relation** R is antisymmetric if and only if, for any a and b, if:

Rab

and:

Rba

then:

a = b.

See also: **Asymmetry, Linear Ordering, Partial Ordering, Strict Ordering, Symmetry, Well-Ordering**

A POSTERIORI see **A Priori**

A PRIORI A **statement** is a priori if and only if it can be known to be **true** independent of any empirical experience (other than those experiences that might be necessary in order to understand the statement). A statement that is not a priori is **a posteriori**.

A-PROPOSITION An A-proposition is a **categorical proposition** asserting that all objects which are **members** of the **class designated** by the **subject term** are members of the class designated by the **predicate term**. In other words, an A-proposition is a categorical proposition whose **logical form** is:

All P are Q.

The **quality** of an A-proposition is **affirmative** and its **quantity** is **universal**. An A-proposition **distributes** its subject term, but not its predicate term.

See also: **E-Proposition, I-Proposition, O-Proposition, Square of Opposition**

ARGUMENT₁ An argument is a **sequence** of **statements** where all but one of the statements (the **premises**) are intended to provide evidence, or support, for the remaining statement (the **conclusion**).
Sometimes, in technical contexts such as the **sequent calculus**, an argument can have more than one **conclusion**.

See also: **Conditionalization, Deductive Argument, Formal Fallacy, Inductive Argument, Inference, Informal Fallacy**

ARGUMENT₂ An argument of a **function** or **relation** is any value that can be input into the function or relation.

See also: **Domain, Field, Range**

ARISTOTELIAN COMPREHENSION SCHEMA   The Aristotelian comprehension schema is the following **formula** in **second-order logic** (for any formula Φ not containing Y **free**):

$$(\exists x)\Phi \rightarrow (\exists Y)(\forall x)(Yx \leftrightarrow \Phi)$$

The Aristotelian comprehension schema guarantees there is a **concept** holding of exactly the objects **satisfying** Φ, as long as at least one object satisfies Φ. Unlike the standard **comprehension schema**, the Aristotelian comprehension schema does not guarantee the existence of an **empty concept**.

See also: **Aristotelian Second-order Logic, Empty Set, Schema**

ARISTOTELIAN LOGIC see **Categorical Logic**

ARISTOTELIAN SECOND-ORDER LOGIC   Aristotelian second-order logic is a variant of **second-order logic** where the **comprehension schema** is replaced by the weaker **Aristotelian comprehension schema**. The main difference between standard second-order logic and Aristotelian second-order logic is that in Aristotelian second-order logic there is no guarantee that the **empty concept** exists.

See also: **Empty Set, Schema**

ARISTOTLE'S SEA BATTLE   Aristotle's sea battle example is meant to challenge what we now call **classical logic**. Aristotle has us consider two **statements**:

(1) There will be a sea battle tomorrow.

(2) There will not be a sea battle tomorrow.

According to classical reasoning, one of these is **true** and the other **false**. But if that is the case, then we have no control over whether there will be a sea battle tomorrow or not – the facts of the matter have already been determined. Since the **argument** generalizes to any statement, we are left with an uncomfortable determinism regarding the future.

See also: **Bivalence, Law of Excluded Middle, Non-Standard Logic**

ARISTOTLE'S THESIS Aristotle's thesis is the following **formula** on **propositional logic**:

$$\sim (\sim A \rightarrow A)$$

This formula is a theorem in **connexive logic**, yet it is not a theorem within **classical logic** – in the classical context Aristotle's thesis is equivalent to $\sim A$.

See also: **Boethius' Theses**

ARITHMETIC Any **theory** regarding the **natural numbers** is an arithmetic. Within **logic**, there are a number of important arithmetic theories, including **Robinson arithmetic**, **Peano arithmetic**, and **non-standard arithmetic**.

See also: **Finitary Arithmetic, Gödel's First Incompleteness Theorem, Gödel's Second Incompleteness Theorem, Hume's Principle, Inconsistent Arithmetic, Intuitionistic Arithmetic**

ARITHMETIC HIERARCHY The arithmetic hierarchy (or **Kleene hierarchy**) is a classification of the **formulas of first-order arithmetic** based on their **complexity**. A formula is designated a Π_0 (or Σ_0) formula if it is, or is **equivalent** to, a formula containing only **bounded quantifiers**. Π_n and Σ_n formulas, for any **natural number** greater than 0, are **defined recursively** as follows:

Φ is Π_{n+1} if and only if Φ is **logically equivalent** to some formula of the form:
$(\forall x_1)(\forall x_2) \ldots (\forall x_m)\Psi$ where Ψ is a Σ_n formula.

Φ is Σ_{n+1} if and only if Φ is logically equivalent to some formula of the form:
$(\exists x_1)(\exists x_2) \ldots (\exists x_m)\Psi$ where Ψ is a Π_n formula.

Every formula of first-order arithmetic is **equivalent** to a formula in **prenex normal form**, guaranteeing that this definition assigns every formula of arithmetic a rank in the arithmetic hierarchy.

See also: **Hierarchy, Π-Formula, Π-Sentence, Σ-Formula, Σ-Sentence, Skolem Normal Form**

ARITHMETIC PREDECESSOR see **Arithmetic Successor**

ARITHMETIC SUCCESSOR The arithmetic successor of a **natural number** is the next natural number. In other words, the arithmetic successor of n is n + 1. If n is the arithmetic successor of m, then m is the **arithmetic predecessor** of n.

See also: **Axiom of Infinity, Cardinal Successor, Inductive Set, Ordinal Successor, Successor Function**

ARITHMETIZATION   Arithmetization is the method by which **numerals** in formalized **arithmetic** are assigned to symbols, **formulas,** and **sequences** of formulas within that system of arithmetic. Various claims about the **syntax, proof theory,** etc. of the arithmetical theory can be formulated and studied within that same theory by using the numerals assigned to expressions by the arithmetization process as proxies for the expressions themselves. **Gödel's first incompleteness theorem** and **Gödel's second incompleteness theorem** are the paradigm instances of using arithmetization in order to study characteristics of **formal systems**.

See also: **Diagonalization, Diagonalization Lemma, Gödel Numbering, Gödel Sentence, Peano Arithmetic**

ARITY see **Adicity**

ASSERTION   Assertion (or **pseudo modus ponens**) is the following principle of **propositional logic**:

$$(A \land (A \to B)) \to B$$

Assertion is the **conditionalization** of the valid argument form **modus ponens**.

ASSOCIATIVE LAW see **Associativity**

ASSOCIATIVITY₁   A **function** f is associative if and only if the following holds for any a, b, and c:

$$f(a, f(b, c)) = f(f(a, b), c)$$

Any function that **satisfies** the above **formula** is said to satisfy the **associative law**.

See also: **Absorbsion, Boolean Algebra, Join, Lattice, Meet**

ASSOCIATIVITY₂   Within **propositional logic**, associativity is the **rule of replacement** that allows one to replace a **formula** of the form:

$(A \land (B \land C))$

with:

$((A \land B) \land C),$

or to replace a formula of the form:

$(A \lor (B \lor C))$

with:

$((A \lor B) \lor C)$

Multiple applications of associativity allow one to rearrange the **parentheses** in long **sequences** of **conjunctions** or in long sequences of **disjunctions**.

See also: **Commutativity, Distributivity**

ASYMMETRY A **relation** R is asymmetric if and only if it is not **symmetric** – that is, if there exist an a and b such that:

Rab

but not:

Rba.

In some contexts asymmetry is understood more strictly, however, so that a relation R is asymmetric if and only if it is nowhere symmetric – that is, if for any x and y, if:

Rxy

then:

$\sim$ Ryx

See also: **Antisymmetry, Strict Ordering**

ATOM₁ Within **mereology**, an atom is any object that has no **proper parts**, that is, no **parts** other than itself. Formally, we can **define** this notion as (where P is the part **relation**):

$Ax \quad = \quad \sim (\exists y)(Pyx \land y \neq x)$

See also: **Gunk, Mereological Nihilism**

ATOM₂ see **Atomic Formula, Atomic Sentence, Propositional Letter**

ATOMIC FORMULA   An atomic formula (or **atom**, or **simple formula**) is a **formula** that consists of a single **n-ary predicate** followed by n **singular terms**. Note that the terms might be simple or **complex**, and might be, or contain, either **constants** or **variables**.

See also: **Atomic Sentence, Compound Formula, Compound Statement, Formation Rules, Propositional Letter, Singular Proposition**

ATOMIC LETTER see **Propositional Letter**

ATOMIC SENTENCE   Within first-order logic, an atomic sentence (or **atom**, or **simple sentence**) is a **formula** that consists of a single **n-ary predicate** followed by n **singular terms** where none of the terms contains any **variables**. In other words, an atomic sentence is an **atomic formula** where all the terms are **constants**, or are **complex terms** containing only constants.

See also: **Compound Formula, Compound Statement, Formation Rules, Propositional Letter, Singular Proposition, Well-Formed Formula**

ATOMLESS GUNK see **Gunk**

ATTRIBUTE see **Concept**

AUSSUNDERONG see **Axiom(s) of Separation**

AUSSONDERONG AXIOM see **Axiom(s) of Separation**

AUTOLOGICAL   A **predicate** is autological if and only if it applies to itself. For example, "polysyllabic" is autological, since "polysyllabic" is polysyllabic, but "unpronounceable" is not autological, since "unpronounceable" is pronounceable. A predicate that is not autological is **heterological**. The **Grelling paradox** arises when one considers whether "heterological" is heterological.

See also: **Liar Paradox, Liar Sentence, Russell Paradox, Russell Set**

AUTOMATON   An automaton is a **finitely** describable abstract machine or computing device. The study of automata is central to computability theory. Examples of automata include **Turing machines** and **register machines**.

See also: **Church-Turing Thesis, Deterministic Turing Machine, Non-Deterministic Turing Machine, Recursive Function Theory, Turing Test**

AUTOMORPHISM An automorphism is an **isomorphism** between a **structure** and itself.

See also: **Endomorphism, Epimorphism, Homomorphism, Monomorphism**

AXIOLOGICAL LOGIC Axiological logic is the **logic** of "good," "bad," and "better than." Typically, axiological logics contain a **binary relation** P where "Pxy" represents "x is preferred to y" or "x is better than y." This relation is usually assumed to be **asymmetric** and **transitive**.

See also: **Modal Logic, Partial Ordering**

AXIOM An axiom is a **formula** used as a starting assumption and from which other **statements** – **theorems** – are **derived**. Thus, many statements are **proved** using axioms, but axioms need not, and given their **definition** cannot, be proved. In the past, axioms were meant to be self-evident and thus in need of no additional support or evidence. Now, however, an axiom is any principle that is assumed without proof.

See also: **Axiom Schema, Axiomatized Theory, Finitely Axiomatizable, Recursively Axiomatizable Theory**

AXIOM OF AUSSONDERONG see Axiom(s) of Separation

AXIOM OF CHOICE The axiom of choice (or **multiplicative axiom**) asserts that, given a **set** containing one or more **pairwise disjoint sets**, there exists a second set containing exactly one **member** of each of the sets contained in the original set – in other words, given a set of non-overlapping sets, the axiom of choice tells us that we can "select" one member from each of the non-overlapping sets and form these into a "new" set. In **first-order logic** supplemented with the membership symbol "∈," this can be formulated as:

$$(\forall x)(((\forall y)(y \in x \rightarrow (\exists z)(z \in y)) \wedge (\forall y)(\forall z)((y \in x \wedge z \in x) \rightarrow$$
$$\sim (\exists w)(w \in y \wedge w \in z))) \rightarrow (\exists y)(\forall z)(z \in x \rightarrow (\exists !t)(t \in z \wedge t \in y)))$$

The axiom of choice is equivalent to **Zorn's lemma**, the **well-ordering principle**, and the **trichotomy law**.

See also: **Axiom of Countable Choice, Axiom of Dependent Choice, Choice Function, Choice Set, Global Choice, Zermelo Fraenkel Set Theory**

AXIOM OF CONSTRUCTIBILITY   The axiom of constructibility is a **set-theoretic** principle that states that the universe of sets (**V**) is identical to the **constructible sets** (**L**). Thus, the axiom can be succinctly stated as:

V = L

The axiom of constructibility is **independent** of **Zermelo Fraenkel set theory**, and Kurt Gödel proved that both the **axiom of choice** and the **continuum hypothesis** are **consistent** with Zermelo Fraenkel set theory by showing that both follow from the axiom of constructibility (which is itself consistent with Zermelo Fraenkel set theory).

See also: **Independence Result, Inner Model**

AXIOM OF COUNTABLE CHOICE   The axiom of countable choice (or **axiom of denumerable choice**) is a weak version of the **axiom of choice**. It states that, given a **countable set** containing one or more **pairwise disjoint sets**, there exists a set containing exactly one **member** of each of the sets contained in the original set.
    The axiom of countable choice is implied by both the full axiom of choice and the **axiom of dependent choice**.

See also: **Choice Function, Choice Set, Global Choice, Trichotomy Law, Well-Ordering Principle, Zorn's Lemma**

AXIOM OF DENUMERABLE CHOICE see **Axiom of Countable Choice**

AXIOM OF DEPENDENT CHOICE   The axiom of dependent choice is a weak version of the **axiom of choice**. It states that, given:

(1) Any non–empty **set** X.

and:

> (2) Any **relation** R on X such that, for any member a of X, there is a member b of X such that Rab (that is, for any **serial relation** R on X).

there is a **sequence** $x_1, x_2, \ldots$ such that, for all n, x_n is in X, and Rx_nx_{n+1}.

The axiom of dependent choice is **implied** by the full axiom of choice and implies the **axiom of countable choice**.

See also: **Choice Function, Choice Set, Global Choice, Trichotomy Law, Well-Ordering Principle, Zorn's Lemma**

AXIOM OF DETERMINATENESS see Axiom of Extensionality

AXIOM OF EMPTY SET   The axiom of empty set (or **axiom of null set**, or **empty set axiom**, or **null set axiom**) asserts that there exists a **set** containing no **members**. In **first-order logic** supplemented with the membership symbol "∈," this can be formulated as:

$$(\exists x)(\forall y)(y \notin x)$$

or:

$$(\exists x)(\forall y)(y \in x \leftrightarrow y \neq y)$$

The **empty set**, the set whose existence is asserted by this **axiom**, is typically **denoted** by "∅."

See also: **Axiom of Infinity, Zermelo Fraenkel Set Theory**

AXIOM OF EXTENSIONALITY   The axiom of extensionality (or **axiom of determinateness**, or **extensionality axiom**) asserts that two **sets** are **identical** if and only if they have exactly the same **members**. In **first-order logic** supplemented with the membership symbol "∈," this can be formulated as:

$$(\forall x)(\forall y)(x = y \leftrightarrow (\forall z)(z \in x \leftrightarrow z \in y))$$

Satisfaction of the axiom of extensionality is often thought to be constitutive of the concept of set – in other words, something cannot be a set unless it satisfies this axiom, regardless of which other set-theoretic axioms are **true**.

See also: **Zermelo Fraenkel Set Theory**

AXIOM OF FOUNDATION   The axiom of foundation (or the **axiom of regularity**, or the **axiom of restriction**, or **foundation axiom**, or **regularity axiom**, or **restriction axiom**), asserts that, given any non-empty **set** A, there is a **member** of A that is **disjoint** from A – in other words, any set that has any members at all has a member that shares no members with the original set. In **first-order logic** supplemented with the membership symbol "∈," this can be formulated as:

$$(\forall x)((\exists y)(y \in x) \rightarrow (\exists z)(z \in x \wedge \sim(\exists w)(w \in z \wedge w \in x)))$$

Although the exact import of the axiom of foundation is difficult to summarize, its main role is to rule out the existence of **non-well-founded sets**.

See also: **Anti-Foundation Axiom, Non-Well-Founded Set Theory, Zermelo Fraenkel Set Theory**

AXIOM OF INFINITY   The axiom of infinity asserts that there exists a **set** A such that (1) the **empty set** is a **member** of A, and (2) for any set that is a member of A, its **ordinal successor** is also a member of A. In **first-order logic** supplemented with the membership symbol "∈" and standard abbreviations, this can be formulated as:

$$(\exists x)(\varnothing \in x \wedge (\forall y)(y \in x \rightarrow y \cup \{y\} \in x))$$

The set whose existence is asserted by this axiom can easily be shown to contain **infinitely** many members.

　　The set-theoretic axiom of infinity should be clearly distinguished from the **infinity axiom**, which merely states that infinitely many objects exist.

See also: **Axiom of Zermelo Infinity, ω, Singleton, Successor, Union, Zermelo Fraenkel Set Theory**

AXIOM OF NULL SET see **Axiom of Empty Set**

AXIOM OF PAIRING   The axiom of pairing (or **pairing axiom**) asserts that, for any two objects A and B, there is a **set** whose **members** are exactly A and B – in other words, for any two objects, the **unordered pair** containing just those two objects as members exists. In **first-order logic** supplemented with the membership symbol "∈," this can be formulated as:

$$(\forall x)(\forall y)(\exists z)(\forall w)(w \in z \leftrightarrow (w = x \vee w = y))$$

The axiom of pairing implies that the **singleton** of every set exists, and it also provides the resources to construct **ordered pairs** and, more generally, **ordered n-tuples**.

See also: **Pairing Function, Zermelo Fraenkel Set Theory**

AXIOM OF POWERSET   The axiom of powerset (or **powerset axiom**) asserts that, given any **set** A, there exists a second set B such that the **members** of B are exactly the **subsets** of A (including the **empty set**, and A itself). B is the **powerset** of A. In **first-order logic** supplemented with the membership symbol "$\in$," this can be formulated as:

$$(\forall x)(\exists y)(\forall z)(z \in y \leftrightarrow (\forall w)(w \in z \rightarrow w \in x))$$

See also: **Cantor's Theorem, Continuum Hypothesis, Generalized Continuum Hypothesis, Zermelo Fraenkel Set Theory**

AXIOM OF REDUCIBILITY   In **ramified type theories**, the axiom of reducibility states that, for any **concept** (of any **type**) of **order** n, there is a concept of order 0 (of the same type) that has the same **extension** – that is, that holds of exactly the same entities. The axiom of reducibility is often **formalized** as:

$$(\forall X_n)(\exists Y_0)(\forall z)(X_n z \leftrightarrow Y_0 z)$$

The axiom of reducibility in effect reduces the ramified theory of types to the **simple theory of types**.

AXIOM OF REGULARITY see **Axiom of Foundation**

AXIOM OF RELATIVITY   The axiom of relativity is the following **theorem** of **Abelian logic**:

$$((A \rightarrow B) \rightarrow B) \rightarrow A$$

This axiom is notable since its addition to most **logics** renders the logic **trivial**. One can see this quite simply in the case of **classical logic**, since **consequential mirabilis**:

$$(\sim A \rightarrow A) \rightarrow A$$

is a theorem of classical logic.

See also: **Paraconsistent Logic, Relevance Logic**

AXIOM OF REPLACEMENT see Axiom(s) of Replacement

AXIOM OF RESTRICTION see Axiom of Foundation

AXIOM OF SEPARATION see Axiom(s) of Separation

AXIOM OF SUMSET see Axiom of Union

AXIOM OF TRICHOTOMY see Trichotomy Law

AXIOM OF UNION   The axiom of union (or **axiom of sumset**, or **sumset axiom**, or **union axiom**) asserts that, given any **set** of sets A, there exists a set B such that B contains all of the **members** of the members of A. B is the **union** of A. In **first-order logic** supplemented with the membership symbol "$\in$," this can be formulated as:

$$(\forall x)(\exists y)(\forall z)(z \in y \leftrightarrow (\exists w)(z \in w \wedge w \in x))$$

The **union** of a set A is typically **denoted** by "$\cup$A."

See also: **Intersection, Zermelo Fraenkel Set Theory**

AXIOM OF ZERMELO INFINITY   The axiom of Zermelo infinity asserts that there exists a set A such that (1) the empty set is a **member** of A, and (2) for any set that is a member of A, its **singleton** is also a member of A. In **first-order logic** supplemented with the **membership** symbol "$\in$" and standard abbreviations, this can be formulated as:

$$(\exists x)(\varnothing \in x \wedge (\forall y)(y \in x \rightarrow \{y\} \in x))$$

This axiom should be clearly distinguished from both the set-theoretic **axiom of infinity** and the **infinity axiom**.

See also: **Ordinal Successor, Zermelo Fraenkel Set Theory**

AXIOM SCHEMA   An axiom schema is a **formula** in the **metatheory** within which one or more **metalinguistic schematic variables** occur. Given an axiom schema, one obtains an **axiom** by systematically replacing each schematic variable with an **object language** formula of the appropriate type. Since there are usually **infinitely** many different object language formulas of the type in question, an axiom schema provides a **finite** formulation of an infinite list of axioms that are similar in structure.

See also: **Axiom(s) of Replacement, Axiom(s) of Separation,**

Comprehension Schema, Mathematical Induction, Substitution Instance, T-schema

AXIOM(S) OF REPLACEMENT   The axiom(s) of replacement (or **axiom of substitution**, or **replacement axiom**) assert that, given any **set** A and any **function** f, there exists a second set B such that the **members** of B are exactly the **image** of the set A under the function f. In other words, an object is a member of B if and only if it is the result of applying the function f to a member of the original set A.

The full import of the axiom(s) of replacement cannot be captured within **first-order logic** by a single **formula**. Instead, in first-order logic supplemented with the membership symbol "$\in$," we can provide the following **axiom schema**, which provides a particular instance of the axiom of replacement for each individual function f:

$$(\forall x)(\exists y)(\forall z)(z \in y \leftrightarrow (\exists w)(w \in x \wedge z = f(w)))$$

Within **second-order logic**, however, we can formulate the axiom(s) of replacement as a single axiom:

$$(\forall f)(\forall x)(\exists y)(\forall z)(z \in y \leftrightarrow (\exists w)(w \in x \wedge z = f(w)))$$

See also: **Zermelo Fraenkel Set Theory**

AXIOM(S) OF SEPARATION   The axiom(s) of separation (or **aussonderong**, or **aussonderong axiom**, or **axiom of aussonderong**, or **separation axiom**) asserts that, given any **set** A and any condition $\Phi(x)$, there exists a second set B such that the **members** of B are exactly the members of A that also **satisfy** the condition $\Phi(x)$. The axiom(s) of separation allows us to form arbitrary **subsets** of any given set, so long as we have to hand some condition that picks out the subset in question.

The full import of the axiom(s) of separation cannot be captured within **first-order logic** by a single **formula**. Instead, in first-order logic supplemented with the membership symbol "$\in$," we can provide the following **axiom schema**, which provides a particular instance of the axiom of separation for each individual **predicate** $\Phi(x)$:

$$(\forall x)(\exists y)(\forall z)(z \in y \leftrightarrow (z \in x \wedge \Phi(z)))$$

Within **second-order logic**, however, we can formulate the axiom(s) of separation as a single axiom:

$$(\forall P)(\forall x)(\exists y)(\forall z)(z \in y \leftrightarrow (z \in x \wedge P(z)))$$

See also: **Russell's Paradox, Zermelo Fraenkel Set Theory**

AXIOMATIC THEORY see **Axiomatized Theory**

AXIOMATIZATION see **Axiomatized Theory**

AXIOMATIZED THEORY   A **theory** is an axiomatized theory if and only if it is the **transitive closure** of some set of **axioms** or **axiom schemata**. Since any theory is axiomatizable in this sense (since we can just take all principles contained in the theory as axioms), logicians are typically interested in theories that can be axiomatized in some convenient manner, such as **finitely axiomatizable theories** or **recursively axiomatizable theories**. A particular set of axioms for an axiomatized theory is (one of) that theory's **axiomatizations**.

B   B (or **Brouwerian Modal Logic**) is the **normal modal logic** whose additional **axioms** are:

T: $\Box P \rightarrow P$
B: $P \rightarrow \Box \Diamond P$

In **possible worlds semantics**, the modal logic B is **valid** on any **frame** in which the **accessibility relation** is **symmetric** and **reflexive**.

B also refers to the **axiom** that is characteristic of the modal logic B (or the **Brouwerian Axiom**). The axiom B is satisfied on any frame in which the accessibility relation is symmetric.

See also: **Kripke Semantics, Kripke Structure, Modality**

ℶ   The second letter of the Hebrew alphabet, ℶ is used to denote a particular type of **infinite cardinal number**. Subscripted **ordinal numbers** are used to distinguish, and order, the ℶ's. $\beth_0$ is **identical** to $\aleph_0$, the first infinite cardinal. $\beth_1$ is identical to $2^{\beth_0}$. $\beth_2$ is identical to $2^{\beth_1}$ ... and generally:

$$\beth_{i+1} = 2^{\beth_i}$$

With the $\beth$ notation in place, we can succinctly express both the **continuum hypothesis** and the **generalized continuum hypothesis**. The continuum hypothesis is the claim that:

$$\aleph_1 = \beth_1$$

The generalized continuum hypothesis is the claim that:

$$(\forall i)(\aleph_i = \beth_i)$$

See also: **c, Cantor's Theorem, Continuum, Cumulative Hierarchy, Rank**

BAD COMPANY OBJECTION   The bad company objection is an objection to **mathematical abstractionism**. According to the bad company objection, the mathematical abstractionist has no reasons for believing that some **abstraction principles**, such as **Hume's Principle,** can play the privileged foundational and epistemological role ascribed to them, since other abstraction principles, such as **Basic Law V,** patently cannot play such a role, being **inconsistent** or otherwise incompatible with Hume's Principle.

See also: **Abstraction, Caesar Problem**

BAG see **Multiset**

BARBARA   A **categorical syllogism** whose **premises** and **conclusion** are all **A-propositions** – that is, whose **syllogistic mood** is AAA – and which is in the first **syllogistic figure** is a "Barbara" **syllogism.**
   The designation comes from a medieval poem which lists all the **valid** syllogistic argument forms in **categorical logic**:

> Barbara, Celerent, Darii, Ferioque, prioris;
> Cesare, Camestres, Festino, Baroco, secundae;
> Tertia, Darapti, Disamis, Datisi, Felapton,
> Bocardo, Ferison, habet: quarta insuper addit
> Bramantip, Camenes, Dimaris, Fesapo, Fresison.

Each name represents a valid form. The vowels in the name represent the syllogistic mood, so Festino is an EIO syllogism, and the syllogistic figure is indicated in Latin (i.e. "prioris," "secundae," "tertia," and "quarta").

See also: **Categorical Proposition, Term Logic, Venn Diagram**

BARCAN FORMULA   The Barcan formula is the following formula of **quantified modal logic**:

$$(\forall x)\Box\Phi \to \Box(\forall x)\Phi$$

The Barcan formula implies that any object that exists in any **possible world accessible** from the **actual world** exists in the actual world – in other words, any object that can **possibly** exist actually exists.

See also: **Converse Barcan Formula, Mere Possibilia, Normal Modal Logic**

BASIC LAW V   Basic Law V is the **abstraction principle**:

$$(\forall X)(\forall Y)(\text{Ext}(X) = \text{Ext}(Y) \leftrightarrow (\forall z)(X(z) \leftrightarrow Y(z)))$$

Basic Law V states that every **concept** has a unique object associated with it, its **extension** (what we would call a **set**). Gottlob Frege used Basic Law V to derive **Hume's Principle**, which can then be used to derive the **Peano axioms** for arithmetic. The **theory** that one obtains from Basic Law V is a form of **naïve set theory**, and, as a result, the **Russell paradox** can be constructed in the theory, showing it to be **inconsistent**.

See also: **Abstraction Operator, Bad Company Objection, Caesar Problem, Frege's Theorem, Mathematical Abstractionism**

BASIS   In a **proof by induction**, the basis is the step in the **proof** where one **demonstrates** that the property in question holds of some initial case(s). For example, if the proof is a **mathematical induction**, then the basis step shows that the property holds of 0, or of some initial segment of the **natural numbers**. In an **induction on the length of well-formed formulas** the basis step typically amounts to demonstrating that the property in question holds of all **atomic formulas** or **propositional letters**.

See also: **Inductive Argument, Transfinite Induction**

BAYES' THEOREM   Within **probability theory**, Bayes' theorem allows us to derive the **probability** of an event occurring in light of new **evidence**. The **theorem** states that:

$$\Pr(A/B) = (\Pr(B/A) \times \Pr(A))/\Pr(B)$$

In other words, the probability of some event A occurring, in light of evidence B, is the probability of the evidence B occurring if A occurs, multiplied by the probability of A occurring *simpliciter*, and then divided by the probability of B occurring *simpliciter*.

See also: **Conditional Probability, Probability Calculus, Probability Logic, Ramsey Test**

BEGGING THE QUESTION   Begging the question is an **informal fallacy** that occurs when a reasoner presents an **argument** for a **conclusion** but omits a crucial **premise**, one whose acceptance would entail prior acceptance of the conclusion.

More generally, the term begging the question (or **petitio principii**) is used for any fallacious argument where the **truth** of the conclusion is already implicit in one or more of the premises.

BERNAYS-GÖDEL SET THEORY see **Von Neumann Bernays Gödel Set Theory**

BERRY PARADOX   The Berry paradox (or **Berry's Paradox**) is the **paradox of denotation** that arises from consideration of the expression:

> The smallest **positive integer** that cannot be uniquely specified in less than 100 characters.

Since there is only a **finite** number of expressions containing no more than 100 characters, there must be a first positive integer which is not denoted by such an expression. Call that integer B. Thus, the offset expression above denotes B. But the expression above contains fewer than 100 characters, so it is, in fact, an expression of fewer than 100 characters that picks out B. **Contradiction**.

Variants of the reasoning underlying the Berry paradox carried out within **first-order arithmetic** have been shown to be intimately connected to **Gödel's first** and **second incompleteness theorems**.

See also: **König Paradox, Richard Paradox**

BERRY'S PARADOX see **Berry Paradox**

BEW see **Provability Predicate**

BHK-INTERPRETATION   On the BHK-interpretation (or **Brouwer-**

Heyting-Kolmogorov interpretation) of the **logical connec-tives** and **quantifiers, truth conditional** clauses are replaced by **proof-theoretic** clauses. The following clauses provide the meaning of the connectives and quantifiers on the BHK interpretation:

A **proof** of A ∧ B is a proof of A and a proof of B.

A proof of A ∨ B is either a proof of A or a proof of B.

A proof of A → B is a construction or procedure which trans-forms a proof of A into a proof of B.

A proof of ~A is a construction or procedure which transforms a proof of A into a proof of **falsum** (that is, ⊥, which by **definition** has no proof).

A proof of (∃x)Φ(x) is a proof of Φ(a) for some a.

A proof of (∀x)Φ(x) is a construction or procedure that provides a proof of Φ(a) for any a.

The BHK-interpretation of the connectives is often used to motivate **intuitionistic logic** or other **constructive logics**.

See also: **Bivalence, Constructive Proof, Excluded Middle, Intuitionism, Logical Antirealism**

BIAS   Any factor that prevents a sample from being representative of the population in question is a bias. More generally, a bias can be any factor that gives preference to a particular outcome or belief independently of any **evidence** for or against that outcome or belief.

See also: **Gambler's Fallacy, Hasty Generalization, Informal Fallacy, Probability Calculus, Probability Theory**

BICONDITIONAL   A biconditional is a **statement** of the form:

A if and only if B

Within **propositional logic**, biconditionals are usually represented as:

A ↔ B

Or as:

A ≡ B

Within **classical logic** the biconditional has the following **truth table**:

P	Q	P ≡ Q
T	T	T
T	F	F
F	T	F
F	F	T

See also: **Deductive Equivalence, Iff, Logical Equivalence, Material Biconditional, Materially Equivalent, T-schema**

BIJECTION   A bijection is a **bijective function**.

See also: **Injection, One-to-One, Onto, Surjection**

BIJECTIVE   A **function** f from a **domain** D to a **range** R is bijective (or **one-to-one onto**) if and only if, for any two distinct **members** of the domain x and y, $f(x) \neq f(y)$ and for any member x of the range there is a y in the domain such that $f(y) = x$. More intuitively, a bijective function maps each member of the domain to exactly one member of the range, and vice versa.

See also: **Injective, Surjective**

BINARY FUNCTION   A binary function (or **dyadic function**) is a **function** that takes two **arguments**, such as "the midpoint between x and y."

See also: **Adicity, Binary Relation**

BINARY RELATION   A binary relation (or **dyadic relation**) is a **relation** that takes two **arguments**, such as "x loves y" or "x is greater than y."

See also: **Adicity, Binary Function**

BIVALENCE   Bivalence (or the **law of bivalence**, or the **principle of bivalence**) is the **metatheoretic** claim that every **statement** is either **true** or **false**. If one is working in a language with a **truth predicate**, bivalence can be expressed in the **metatheory** as:

$$(\forall P)(T(P) \vee T(\sim P))$$

(assuming we read "T(~P)," that is, "the **negation** of P is true," as **equivalent** to "P is false"). Bivalence should not be confused with the **object language** principle of **excluded middle**, although the two are intimately connected.

See also: **Classical Logic, Law of Non-Contradiction, Semantically Closed Language, Weak Excluded Middle**

BOETHIUS' THESES   The following **formulas** in **propositional logic** are Boethius' theses:

$$(A \rightarrow B) \rightarrow \sim (A \rightarrow \sim B)$$

$$(A \rightarrow \sim B) \rightarrow \sim (A \rightarrow B)$$

These formulas are theorems of **connexive logic,** yet are not theorems within **classical logic** – in the classical context Boethius' theses are both equivalent to A.

See also: **Aristotle's Thesis**

BOOLEAN ALGEBRA   A Boolean algebra is a type of lattice consisting of a **set** of **objects** A which contains two distinguished **members** (typically represented by 1 and 0) along with two **binary functions** on A (typically represented by ∩ and ∪) and a **unary function** on A (typically represented by ~) which **satisfy** the following **axioms:**

Associativity:	$A \cap (B \cap C) = (A \cap B) \cap C$
	$A \cup (B \cup C) = (A \cup B) \cup C$
Commutativity:	$A \cap B = B \cap A$
	$A \cup B = B \cup A$
Absorbsion:	$A \cap (A \cup B) = A$
	$A \cup (A \cap B) = A$
Distributivity:	$A \cap (B \cup C) = (A \cap B) \cup (A \cap C)$
	$A \cup (B \cap C) = (A \cup B) \cap (A \cup C)$
Complement:	$A \cup \sim A = 1$
	$A \cap \sim A = 0$

The function ∩ is **meet,** the function ∪ is **join,** the **function** ~ is **complement,** 0 is the minimal element, or the **bottom,** and 1 is the maximal element, or the **top.** The top and bottom of a Boolean algebra are also sometimes represented as T and ⊥ respectively.

Boolean algebras are used to provide **formal semantics** for various logics and are used in the **set theoretic** method of **forcing.**

See also: **Algebraic Logic, Boolean Operator, Logic Gate, Partial Order**

BOOLEAN NEGATION   Boolean negation is the **negation operator** characterized by the following rules:

> ~A is **true** if and only if A is not **true**.

> ~A is **false** if and only if A is not **false**.

Boolean negation is **equivalent** to other versions of negation (such as **DeMorgan negation**) in the context of **classical semantics**, but these negations are non-equivalent in **many-valued logics** such as **first-degree entailment**.

See also: **Boolean Operator, Choice Negation, Exclusion Negation**

BOOLEAN OPERATOR   A Boolean operator is any **function** mapping **n-tuples** of **members** of a **Boolean algebra** onto members of the Boolean algebra. Often within logic we are interested in the 2 **element** Boolean algebra. In this case we can interpret the **top** element as **true**, the **bottom** element as **false**, and the Boolean operations **meet** (∩), **join** (∪), and **complement** (~) correspond to the **classical truth functions** for **conjunction, disjunction**, and **negation**.

See also: **Boolean Negation, Dagger, Sheffer Stroke**

BORDERLINE CASE   An object x is a borderline case of a **predicate** Φ if and only if x is not a clear case of Φ and x is not a clear case of ~Φ. Borderline cases are often associated with **vagueness**.

See also: **Forced March Sorites, Higher-Order Vagueness, In Rebus Vagueness, Semantic Vagueness, Sorites Paradox, Sorites Series**

BOTTOM   The minimal **element** in a **lattice** or **Boolean algebra** is the bottom, and is usually symbolized as "0" or "⊥."

See also: **Falsum, Partial Ordering, Top, Verum**

BOUND VARIABLE   In a **formula** of **first-, second-,** or **higher-order logic**, a **variable** x is a bound variable if it occurs within the **scope** of a **quantifier**. A variable that is not bound by a quantifier is a **free variable**.

See also: **Existential Quantifier, Generalized Quantifier, Universal Quantifier**

BOUNDED QUANTIFIER   In **arithmetic**, a bounded quantifier is a **quantifier** whose instances are restricted to some **initial segment** of the **natural numbers**. Thus, while a **statement** beginning with the standard **universal quantifier**:

$$(\forall x)\Phi x$$

says that all natural numbers **satisfy** Φ, a statement beginning with a bounded universal quantifier:

$$(\forall x < n)\Phi x$$

says that all natural numbers less than n satisfy Φ.

See also: **Finitary Arithmetic, Π-formula, Π-sentence, Σ-formula, Σ-sentence**

BRANCHING QUANTIFIER   A branching quantifier (or **Henkin quantifier**) is a matrix of **first-order quantifiers** that allows for **variable dependencies** that cannot be **expressed** in standard **first-order logic**, which is written with a **linear** notation. For example, in the branching quantifier:

$$\begin{pmatrix}(\forall x)(\exists y)\\(\forall z)(\exists w)\end{pmatrix}\Phi$$

the **existential variable** y **depends** on **the universal variable** x, but not on the universal variable z, and the existential variable w depends on the universal variable z, but not on the universal variable x.

A **logic** which allows branching quantifiers is **expressively** stronger than standard first-order logic, but expressively weaker than **second-order logic**. Certain **statements** in **natural language**, such as the **Geach-Kaplan sentence**, cannot be adequately **formalized** using first-order logic, but can be formalized using branching quantifiers. **Independence-friendly logic** provides a linear notation for branching quantifiers.

See also: **Geach-Kaplan Sentence, Generalized Quantifier, Higher-order Logic, Higher-order Quantifier, Higher-order Variable, Independence-Friendly Logic, Plural Quantification, Second-order Logic**

BROUWER-HEYTING-KOLMOGOROV INTERPRETATION see
   BHK-Interpretation

BROUWERIAN AXIOM see **B**

BROUWERIAN MODAL LOGIC see **B**

BURALI-FORTI PARADOX   The Burali-Forti paradox (or **Burali-Forti's paradox**) shows that the **order-type** of all **ordinal numbers** cannot be an ordinal number or, equivalently, there can be no set of all ordinal numbers. The **paradox** can be easily **derived** once we have the following principle, which is **provable** in most formulations of **set theory**:

   (1) For any ordinal number γ, the order-type of the ordinal numbers less than γ, on the standard **ordering**, is γ.

To derive the paradox, assume that there was an order-type of all ordinal numbers, that is, an ordinal number corresponding to the standard ordering on the collection of all ordinal numbers. Call this order-type Γ. Then, by the principle above, the order-type of the ordinal numbers less than Γ is Γ. So the order-type of the ordinal numbers less than or equal to Γ, that is, the order-type of all the ordinal numbers, is $\Gamma+1$. But this contradicts our assumption that the order-type of all the ordinal numbers is Γ, since $\Gamma \neq \Gamma+1$.

See also: **Iterative Conception of Set, Limitation-of-Size Conception of Set, Russell Paradox, Set-Theoretic Paradox**

BURALI-FORTI'S PARADOX see **Burali-Forti Paradox**

BURIDAN'S SOPHISMATA   Burdian's sophismata is a series of puzzles involving **self-reference** posed by the medieval logician **John Buridan**. Notable among them is a second **sophisma**:

   No **proposition** is **negative**, thus some proposition is negative.

which seems both **valid** and **invalid** at the same time, and his ninth sophisma:

   Plato says: "What Socrates is saying is **true**."
   Socrates says: "What Plato is saying is **false**."

which demonstrates that direct **self-reference**, of the sort found in the **Liar paradox**, is not necessary in order to generate **semantic paradoxes**.

BUSY BEAVER FUNCTION see **Busy Beaver Problem**

BUSY BEAVER MACHINE see **Busy Beaver Problem**

BUSY BEAVER PROBLEM   The busy beaver problem concerns **Turing machines**, which carry out complex **computations** and then halt. Consider Turing machines that begin on a blank tape and eventually halt while scanning the leftmost cell in an unbroken **sequence** of "1"s. For any **natural number** n, let p(n) be the longest such sequence that can be generated by such a Turing machine consisting of n distinct states. (Note that the machine must halt at the end of the sequence of "1"s and, since there are only **finitely** many distinct Turing machines with n states, p(n) must be finite.) The question is, can we design a Turing machine that can compute p(n) (given n as input)? Computing p(n) is the **busy beaver function**, and the hypothetical Turing machine that computes p(n) would be the **busy beaver machine**.

    The answer to our question, however, is "no." The busy beaver function p(n) is not **computable** by a Turing machine, and thus is not **recursive**.

See also: **Automaton, Deterministic Turing Machine, Effectively Computable Function, Halting Problem, Non-Deterministic Turing Machine**

c   c is sometimes used to denote the **cardinality** of the **continuum** – that is, the cardinality of the **set** of **real numbers**. Thus:

$$c = 2^{\aleph_0}$$

See also: **ℶ, Cantor's Theorem, Continuum Hypothesis, Generalized Continuum Hypothesis**

CAESAR PROBLEM   The Caesar problem is an objection to **mathematical abstractionism**. The mathematical abstractionist wishes to use **Hume's Principle**:

$$(\forall P)(\forall Q)(NUM(P) = NUM(Q) \leftrightarrow P \approx Q)$$

as an **implicit definition** of the concept "**cardinal number**." If Hume's Principle is a definition of number, however, then it should tell us which objects in particular the cardinal numbers are. Hume's Principle alone fails to achieve this; although it provides a test for determining whether or not two cardinal numbers are **identical**, it is silent on the issue of whether the numbers might be identical to other familiar objects. In particular, Hume's Principle is **consistent** with the claim that one of the numbers is identical to Julius Caesar.

See also: **Abstraction, Abstraction Operator, Abstraction Principle, Bad Company Objection**

CALCULUS see **Formal System**

CALCULUS OF INDIVIDUALS   The calculus of individuals is theory of **mereology** developed by Nelson Goodman and Henry Leonard. The theory was intended to replace **set theory** within science and philosophy, providing these disciplines with a **nominalistically** respectable foundation.

See also: **Atom, Classical Mereology, Individual, Parthood**

CANTOR PARADOX   The Cantor paradox shows that there cannot be a **set** of all sets – a **universal set** – and depends on **Cantor's theorem**, which demonstrates that the **powerset** of a set cannot be placed into **one-to-one** correspondence with that set itself. To derive the **paradox**, assume that there is a set of all sets. Then that set must contain, as **members**, all of its **subsets**. The **identity function**, mapping each set to itself, would then provide a one-to-one mapping from the members of the powerset of the universal set to the members of the universal set itself, violating Cantor's theorem. **Contradiction**.

See also: **Burali-Forti Paradox, New Foundations, Russell Paradox**

CANTOR'S DIAGONALIZATION THEOREM see **Cantor's Theorem**

CANTOR'S PARADOX see **Cantor Paradox**

CANTOR'S THEOREM   Cantor's theorem (or **Cantor's Diagonalization Theorem**) states that the **cardinal number** of the

powerset of a **set** is strictly greater than the cardinal number of the set itself. The **theorem** can be **proved** as follows. First, the cardinal number of the powerset of a set A is clearly greater than, or equal to, the cardinal number of A itself, since there is a **one-to-one function** from the powerset of A to A – merely map each object onto its **singleton**. We can show that no **function** can map A **onto** the powerset of A, and that the cardinal number of the powerset of A is not equal to the cardinal number of A.

Let f be any function from A to the powerset of A. Consider the following set B:

$$B = \{x \in A : x \notin f(x)\}$$

that is, the set of all objects in A that are not **members** of their **image** under the function f. The function f cannot "hit" B. Assume that it did, that is, that there is some m in A such that f(m) = B. Now, by the **definition** of B, m is a member of B if and only if m is a member of A and m is not a member of f(m). We know m is a member of A, so this simplifies to: m is a member of B if and only if m is not a member of f(m). Since f(m) = B, this is then **equivalent** to m is a member of B if and only if m is not a member of B. This is a **contradiction**, so by **reductio ad absurdum** we know that there is no m such that f(m) = B. In other words, f "misses" B, and is not onto. Since f was completely arbitrary, this shows that there can be no onto function from A to the powerset of A. Thus, the cardinal number of the powerset of A is greater than the cardinal number of A.

This proof is an example of a **diagonalization proof**.

See also: **c, Continuum Hypothesis, Fixed Point, Generalized Continuum Hypothesis**

CARDINAL see **Cardinal Number**

CARDINAL ARITHMETIC Cardinal arithmetic is the **theory** governing the extension of the standard **functions** of **arithmetic**, such as addition and multiplication, to **infinite cardinal numbers**.

See also: **König's Lemma, Ordinal Arithmetic**

CARDINAL NUMBER A cardinal number (or **cardinal**) is the **number** assigned to a **set**. For **finite sets**, the cardinal number will be the same as the **ordinal number** and is just a **natural number**. For example, the cardinal number of the set {a, b, c} is 3.

Infinite sets receive cardinal numbers as well. The cardinal number of the set of **natural numbers** (i.e. $\{0, 1, 2, 3 \ldots\}$) is $\aleph_0$, and is the first **infinite** cardinal number. The cardinal number of the set of **countable ordinal numbers** is $\aleph_1$, and is the next cardinal number. The next cardinal number after that is $\aleph_2$, and so on.

See also: $\aleph$, **Cardinal Successor, Large Cardinal, Limit Cardinal, Regular Cardinal**

CARDINAL PREDECESSOR see **Cardinal Successor**

CARDINAL SUCCESSOR   The cardinal successor of a **cardinal number** is the next greater cardinal number. In "$\aleph$" notation, the cardinal successor of $\aleph_\gamma$ is $\aleph_{\gamma+1}$. Given an arbitrary cardinal number κ, the cardinal successor of κ can also be written $\kappa+$. If n is the cardinal successor of m, then m is the **cardinal predecessor** of n.

See also: **Limit Cardinal, Ordinal Successor, Transfinite Induction, Transfinite Recursion**

CARDINALITY   The cardinality (or **power**) of a **set** is the **cardinal number** associated with that set. Two sets have the same cardinality if and only if they receive the same cardinal number – that is, if they have the same number of **members**.

See also: $\aleph$, $\beth$, c, **Cardinal Successor, Large Cardinal, Limit Cardinal**

CARNAP-RAMSEY SENTENCE see **Ramsey Sentence**

CARTESIAN PRODUCT   The Cartesian product (or **product**) of two **sets** A and B is the set of all **ordered pairs** <x, y> such that x is a **member** of A and y is a member of B. The **cardinal number** of the Cartesian product of A and B is the product (that is, multiplication) of the cardinal numbers of A and B. The Cartesian product of A and B is usually denoted A × B.

See also: **Cardinal Arithmetic, Ordered N-tuple, Unordered Pair**

CATEGOREMATIC TERM see **Syncategorematic Term**

CATEGORICAL   A **theory** is categorical if all of its **models** are

isomorphic. In other words, a categorical theory is one such that any two of its models have the same structure.

See also: **Downward Lowenheim-Skolem Theorem, κ-Categorical, Non-Standard Arithmetic, Non-Standard Analysis, Non-Standard Model, Upward Lowenheim-Skolem Theorem**

CATEGORICAL IN κ see **κ-Categorical**

CATEGORICAL LOGIC₁   Categorical logic (or **Aristotelian logic**) is a **formal system** developed by Aristotle in ancient Greece. Categorical logic studies the **valid** and **invalid syllogisms**, or two-**premise arguments**, formed out of various combinations of the four types of **categorical proposition**: **A-propositions, E-propositions, I-propositions**, and **O-propositions**. Categorical logic was the main focus within **logic** until the introduction of **quantificational** logic in the late nineteenth century.

See also: **Square of Opposition, Term Logic, Venn Diagram**

CATEGORICAL LOGIC₂   Categorical logic is a **non-standard logic** developed by treating both the **semantics** and the **deductive system** of the logic as **categories** (in particular, as **topoi**). There are fundamental connections between categorical logic and **intuition-istic logic**.

See also: **Category Theory, Constructive Logic, Constructive Proof, Topos Theory**

CATEGORICAL PROPOSITION   A categorical proposition is any **statement** of the **form**:

   [**quantifier**] P [**copula**-phrase] Q

where P and Q are **predicates**, and where the quantifier is either "all" or "some," and the copula-phrase is either "are" or "are not." If the quantifier is "all," then the proposition is **universal**, and if the quantifier is "some," then the proposition is **particular**. If the copula-phrase is "are," then the proposition is **affirmative**, and if the copula-phrase is "are not," then the proposition is **negative**. The first predicate (P) is the **subject term** of the proposition and the second predicate (Q) is the **predicate term**.

   The **logical form** of a categorical proposition is denoted by a vowel:

A-Proposition: All P are Q.

E-proposition: All P are not Q.

I-proposition: Some P are not Q.

O-proposition: Some P are not Q.

E-propositions are often written as "No P are Q."

See also: **Distribution, Existential Import, Quality, Quantity, Square of Opposition**

CATEGORICAL SYLLOGISM A categorical syllogism is an **argument** in **categorical logic** which has two **premises**, and where each **term** occurs twice. Categorical syllogisms are characterized in terms of **syllogistic figure** and **syllogistic mood**. The mood of a categorical syllogism is determined by which type of **categorical proposition** (**A-proposition, E-proposition, I-proposition,** or **O-proposition**) occurs as first premise, second premise, and **conclusion**. The figure of a categorical syllogism is determined by how the three terms are distributed within the argument.

See also: **Fallacy of Four Terms, Major Premise, Major Term, Middle Term, Minor Premise, Minor Term**

CATEGORY A category is one of the **structures** or **classes** of structures studied by **category theory**. There are different presentations of category theory, but the most common one **defines** a category to be a **set** of objects C, supplemented with a binary operation Hom(X, Y) where:

(1) For any X, Y in C, Hom(X, Y), the morphisms from X to Y is a set of mappings (or **functions**) from X to Y. If f is a morphism from X to Y, then we write f: $X \to Y$.

(2) For any X, Y, and Z in C, and any f: $X \to Y$ in Hom(X, Y) and g: $Y \to Z$ in Hom(Y, Z), the **composition** of f and g exists; that is, there is a binary mapping $\circ$ from Hom(X, Y) × Hom (Y, Z) to Hom(X, Z). The composition of f and g is g $\circ$ f, and is in Hom(X, Z).

(3) For any object X in C, there is a morphism id_X in Hom(X, X), the **identity** on X, such that $id_X \circ f = f = f \circ id_X$.

(4) Composition of morphisms is **associative**: For any f: $X \to$

Y, g: Y → Z, and h: Z → W, we have:
h $\circ$ (g $\circ$ h) = (f $\circ$ g) $\circ$ h.

Two of the most important categories are the category of **sets** and the category of categories.

See also: **Categorical Logic, Set Theory, Topos, Topos Theory**

CATEGORY THEORY   Category theory is the **mathematical** study of **structures**, systems of structures, and their interrelations – all of which are **categories**. Thus, category theory is the study of categories. Category theory has been suggested as an alternative to **set theory** as the appropriate framework within which to study the **foundations of mathematics** and **logic**.

See also: **Categorical Logic, Topos, Topos Theory**

CAUSAL LOGIC see **Causal Modal Logic**

CAUSAL MODAL LOGIC   Causal modal logic (or **causal logic**) is the branch of **modal logic** that studies the **unary modal operator** "it is casually necessary that ...," which is usually **formalized** as "$\boxed{c}$."

See also: **Alethic Modal Logic, Kripke Semantics, Kripke Structure, Normal Modal Logic**

CHARACTERISTIC FUNCTION$_1$ Given a **set** A, the characteristic function of A is the **unary function** f such that $f(x) = 1$ if x is a **member** of A, and $f(x) = 0$ if x is not a member of A.

See also: **Primitive Recursive Set, Recursive Set**

CHARACTERISTIC FUNCTION$_2$ Given a **n-ary relation** R, the characteristic function of R is the **n-ary function** f such that $f(x_1, x_2, \dots x_n) = 1$ if $Rx_1, x_2, \dots x_n$ is **true**, and $f(x_1, x_2, \dots x_n) = 0$ if $R\ x_1, x_2, \dots x_n$ is **false**.

See also: **Primitive Recursive Relation, Recursive Function Theory, Recursive Relation, Recursive Set**

CHOICE see **Axiom of Choice, Choice Function, Choice Set**

CHOICE FUNCTION   A choice function on a **set** S is a **function** mapping S to the **union** of S such that, for any x in S, f(x) is a

member of x. Essentially, given a set of sets, a choice function maps each set to one of its members. The **axiom of choice** can be understood as asserting that for every non-empty set of sets S there is a choice function on S.

See also: **Axiom of Countable Choice, Axiom of Dependent Choice, Choice Set, Global Choice, Zorn's Lemma**

CHOICE NEGATION Within **three-valued logic**, choice negation (or **internal negation**) is the **unary logical connective** whose associated **truth function** outputs **true** if the **statement** being negated is **false**, outputs false if the statement being negated is true, and outputs the third value (whatever that is – for example, a **truth value gap** or **truth value glut**) whenever the sentence being negated takes the third value. Thus, the **truth table** for choice negation (where N is the third value) is:

A	~ A
T	F
N	N
F	T

See also: **Boolean Negation, Bottom, DeMorgan Negation, Exclusion Negation, Falsum**

CHOICE SEQUENCE see **Free Choice Sequence**

CHOICE SET A choice set for a set S is a **set** containing exactly one **member** from each set contained in S. The **axiom of choice** can be understood as asserting that for each non-empty set of sets S there is a choice set for S.

See also: **Axiom of Countable Choice, Axiom of Dependent Choice, Choice Function, Global Choice, Zorn's Lemma**

CHRONOLOGICAL LOGIC see **Temporal Modal Logic**

CHURCH'S THEOREM Church's Theorem states that **validity** in **first-order logic** is not **decidable** – that is, there is no **decision procedure** for determining, of an arbitrary **formula** from a **first-order language**, whether or not it is a **logical truth**.

See also: **Entscheidungsproblem, Limitation Result, Meta-**

theorem, **Recursively Axiomatizable Theory, Semi-Decidable Theory**

CHURCH'S THESIS see **Church-Turing Thesis**

CHURCH-TURING THESIS The Church-Turing thesis (or **Church's thesis**, or **Turing's thesis**) is the hypothesis that any **effectively computable function** can be computed by a **Turing machine**. Later results showed that this is **equivalent** to the claims that: (i) any effectively computable function is a **recursive function**, (ii) any effectively computable function is **definable** in the λ-**calculus**, and (iii) any effectively computable function is **register computable**.

See also: **Decision Procedure, Deterministic Turing Machine, Effective Procedure, Non-Deterministic Turing Machine, Recursive Function Theory, Turing Computable Function**

CLASS A class is any collection of objects. Some classes correspond to **sets** (that is, they are collections that can be coherently treated as objects, and thus can be **members** of other classes and sets), but the **Russell paradox** shows that not all classes can be sets. Those classes that are too large, or otherwise too ill-behaved, to be treated as sets are **proper classes**.

See also: **Absolute Infinite, Element, Von Neumann Bernays Gödel Set Theory**

CLASS COMPREHENSION SCHEMA Within **Von Neuman Bernays Gödel Set Theory**, the class comprehension schema is the following **axiom schema** guaranteeing the existence of **proper classes**:

If Φ is a **formula** with all **quantifiers** restricted to **sets**, and Φ contains x as a **free variable**, then:

$$(\exists y)(\forall x)(x \in y \leftrightarrow \Phi)$$

is an **axiom**.

One obtains **Morse-Kelley set theory** by lifting the restriction on the type of formulas that can occur in the class comprehension schema.

See also: **Kripke-Platek Set Theory, New Foundations, Positive**

Set Theory, Ramified Type Theory, Simple Type Theory, Zermelo Fraenkel Set Theory

CLASSICAL DILEMMA Classical dilemma (or **proof by cases**) is the **rule of inference** that allows one to move from a **proof** that A **entails** B and a second proof that ~ A entails B to **concluding** that B is the case. In symbols, we have:

$$
\begin{array}{cc}
\overline{A} & \overline{\sim A} \\
\vdots & \vdots \\
\vdots & \vdots \\
B & B \\
\hline
B &
\end{array}
$$

where the horizontal lines above A and ~ A indicate that these assumptions have been **discharged** – that is, that the proof no longer depends on them.

See also: **Classical Reductio ad Abusurdum, Conditional Proof, Excluded Middle, Natural Deduction, Reductio ad Absurdum**

CLASSICAL LOGIC Classical logic contains all of the following **theorems** and **rules of inference**:

Double Negation:	$A \leftrightarrow (\sim \sim A)$
Excluded Middle:	$(A \vee \sim A)$
Non-Contradiction:	$\sim (A \wedge \sim A)$
DeMorgan's Laws:	$\sim (A \wedge B) \leftrightarrow (\sim A \vee \sim B)$
	$\sim (A \vee B) \leftrightarrow (\sim A \wedge \sim B)$
Explosion:	$(B \wedge \sim B) \rightarrow A$
Monotonicity:	If Δ entails A, then Δ, Φ entails A.

While the above list is not sufficient to pick out exactly one **formal logic**, the vast majority of **non-classical logics** of interest to logicians reject one or more of the above principles.

From a **semantic** perspective, classical logic accepts both **bivalence** and the **law of non-contradiction** – that is, classical logic assumes that each statement receives exactly one of the **true** and the **false** as its **semantic value**. Classical logic also requires **truth functionality** – that is, that each **compound statement** receives its semantic value as a **function** of the semantic values of its constituent statements.

Typically, when the term "classical logic" is used without modification it is classical **propositional** or classical **first–order logic** that is being referred to. Extensions of classical logic, such as **normal modal logics,** are also sometimes referred to as classical logics (e.g. classical modal logic) in order to distinguish them from logics obtained by similarly extending non–classical logics (e.g. **intuitionistic** modal logic).

See also: **Classical Dilemma, Classical Reductio ad Absurdum, Model Theory, Truth Tables**

CLASSICAL MEREOLOGY Classical mereology (or **general mereology**) is the **mereological** theory obtained by assuming that the **parthood relation** is a **partial ordering**:

> **Reflexive:** $\quad\quad\quad (\forall x)(Pxx)$
>
> **Transitive:** $\quad\quad\quad (\forall x)(\forall y)(\forall z)((Pxy \land Pyz) \to Pxz)$
>
> **Antisymmetric:** $\quad (\forall x)(\forall y)((Pxy \land Pyx) \to x = y)$

and that the **unrestricted fusion** principle (where O is the defined **overlap relation**):

> $(\exists x)\Phi(x) \to (\exists y)(\forall z)(Ozy \to (\exists w)(\Phi(w) \land Ozw))$

holds.

See also: **Composition, Mereological Extensionality, Mereological Fusion, Proper Parthood, Underlap**

CLASSICAL REDUCTIO see **Classical Reductio ad Absurdum**

CLASSICAL REDUCTIO AD ABSURDUM Classical reductio ad absurdum (or **classical reductio**) is the **rule of inference** that allows one to **infer** a **formula** from a derivation whose assumption is the **negation** of the formula in question, and which terminates in a **contradiction**. In symbols we have:

$$\overline{\sim P}$$
$$\vdots$$
$$\vdots$$
$$\frac{Q \land \sim Q}{P}$$

where the horizontal line above ~ P indicates that this assumptions has been **discharged** – that is, that the proof no longer depends on it. Classical reductio ad absurdum should be distinguished from the weaker rule of inference known merely as **reductio ad absurdum**.

See also: **Classical Dilemma, Double Negation, Double Negation Elimination, Double Negation Introduction**

CLAVIUS' LAW see **Consequentia Miribilis**

CLOSED FORMULA see **Open Formula**

CLOSED TERM see **Open Term**

CLOSURE see **Transitive Closure**

CO-DOMAIN see **Range**

CO-EXTENSIVE   Two **sets** are co–extensive if and only if they contain exactly the same objects as **members**. Given the **axiom of extensionality**, this amounts to saying that two sets are co–extensive if and only if they are **identical**.

See also: **Extension**

COFINALITY   The cofinality of an **ordinal number** γ (written as $\text{co}(\gamma)$) is the least ordinal number that can be mapped unboundedly into γ – in other words, the cofinality of γ is the least ordinal number δ such that there is a **function** f from δ to γ such that, for any α that is a member of γ, there is a β in δ such that $f(\beta)$ is greater than or equal to α.

See also: **Axiom of Replacement, Regular Cardinal, Regular Ordinal, Strongly Inaccessible Cardinal, Weakly Inaccessible Cardinal**

COFINITE   A **set** is cofinite if and only if the collection of objects not in the set (its **complement**) is **finite**.

See also: **Relative Complement, Symmetric Difference**

COGENT INDUCTIVE ARGUMENT   A cogent inductive argument is a **strong inductive argument** where all of the **premises** are **true**.

See also: **Abduction, Fallacy, Informal Fallacy, Strong Inductive Argument**

COHERENCE THEORY OF TRUTH   The coherence theory of truth is the view that a **statement** is **true** if and only if it coheres with the **set** of all truths. Thus, on this view, the **statement** "The cat is on the mat" is true if and only if it coheres (better than its **negation**, at least) with the set of all other truths (which themselves are true in virtue of coherence). Unlike the **correspondence theory of truth**, which treats truth as a **relation** between individual statements and the world, the coherence theory of truth is best understood as attributing truth, not to individual sentences, but to **theories** as a whole.

See also: **Deflationism, Disquotationalism, Minimalism, Prosentential Theory of Truth, Redundancy Theory of Truth**

COLLECTIVE PREDICATION see **Distributive Predication**

COMBINATOR   A combinator is a **higher–order** functional expression which contains no **free variables**. Within **combinatory logic, combinatory terms** are formed by applying combinators to previously **defined** combinatory terms (which include **unbound variables** and primitive combinators).

See also: **Function, λ-Calculus, Singular Term**

COMBINATORIAL SET THEORY   Combinatorial set theory is the branch of **set theory** dealing with combinatorial problems and methods. Of particular interest within combinatorial set theory is the study of trees and of **partitions** on **infinite sets**.

See also: **Axiom of Constructibility, Axiom of Powerset, Axiom of Replacement, Descriptive Set Theory, König's Lemma, Zorn's Lemma**

COMBINATORIALISM   Combinatorialism is the view that any arbitrary combination of **elements** constitutes a legitimate mathematical **structure**, whether that structure is **definable** or not – in other words, combinatorialists accept the existence of absolutely arbitrary **functions, sets**, etc. Combinatorialism is contrasted with **definibilism**, where all mathematical objects are definable. Definibilism was the default view throughout much of the history of mathematics, although in the last century and a half there has been a decided turn in favor of combinatorialism.

See also: **Axiom of Constructibility, Combinatorial Set Theory, Constructible Set, Definable Set, Hierarchy**

COMBINATORY LOGIC Combinatory logic is a **logic** which eliminates the need for **bound variables** by making use of a special sort of functional expression called a **combinator**. Combinatory logics are **expressively** and **deductively** stronger than standard **first-order logic**, and the standard presentation of combinatory logic is **equivalent** in strength to the λ-**calculus**.

COMBINATORY TERMS see **Combinator**

COMMUTATIVITY   A **binary relation** R is commutative if and only if, for all a and b:

R(a, b)

holds if and only if:

R(b, a)

holds. Similarly, a two–place **function** f is commutative if and only if, for all a and b, we have:

f(a, b) = f(b, a)

See also: **Associativity, Boolean Algebra, Distributivity, Join, Lattice, Meet**

COMMUTATIVITY$_2$ Within **propositional logic**, a **connective** * is commutative if and only if:

A * B

and:

B * A

are **logically equivalent. Conjunction** and **disjunction** are typically commutative, while the **conditional** is not.

See also: **Abelian Logic, Classical Logic, Non-Commutative Logic, Permutation**

COMPACT CARDINAL   A compact cardinal is type of **large cardinal number**.

See also: **Large Cardinal Axiom, Strongly Inaccessible Cardinal, Weakly Inaccessible Cardinal**

COMPACTNESS   A **logic** is compact if and only if, whenever there is a **set** of **premises** Δ and a **conclusion** Φ such that Φ is a **logical consequence** of Δ, there is a **finite subset** Δ^* of Δ such that Φ is a logical consequence of Δ^*. The term "compactness" has its origin in the idea of treating the collection of **sets** of **logical formulas** as a topological space, in which case the logical notion of compactness is a specific instance of the more general topological notion.

See also: **Categorical, Downward Lowenheim-Skolem Theorem, Limitation Result, Metatheorem, Model Theory, Upward Lowenheim-Skolem Theorem**

COMPARABILITY see **Trichotomy**

COMPLEMENT₁   The complement of a set A is the **set** that contains, as **members**, exactly the objects that are not members of A. In other words, the complement of A is:

$$\{x : x \notin A\}$$

In most familiar formulations of **set theory** if a set exists, then its complement does not.

See also: **Anti-extension, Disjoint, Exclusive, Exhaustive, Relative Complement, Symmetric Difference**

COMPLEMENT₂   Within **Boolean algebra** or the theory of **lattices**, complement is the **unary function** "~" which satisfies:

$$A \cup \sim A = 1$$

$$A \cap \sim A = 0$$

See also: **Absorbsion, Associativity, Commutativity, Distributivity, Join, Meet**

COMPLETE INDUCTION see **Strong Mathematical Induction**

COMPLETE INFINITY   A complete infinity (or **actual infinity**) is an **infinite** collection that exists as a finished totality. Complete infinities are contrasted with **potentially infinite** collections, which are always **finite** (at a time), but which can be extended without limit. The distinction, attributed to Aristotle, was intended to help clear up confusions about infinity brought about by puzzles such as the **Zeno paradoxes**.

See also: **Absolute Infinite, Dedekind Infinite, Indefinite Extensibility, Simply Infinite**

COMPLETE SET OF CONNECTIVES see **Expressive Completeness**

COMPLETE THEORY see **Negation Completeness, Strong Completeness, Weak Completeness**

COMPLETENESS₁ see **Expressive Completeness, Negation Completeness, Strong Completeness, Weak Completeness**

COMPLETENESS₂ A **partial ordering** is complete if and only if every set of **elements** in the order that has an **upper bound** has a **least upper bound**, and every set of **elements** that has a **lower bound** has a **greatest lower bound**.

See also: **Boolean Algebra, Join, Lattice, Meet**

COMPLETENESS₃ see **Connected**

COMPLEX EXPRESSION see **Compound Statement**

COMPLEX STATEMENT see **Compound Statement**

COMPLEXITY CLASS **Recursive functions** are categorized into complexity classes based on the relative difficulty of **computing** values of those **functions**. The most important complexity classes are **P**, **NP**, and **NP-complete**.

See also: **Automaton, Deterministic Polynomial Time, Non-Deterministic Polynomial Time, Recursive Function Theory**

COMPLEXITY THEORY Complexity theory is the mathematical study of the relative **computational** difficulty of computing values of **recursive functions**. Recursive functions are organized into **complexity classes**, the most important of which are **P**, **NP**, and **NP-complete**. In addition to categorizing **classes** of **functions** into complexity classes, complexity theory also analyzes the **relations** between these classes.

See also: **Automaton, Deterministic Polynomial Time, Non-Deterministic Polynomial Time, Recursive Function Theory**

COMPOSITION₁   The composition of two **functions** f and g is the function h such that, for all inputs x:

$$h(x) = g(f(x))$$

In other words, the composition of f and g is the function resulting from applying f and then g to an **argument**. The composition of f and g is usually written as:

$$(g \circ f)$$

See also: **Domain, Field, Image, Inverse, Range**

COMPOSITION₂   Composition is one of the simple **function**-building operations of **recursive function theory**. Given a **computable** n-ary function f and a series of n computable m-ary functions $g_1, g_2, \ldots g_n$, the composition of f and the g_i's is the function h such that:

$$h(x_1, x_2, \ldots x_m) = f(g_1(x_1, x_2, \ldots x_m), g_2(x_1, x_2, \ldots x_m), \ldots g_n(x_1, x_2, \ldots x_m))$$

See also: **Identity Function, Minimization, Primitive Recursion, Successor Function, Zero Function**

COMPOSITION₃   Composition is the **relation** that holds between an object and its **parts**. If $a_1, a_2, a_3 \ldots$ are all of the parts of object d, then d is composed of $a_1, a_2, a_3 \ldots$ (or d is composed of some suitably comprehensive sub-collection of $a_1, a_2, a_3 \ldots$).

See also: **Calculus of Individuals, Fallacy of Composition, Fallacy of Division, Mereological Extensionality, Mereology, Proper Parthood**

COMPOSITION see **Fallacy of Composition**

COMPOSITIONALITY   Compositionality is the view that the meaning of a complex expression, such as a **compound statement**, is a **function** solely of the meaning of its constituent **parts** and the manner in which those constituents are combined to form the complex expression – that is, its **logical form**. Compositionality is often contrasted with views of meaning where additional factors contribute to the meaning of expressions, such as **contextualism** or **holism**.

See also: **Compound Formula, Connective, Formation Rules, Quantifier, Semantics, Truth Functionality**

COMPOUND EXPRESSION see **Compound Statement**

COMPOUND FORMULA A compound formula (or **complex formula**, or **molecule**) is a formula that is composed of other, simpler **formulas**. Compound formulas are typically formed by prefixing a formula with **negation** (~), joining two or more statements together with a binary **connective** such as **conjunction** (∧), **disjunction** (∨), or **material implication** (→), or by prefixing a formula with a **quantifier** (∃, ∀) or **modal operator** (□, ◇).

See also: **Atomic Formula, Atomic Sentence, Compound Statement, Formation Rules, Well-Formed Formula**

COMPOUND STATEMENT A compound statement (or **complex statement**, or **complex expression**, or **compound expression**) is a **statement** that is **composed** of other, simpler statements.

See also: **Atomic Formula, Atomic Sentence, Compound Formula, Formation Rules, Well-Formed Formula**

COMPREHENSION SCHEMA₁ The comprehension schema (or **naïve comprehension schema**) states that, for any **predicate** $\Phi(x)$, there exists a **set** that contains as **members** exactly the objects that **satisfy** $\Phi(x)$.

In **first-order logic** supplemented with the membership symbol "∈," we can provide the following **axiom schema**, which provides a particular instance of the comprehension schema for each individual predicate Φ not containing x as a **free variable**:

$$(\exists x)(\forall y)(y \in x \leftrightarrow \Phi(y))$$

The **set-theoretic** comprehension schema is **inconsistent** – one can derive the **Russell paradox** from it.

See also: **Burali-Forti Paradox, Indefinite Extensibility, Iterative Conception of Set, Limitation-of-Size Conception of Set**

COMPREHENSION SCHEMA₂ Within **second-order logic**, the comprehension schema is an **axiom schema** asserting that, for every predicate $\Phi(x)$, there is a **concept** that holds of exactly the objects that satisfy $\Phi(x)$. This can be expressed formally as:

$$(\exists X)(\forall y)(X(y) \leftrightarrow \Phi(y))$$

See also: **Geach-Kaplan Sentence, Higher-order Quantifier, Higher-order Logic, Higher-order Variable, Plural Quantification**

COMPUTABILITY THEORY see **Recursive Function Theory**

COMPUTABLE FUNCTION see **Effectively Computable Function, Recursive Function**

COMPUTABLE SET see **Effectively Computable Set, Recursive Set**

COMPUTABLY ENUMERABLE SET see **Effectively Enumerable Set, Enumerable Set, Recursively Enumerable Set**

COMPUTATION A computation is any (usually **finite**) process that can be represented mathematically. Alternatively, a computation is the result of following an **algorithm**. **Recursive function theory** is the branch of **mathematical logic** that studies (among other things) which **functions** are **computable** – that is, which functions are such that we can determine the value of that function for particular **arguments** based on certain sorts of computation.

See also: **Automaton, Church-Turing Thesis, Complexity Class, Effectively Computable Function, Recursive Function**

CONCEPT A concept (or **attribute**, or **property**) is either an abstract object or a mental entity (often called an "idea") which is, or corresponds to, the meaning of a **predicate**.

Within logic, however, concepts are more often thought of as the **referent** (if there are such) of **predicates** (note that this latter understanding could just be a special case of the former). Along these lines the concept "redness" would be the referent of the predicate "is red." As a result, the **second-order quantifiers** are often interpreted as ranging over concepts.

See also: **Comprehension Schema, Empty Concept, Higher-**

order Logic, Indefinite Extensibility

CONCLUSION In an **argument**, the conclusion is that **statement** for which the other **statements** (the **premises**) are intended to provide evidence or support.

See also: **Deductive Argument, Double Turnstile, Inductive Argument, Logical Form, Single Turnstile**

CONCRETE OBJECT see **Abstract Object**

CONDITIONAL A conditional is a **statement** of the form:

If A then B

Within **propositional logic**, conditionals are usually represented as:

A → B

Or:

A ⊃ B

The term "conditional" is also used to **denote**, not the entire **statement**:

A → B

but rather the **logical operator** represented by "→."

Within classical logic the conditional (the **material conditional**) has the following **truth table**:

P	Q	P → Q
T	T	T
T	F	F
F	T	T
F	F	T

See also: **Antecedent, Consequent, Counterfactual Conditional, Indicative Conditional, Subjunctive Conditional, Strict Conditional**

CONDITIONAL ELIMINATION see **Modus Ponens**

CONDITIONAL INTRODUCTION see **Conditional Proof**

CONDITIONAL LOGIC Conditional logic (or the **logic of conditionals**) refers to any of a number of **formal systems** which attempt to eliminate the defects of the **material conditional** by supplementing or replacing it with a **conditional** whose **truth conditions** are given using **possible worlds semantics**. Thus, conditional logics are a form of **modal logic** where, instead of using **unary sentential operators** such as **necessity** ($\Box$) and **possibility** ($\Diamond$), the primary **modal operator** is a **binary operator**, the conditional.

See also: **Alethic Modal Logic, Kripke Semantics, Kripke Structure**

CONDITIONAL PROBABILITY The conditional probability of A given that B, where A and B are **statements,** is the **probability** that A will occur in light of the fact that B has occurred. The conditional probability of A given that B is usually written **Pr(A/B)** or P(A/B).

See also: **Bayes' Theorem, Probability Calculus, Probability Logic, Probability Theory, Ramsey Test**

CONDITIONAL PROOF Conditional proof (or **conditional introduction**) is the **rule of inference** that allows one to **infer** a **conditional** from a **derivation** whose assumption is the **antecedent**, and which terminates at the **consequent** of that **conditional**. In symbols we have:

$$
\begin{array}{c}
\overline{P} \\
\vdots \\
\vdots \\
\underline{Q} \\
P \rightarrow Q
\end{array}
$$

where the horizontal line above P indicates that this assumptions has been **discharged** – that is, that the proof no longer depends on it.

See also: **Affirming the Consequent, Deduction Theorem, Denying the Antecedent, Introduction Rule, Modus Ponens, Modus Tollens**

CONDITIONALIZATION The conditionalization (or **corresponding conditional**) of an **argument** is the **conditional** obtained by taking the **conjunction** of the **premises** of the argument as **antecedent** and the **conclusion** of the argument as **consequent**.

Thus, the conditionalization of **modus ponens**:

A
A → B
B

is:

(A ∧ (A → B)) → B

See also: **Consequence Relation, Deduction Theorem, Exportation, Material Conditional**

CONGRUENCE RELATION₁ A **relation** R is a congruence relation on a **set** of objects S with an n-ary **function** f if and only if R is an **equivalence relation** on S and, for any members x_1, x_2, ... x_n, y_1, y_2, ... y_n of S, if $R(x_1, y_1)$, $R(x_2, y_2)$, ... $R(x_n, y_n)$, then $f(x_1, x_2, ... x_n) = f(y_1, y_2, ... y_n)$.

See also: **Automorphism, Elementary Equivalence, Equivalence Class, Isomorphism**

CONGUENCE RELATION₂ A **relation** R is a congruence relation on a **set** of objects S with an n-ary **relation** P if and only if R is an **equivalence relation** on S and, for any members x_1, x_2, ... x_n, y_1, y_2, ... y_n of S, if $R(x_1, y_1)$, $R(x_2, y_2)$, ... $R(x_n, y_n)$, then $P(x_1, x_2, ... x_n)$ is **true** if and only if $P(y_1, y_2, ... y_n)$ is true.

See also: **Automorphism, Elementary Equivalence, Equivalence Class, Isomorphism**

CONJUNCT The conjuncts of a **conjunction** are the **subsentences** of that **conjunction** that occur to either side of the "and" (or to either side of the **formal language** counterpart to "and," e.g. "∧").

See also: **Conjunction Elimination, Conjunction Introduction, Conjunctive Normal Form, Wedge**

CONJUNCTION A conjunction is a **statement** of the form:

A and B

Within **propositional logic**, conjunctions are usually represented as:

A ∧ B

or:

A · B

or:

A & B

The term "conjunction" is also used to **denote**, not the entire statement:

A ∧ B

but the **logical operator** represented by "∧."

Sometimes the term conjunction is used to designate a **sequence** of formulas linked by the conjunction operator, such as:

P ∧ Q ∧ R ∧ S

Within **classical logic** conjunction has the following **truth table**:

P	Q	P ∧ Q
T	T	T
T	F	F
F	T	F
F	F	F

See also: **Associativity, Conjunct, Conjunction Elimination, Conjunction Introduction, Conjunctive Normal Form, Wedge**

CONJUNCTION ELIMINATION   Conjuction elimination (or **and elimination,** or **simplification**) is the **rule of inference** that allows one to **infer** either **conjunct** of a conjunction from the conjunction itself. In symbols we have:

$$\frac{A \wedge B}{A}$$

or:

$$\frac{A \wedge B}{B}$$

See also: **Conjunction Introduction, Elimination Rule, Natural Deduction**

CONJUNCTION INTRODUCTION   Conjuction introduction (or **and introduction,** or **adjunction**) is the **rule of inference** that allows one to **infer** a conjuction from both of the conjuncts individually. In symbols we have:

$$\frac{A \quad B}{A \wedge B}$$

See also: **Conjunction Elimination, Introduction Rule, Natural Deduction**

CONJUNCTIVE NORMAL FORM   A **formula** is in conjunctive normal form if and only if it is a **conjunction** of **disjunctions**, where each **disjunct** of each disjunction is either an **atomic formula** or the **negation** of an **atomic formula**. For example, if A, B, and C are atomic formulas, then:

$$(\sim A \vee \sim B \vee C) \wedge (B \vee \sim C) \wedge (A \vee \sim C)$$

is in conjunctive normal form.

In **classical propositional logic**, every **formula** is **logically equivalent** to one in conjunctive normal form.

See also: **Disjunctive Normal Form, Negation Normal Form, Prenex Normal Form, Skolem Normal Form**

CONNECTED   A relation R is connected (or **complete**) if and only if, for any x and y such that:

$$x \neq y$$

we have either:

Rxy

or:

Ryx

See also: **Strongly Connected, Trichotomy**

CONNECTIVE see **Logical Connective**

CONNEXIVE LOGIC   Connexive logic is a **nonstandard logic** that is motivated, in large part, by the idea that no **formula** should entail, or be entailed by, its own **negation**. As a result, connexive logics are neither **sublogics** nor **extensions** of **classical logic** – instead, there are **theorems** of each logic that fail to be theorems of the other. In particular, both **Aristotle's thesis** and **Boethius' theses** are theorems of connexive logic, but not of classical logic.

See also: **Deviant Logic**

CONSEQUENCE RELATION   The consequence relation is the relation that holds between the **premises** and **conclusion** of a valid **argument**. Typically, a consequence relation is thought to be both **necessary** and **formal**: it is **impossible** for the premises to be **true** and the conclusion to be **false**, and this impossibility arises merely from the **logical form** of the **statements** involved.

The consequence relation can be formalized either **deductively** or **logically** (i.e. **semantically**). Typically, a deductive formalization of the consequence relation asserts that A is a consequence of B, C, D … if and only if there is a **proof** of A from B, C, D … in a particular **deductive system**. A semantic formalization of the consequence relation typically asserts that A is a consequence of B, C, D … if and only if there is no **interpretation** in which B, C, D … are all true, but A fails to be true.

See also: **Double Turnstile, Formal Consequence, Material Consequence, Single Turnstile**

CONSEQUENT   The consequent of a **conditional** is the **subformula** of the conditional occurring after the "then," or, if the conditional is not in strict "If … then …" form, then the consequent is the subformula occurring after the "then" in the "if … then …" statement **logically equivalent** to the original conditional.

See also: **Affirming the Consequent, Antecedent, Denying the Antecedent, Modus Ponens, Modus Tollens**

CONSEQUENTIA MIRABILIS   Consequentia mirabilis (from the Latin "following as an extraordinary logical consequence;" or **Clavius' Law**) is the following theorem of **classical logic**:

$$(\sim A \rightarrow A) \rightarrow A$$

Consequentia mirabilis is the **conditionalization** of the **classical reductio rule of inference**.

See also: **Conditional, Double Negation, Negation**

CONSERVATIVE EXTENSION   Given a **language** L and an extension of that language L*, a **theory** T* in L* is a conservative extension of a theory T in L if and only if, for any **statement** Φ in

L, T* entails Φ if and only if T entails Φ. In other words, a new theory T* is a conservative extension of an old theory T if and only if T* does not prove any statement in the language of T that T does not already prove.

See also: **Sublanguage, Sublogic, Subtheory**

CONSISTENCY see **Maximal Consistent Set, Negation Consistency, Post Consistency**

CONSTANT Within **logic**, a constant is a simple **expression** within a **formal language** that **denotes** an object. Typically, within **first-order logic** (and **extensions** of it), lower-case letters from the beginning and middle of the alphabet are used as constants in order to distinguish them from **first-order variables** (for which lower-case letters from the end of the alphabet are typically used). Within **formalizations** of mathematical **theories**, however, other, more traditional symbols are often used for constants (such as "0" for zero, "1" for one, etc.).

The word "constant" is also sometimes used to refer to **logical constants**.

See also: **First-order Variable, Formation Rules, Individual, Singular Proposition, Singular Term, Variable**

CONSTANT FUNCTION A **function** f is a constant function if and only if it produces the same output for every **argument**. In other words, f is a constant function if and only if there is some y such that, for any x:

$$f(x) = y$$

See also: **Characteristic Function, Idempotent, Identity Function, Pairing Function, Total Function, Unary Function**

CONSTRUCTIBLE SET The constructible sets are obtained as follows: At the first **stage** of the construction, the **class** of constructible sets is empty. At each **succeeding** stage, one adds to the stock of constructible sets any **set** that can be **defined** within the **language** of **first-order set theory** where (1) the **quantifiers** in the defining **formula** are understood to range only over those sets that have been added to the constructible sets in previous stages, and (2) the formula is allowed to contain **parameters denoting** particular sets that have been added to the constructible sets at previous stages.

The class of constructible sets (the **constructible universe**, or **L**) is an **inner model** of **Zermelo Fraenkel set theory**. Kurt Gödel showed that the class of constructible sets also satisfies the **axiom of choice** and the **continuum hypothesis**, demonstrating that both of these principles are **consistent** with **Zermelo Fraenkel set theory**.

See also: **Cumulative Hierarchy, Independence Result, Rank**

CONSTRUCTIBLE UNIVERSE   The constructible universe (often denoted **L**) is the **class** of all **constructible sets**. Both the **axiom of choice** and the **generalized continuum hypothesis** are satisfied in the constructible universe, which demonstrates that they are both consistent with **Zermelo Fraenkel set theory**.

See also: **Cumulative Hierarchy, Independence Result, Zermelo Fraenkel Set Theory**

CONSTRUCTIVE CHOICES see **Markov's Principle**

CONSTRUCTIVE DILEMMA   Constructive dilemma is the **rule of inference** which, given two **conditionals** and the **disjunction** of the **antecedents** of those conditionals, allows us to **infer** the disjunction of the **consequents** of those conditionals. In symbols:

$$A \vee B$$
$$A \to C$$
$$\underline{B \to D}$$
$$C \vee D$$

See also: **Classical Dilemma, Destructive Dilemma, Dilemma**

CONSTRUCTIVE EXISTENCE PROOF see **Constructive Proof**

CONSTRUCTIVE LOGIC   A constructive logic is a **non-standard logic** which equates the **truth** of a **statement** with its **provability**. In addition, constructive logics typically require that a proof of a **disjunction**:

$$A \vee B$$

requires an explicit proof of one or the other of the **disjuncts** (here, either A or B), and that a proof of an **existential generalization**:

$$(\exists x)\Phi(x)$$

requires an explicit proof of $\Phi(a)$, for some particular instance a.

Intuitionistic logic is the most extensively studied constructive logic, but it should not be confused with the notion of constructive logic more generally, since it represents just one of a number of ways in which constructive logic can be developed.

See also: **BHK-Interpretation, Constructive Mathematics, Constructive Proof, Disjunction Property, Excluded Middle, Logical Antirealism**

CONSTRUCTIVE MATHEMATICS   Constructive mathematics is a project of reconstructing current mathematical practice (as far as is possible) using only **constructive logic**.

Constructive mathematics should be distinguished from **intuitionistic mathematics**, which is merely one way among many of developing a constructive mathematics. Intuitionistic mathematics is characterized not only by constructive proofs, but also by a rejection of **uncountably infinite** collections. Errett Bishop, on the other hand, has developed an alternative version of constructive mathematics which requires **constructive proof**, but which retains the standard mathematical structures studied by classical mathematicians (or at least their **axiomatizations**).

See also: **BHK-Interpretation, Excluded Middle, Intuitionism, Logical Antirealism, Markov's Principle**

CONSTRUCTIVE METHODS OF PROOF see **Constructive Proof**

CONSTRUCTIVE PROOF   A constructive proof is a **proof** based on the underlying notion that the phrase "there exists" is **equivalent** to the phrase "we can **construct**," and that the phrase "is **true**" is equivalent to the phrase "we can know to be true." As a result, a constructive proof of an **existential claim** of the form:

$$(\exists x)\Phi(x)$$

will consist of either an explicit presentation of a particular object a such that $\Phi(a)$, or of an **algorithm** for obtaining such an object. Such a proof is called a **constructive existence proof**. Similarly, a constructive proof of a **disjunction**:

$$A \vee B$$

will consist of either a proof that A is true, or a proof that B is true, or an algorithm for determining which of A and B is true.

One defining characteristic of constructive proof is that it rejects the **rule of inference classical reductio ad absurdum** – in other words, it is not enough to prove Φ that we assume that Φ is false and obtain a **contradiction**.

See also: **BHK-Interpretation, Constructive Logic, Constructive Mathematics, Excluded Middle, Intuitionistic Logic, Logical Antirealism**

CONTEXTUALISM Contextualism is the view that the **meaning** of an **expression** is a **function** of more than just the meaning of its constituent **parts** and the manner in which those constituents are combined to form the **complex expression** – in particular, the context within which that expression occurs contributes to its meaning.

See also: **Pragmatics, Semantics**

CONTINGENCY A **statement** is contingent if it is both **possible** that it be **true** and possible that it be **false**. Contingent statements are contrasted with both **necessary** statements, which must be true, and **impossible** statements, which must be false.

Within **modal logic**, where possibilities are represented by **possible worlds**, a contingent statement is one where there is an accessible possible world in which it is true, and another accessible possible world in which it is false. This can be represented in the **language** of modal logic as:

$$\Diamond A \wedge \Diamond \sim A$$

See also: **Accessibility Relation, Actual World, Alethic Modal Logic, Mere Possibilia**

CONTINUUM Generally speaking, a continuum is any entity that is "smooth," "has no gaps," "is unbroken," etc. Within **logic**, however, a continuum is any **structure** that has certain **properties** that are characteristic of the **real numbers** – in particular, **density** and **completeness**. Additionally, the real numbers themselves are often referred to as the continuum.

See also: **c, Cantor's Theorem, Continuum Hypothesis, Continuum Many**

CONTINUUM HYPOTHESIS George Cantor proved that the **cardinality** of the **powerset** of any **set** is strictly greater than the cardinality of the set itself – this is **Cantor's theorem**. In particular, the cardinality of a set of **natural numbers** (whose cardinality is the smallest infinite **cardinal number**), which we represent as $\aleph_0$, is strictly less than the cardinality of the powerset of the natural numbers, which we represent as $2^{\aleph_0}$.

Since $\aleph_1$ is the second largest infinite cardinality, that is, it is the cardinal number of an infinite set which is bigger than the set of natural numbers, but for which there is no set intermediate between it and the set of natural numbers, Cantor's result can be stated as:

$$2^{\aleph_0} \geq \aleph_1$$

Cantor's continuum hypothesis is the claim that the cardinal number of the powerset of the set of natural numbers is, in fact, the next largest cardinal number, that is:

$$2^{\aleph_0} = \aleph_1$$

Standard **set theories**, such as **Zermelo Fraenkel set theory (ZFC)**, do not settle the continuum hypothesis. Kurt Gödel used his **inner model** method to **demonstrate** that one can **consistently** add Cantor's continuum hypothesis to ZFC set theory. Paul Cohen used his **forcing** method, however, to show that one can consistently add the **negation** of Cantor's continuum hypothesis to ZFC set theory. Thus, ZFC neither **proves** nor **refutes** the continuum hypothesis, and its **truth value** remains one of the mysteries of modern set theory. The question regarding the relationship between the cardinality of the set of natural numbers and the cardinality of its powerset (or between the cardinality of any set and the cardinality of its powerset) has come to be called the **continuum problem**.

See also: $\beth$, **c, Constructible Universe, Generalized Continuum Hypothesis, Independence Result**

CONTINUUM MANY   A **set** has continuum many **members** if it can be put into a **one-to-one onto correspondence** with the set of **real numbers**. Equivalently, a set has continuum many members if and only if its **cardinal number** is **c** or $2^{\aleph_0}$.

See also: **Cantor's Theorem, Continuum, Continuum Hypothesis, Transfinite Cardinal Number**

CONTINUUM PROBLEM see **Continuum Hypothesis, Generalized Continuum Hypothesis**

CONTRACTION₁   Contraction is the following principle of propositional logic:

$$(A \rightarrow (A \rightarrow B)) \rightarrow (A \rightarrow B)$$

This law is also sometime called **absorbsion**.

See also: **Conditional, Conditional Proof, Conditionalization**

CONTRACTION₂   Contraction is the following **structural rule**. If we have a **sequent** of the form:

$$\Delta, A, A \Rightarrow B, \Gamma$$

then we can write down a sequent of the form:

$$\Delta, A \Rightarrow B, \Gamma$$

And if we have a sequent of the form:

$$\Delta, A \Rightarrow B, B, \Gamma$$

then we can write down a sequent of the form:

$$\Delta, A \Rightarrow B, \ \Gamma$$

In other words, contraction allows us to eliminate multiple occurrences of a **premise** or **conclusion**.

See also: **Abelian Logic, Affine Logic, Linear Logic, Permutation, Weakening**

CONTRADICTION₁   A **statement** is a contradiction (or is **self-contradictory**) if it is **impossible** that it be true.

See also: **Impossible World, Law of Non-Contradiction, Triviality**

CONTRADICTION₂   A contradiction is a **statement** of the form:

$$P \wedge \sim P$$

In **classical logic** and most **non-standard logics** – but not in some **paraconsistent logics** such as the **logic of paradox** – a contradiction cannot be **true**.

See also: **Dialethic Logic, Ex Falso Quodlibet, Law of Non-Contradiction, Triviality, Truth Value Gap, Truth Value Glut**

CONTRADICTORIES see **Contradictory**

CONTRADICTORY A pair of **statements** are contradictory (or **contradictories**) when it is **impossible** for them simultaneously to be **true**, but it is also impossible for them simultaneously to be **false**. Within **classical logic**, two statements are contradictory if and only if each one is **logically equivalent** to the **negation** of the other.

Within **categorical logic** contradictory is a term of art, expressing the relationship that holds between an **A-proposition** and the corresponding **O-proposition**, or between an **E-proposition** and the corresponding **I-proposition**. This is just a special case of the more general usage, however.

See also: **Antilogism, Antimony, Contrary, Contradiction, Paradox**

CONTRAPOSITION Contraposition is the process of taking the **contrapositive** of a **categorical proposition**, or of taking the contrapositive of a **conditional**. It also refers to the **immediate inference**, within **categorical logic**, where one infers, from an **A-proposition** or an **O-proposition**, the contrapositive of that **proposition**.

See also: **Contradictory, Contrary, Conversion, Obversion, Subalternation**

CONTRAPOSITIVE₁ Within **categorical logic**, the contrapositive of a **categorical proposition** is obtained by switching the **subject term** and **predicate term** of the **proposition**, and replacing the subject term and the predicate term with their **complements**. For example, the contrapositive of the **A-proposition**:

All men are mortal.

is:

All non–mortals are non–men.

In **categorical logic**, the contrapositive of A-propositions and O-propositions must have the same **truth values** as the original **propositions**, although the truth values of **E-propositions** and **I-propositions** and their respective contrapositives are, in general, unrelated.

See also: **Contraposition, Conversion, Immediate Inference, Obversion, Subalternation**

CONTRAPOSITIVE$_2$ The contrapositive of a **conditional** is the result of switching the **antecedent** and **consequent** of the conditional, and replacing the antecedent and consequent of the conditional with their **negations** For example, the contrapositive of:

>   If snow is white, then the grass is green.

is:

>   If grass is not green then snow is not white.

In symbols, the former is:

>   S → G

and its contrapositive is:

>   ~ G → ~ S

Within **classical logic**, the contrapositive of a conditional has the same **truth value** as the original conditional.

See also: **Conditional Proof, Modus Ponens, Modus Tollens, Transposition**

CONTRARY   A pair of **statements** are contrary (or **contraries**, or **mutually exclusive**) when it is **impossible** for them to simultaneously be **true**, but it is **possible** for them to simultaneously be **false**.

   Within **categorical logic** contrary is a term of art, expressing the relationship that holds between an **A-proposition** and the corresponding **E-proposition**. This is just a special case of the more general usage, however.

See also: **Contradictory, Converse, Obverse, Subalternation, Subcontrary**

CONTRARY TO FACT CONDITIONAL   see **Counterfactual Conditional**

CONVENTION T   Convention T (or **Tarski's Convention T**) is an adequacy condition on attempted **definitions** of the **truth predicate**. Convention T states that a definition of a **predicate** "T(x)" is an adequate definition for a **language** L if and only if:

   (1)   "T(x)" only applies to **names** of **statements** of L.

   (2)   For any statement A in L, and n a name of A, the definition

allows us to **prove**:

$$T(n) \leftrightarrow P$$

The formula:

$$T(n) \leftrightarrow P$$

is known as the **T-schema**. Thus, Convention T requires that an adequate definition of the truth predicate must allow us to prove all instances of the **T-schema**. The idea that an adequate definition of the truth predicate is one that satisfies Convention T is the **semantic conception of truth**.

See also: **Disquotationalism, Minimalism, Redundancy Theory of Truth, Schema, Semantically Closed Language, Tarski's Indefinability Theorem**

CONVERSE₁ The converse of a **categorical proposition** is obtained by switching the **subject term** and **predicate term** of the **proposition**. For example, the converse of the **A-proposition**:

All men are mortal.

is:

All mortals are men.

In **categorical logic**, the converse of **E-propositions** and **I-propositions** must have the same **truth value** as the original proposition, although the **truth values** of **A-propositions** and **O-propositions** and their respective converses are, in general, unrelated.

See also: **Contrapositive, Conversion, Immediate Inference, Obversion, Subalternation**

CONVERSE₂ The converse of a **conditional** is the result of switching the **antecedent** and **consequent** of the conditional. For example, the converse of:

If snow is white, then the grass is green.

is:

If grass is green, then snow is white.

In symbols, the former is:

$$S \rightarrow G$$

and its converse is:

$$G \rightarrow S$$

Within **propositional logic**, the **truth value** of a conditional and its converse are, in general, unrelated.

See also: **Contraposition, Exportation, Transposition**

CONVERSE ACCIDENT see **Hasty Generalization**

CONVERSE BARCAN FORMULA   The converse Barcan formula is the following formula of **quantified modal logic**:

$$\Box(\forall x)\Phi \rightarrow (\forall x)\Box\Phi$$

The converse Barcan formula implies that any object that exists in the **actual world** exists in any **possible world accessible** from the actual world – in other words, any object that actually exists must exist in all **possibilities**.

See also: **Barcan Formula, Mere Possibilia, Normal Modal Logic**

CONVERSE DOMAIN see **Range**

CONVERSE OF A RELATION see **Inverse**

CONVERSE-WELL-FOUNDED   A **relation** R is converse-well-founded if and only if, for any **set** X, there is an R-maximal **member** of X – that is, there is a y in X such that there is no z in X such that Ryz. In other words, a relation R is converse-well-founded if and only if its **inverse** is **well-founded**.

See also: **Well-Ordered**

CONVERSION   Conversion is the process of taking the **converse** of a **categorical proposition**, or of taking the **converse** of a **conditional**. It also refers to the **immediate inference**, within **categorical logic**, where one infers, from an **E-proposition** or an **I-proposition**, the converse of that **proposition**.

See also: **Contraposition, Contrary, Obversion, Subalternation, Subcontrary**

COPULA see **"Is" of Predication**

CO-REFERENTIAL   Two expressions are co-referential if and only if they **refer** to the same object.

See also: **Denotation, Referential Opacity, Semantic Value, Slingshot Argument**

COREFLEXIVITY   A **binary relation** R is coreflexive if and only if, for any objects x and y, if:

Rxy

then:

x = y

See also: **Irreflexivity, Reflexivity**

COROLLARY   A corollary is a result that immediately follows from, or is easily **deduced** from, a main result (i.e. a **theorem**).

See also: **Lemma**

CORRESPONDENCE THEORY OF TRUTH   The correspondence theory of truth is the view that a **statement** is **true** if and only if there is an appropriate fact to which it corresponds. Thus, the statement "The cat is on the mat" is true if and only if there exists in the world a fact whose structure is something like <cat, on, mat> – that is, a complex object somehow **composed** of the cat, the mat, and the "is on" **relation**.

See also: **Coherence Theory of Truth, Disquotationalism, Minimalism, Prosentential Theory of Truth, Redundancy Theory of Truth, Truthmaker**

CORRESPONDING CONDITIONAL see **Conditionalization**

COUNTABLE   A **set** is countable (or **denumerable**) if and only if it is either **finite**, or it is **infinite** and its **cardinal number** is $\aleph_0$, the first **infinite cardinal number**. The term "countable" refers to the idea that a set of this size can be counted by the **natural numbers** (in a loosened sense of "count" in the case of **countably infinite** sets).

See also: **Absolute Infinite, Countable Cardinal, Countable**

Ordinal, Dedekind Infinite, Simply Infinite, Transfinite Cardinal Number

COUNTABLE CARDINAL   A countable cardinal is a **cardinal number** of a **countable set**.

See also: **Cardinal Successor, Countable Ordinal, Countably Infinite, Limit Cardinal, Regular Cardinal**

COUNTABLE CHOICE see **Axiom of Countable Choice**

COUNTABLE ORDINAL   A countable ordinal is an **ordinal number** that is the **order type** of an **ordering** on a **countable set**.

See also: **Countable Cardinal, Countably Infinite, Limit Ordinal, ω, Ordinal Successor, Regular Ordinal**

COUNTABLY INFINITE   A **set** is countably infinite (or **denumerably infinite**) if its **cardinal number** is $\aleph_0$. In other words, a countably infinite **set** is an **infinite** set that is the same size as the **natural numbers**.

See also: **Countable Cardinal, Countable Ordinal, Dedekind Infinite, Simply Infinite, Transfinite Cardinal Number, Transfinite Ordinal Number**

COUNTERDOMAIN see **Range**

COUNTEREXAMPLE   A counterexample is a scenario, actual or merely **possible**, which **demonstrates** the **invalidity** of an **argument** by showing that it is possible for the **premises** to be **true** and the **conclusion false**. For example, we can show that:

> All grapes are fruits.
> Some fruits are red.
> Some grapes are red.

is invalid by imagining a **possible world** where red apples exist, but where the only grapes to exist are green. As this example demonstrates, counterexamples are critical in demonstrating that an argument is invalid when the conclusion of the argument is true.

See also: **Countermodel, Deductive Argument, Deductive Validity, Fallacy, Formal Fallacy, Refutation**

COUNTERFACTUAL CONDITIONAL A counterfactual conditional (or **contrary to fact conditional**) is a **conditional** that
expresses what would have been the case had the **antecedent**
been **true**. Counterfactual conditionals thus should be distinguished
from **material conditionals** and **indicative conditionals** which
express what is the case if, in fact, the antecedent is true. For example,
the counterfactual conditional:

> If Plato had not been a philosopher, then he would have been an
> accountant.

is **false**, since if Plato had not been a philosopher, accountancy would
not have been his next choice in careers. The similar material
conditional:

> If Plato is not a philosopher, then he is an accountant.

is true, however, merely because the antecedent is false.

Typically, counterfactual conditionals are equated with
subjunctive conditionals, although occasionally the term
counterfactual conditional is reserved for subjunctive conditionals
with false antecedents (i.e. those that actually are counter-factual).

See also: **Conditional Logic, Conditionalization, Counterfactual Logic, Counternecessary Conditional, Strict
Conditional**

COUNTERFACTUAL LOGIC Counterfactual logic refers to any of
a number of **formal systems** which attempt to formalize the
notion of a **counterfactual conditional** using **possible worlds
semantics**. Thus counterfactual logics are a form of **modal logic**
where, instead of using **unary sentential operators** such as
necessity ($\Box$) and **possibility** ($\Diamond$), the primary **modal operator** is
a **binary operator**, the conditional. Counterfactual logics differ
from other **conditional logics** in that they typically reject
contraposition as a **valid inference**.

See also: **Alethic Modal Logic, Counternecessary Conditional,
Kripke Semantics, Subjunctive Conditional**

COUNTERMODEL A countermodel is a **model** that is used to
demonstrate the **invalidity** of an **argument** in **first-order
logic** (or **logics** extending first-order logic) by providing an
interpretation that makes the **premises** of the argument **true**
in the model and the **conclusion false** in the model. Thus,

countermodels are the formal analogue of **counterexamples**.

See also: **Deductive Argument, Deductive Validity, Fallacy, Formal Fallacy, Model Theory, Refutation**

COUNTERNECESSARY CONDITIONAL   A counternecessary conditional is a **counterfactual conditional** with a **necessarily false antecedent**. For example:

> If 2 were not odd, then 2 would be even.

is a counternecessary conditional.

See also: **Conditional Logic, Counterfactual Logic, Indicative Conditional, Material Conditional, Strict Conditional, Subjunctive Conditional**

COUNTERPART see **Counterpart Theory**

COUNTERPART THEORY   Counterpart theory is a framework that allows us to interpret modal claims about objects as actually applying to modal **counterparts** of those objects. To see the puzzle at hand, consider the **statement**:

> Roy is a mathematician.

This statement, while **false** (assuming it is about the author), is certainly not **impossible**. Thus, according to **possible worlds semantics**, there must be a **possible world** in which it is **true**. Taken at face value, this would mean that, in that possible world, Roy exists and is a mathematician. But this is absurd, since Roy exists solely in the **actual world**, and cannot also exist in the possible one.

The counterpart theorist solves this problem by denying that Roy inhabits the possible world in question. Rather, it is a distinct object (a **counterpart** of Roy) that is in that possible world, and that is a mathematician.

See also: **Mere Possibilia, Trans-World Identity**

COURSE OF VALUES INDUCTION see **Strong Mathematical Induction**

COURSE OF VALUES RECURSION   Course of values recursion is a method for **defining functions** on the **natural numbers**. Using course of values recursion, we define the value of f applied to $n+1$

(that is, $f(n+1)$) in terms of the values of f for all natural numbers less than $n+1$. For example, the function g such that:

$$g(0) \quad = \quad 2$$

$$g(n+1) \quad = \quad g(n) \times g(n-1) \times \ldots \times g(1) \times g(0)$$

(i.e. the value of $g(m)$ is the result of multiplying together all $g(i)$'s where i is less than m) is a function defined in terms of course of values recursion, since **computing** the value of $g(m)$ requires knowing all previous values of g.

The functions that can be defined using the **primitive recursive functions** plus course of values recursion are exactly those that can be obtained using merely the primitive recursive functions.

See also: **Primitive Recursion, Recursive Function, Recursive Function Theory, Transfinite Recursion**

CRAIG'S INTERPOLATION THEOREM see **Interpolation Theorem**

CROSS-WORLD IDENTITY see **Trans-World Identity**

CUMULATIVE HIERARCHY The cumulative hierarchy (or **set-theoretic hierarchy**, or **V, Von Neumann hierarchy**, or **Von Neumann universe**) is the **class** of all **sets**. This class is divided into a **transfinite hierarchy** in the following **recursive** manner:

$$V_0 \quad = \quad \varnothing$$

$$V_{\alpha+1} \quad = \quad \wp(V_\alpha)$$

$$V_\lambda \quad = \quad \bigcup_{\gamma > \lambda} V_\gamma$$

In other words, the initial stage of the hierarchy is empty. At each successor stage, we take the **powerset** of the previous stage. And at limit stages – that is, those stages indexed by **limit ordinals** – we take the **union** of all previous stages.

The entire cumulative hierarchy can be obtained by taking the **union** of all stages in the hierarchy:

$$V \quad = \quad \bigcup V_\alpha$$

See also: **Absolute Infinite, Ad Infinitum, Constructible Universe, Iterative Conception of Set, Limitation-of-Size Conception of Set, Rank**

CURRY PARADOX   The Curry paradox (or **Curry's Paradox**, or the **Löb paradox**) is a variant of **semantic paradox** which can be formulated without the use of **negation** or **falsity**. Consider the **statement**:

> If this **conditional** is true, then Santa Claus exists.

We can reason as follows. The conditional must be **true**, since, if it were false, then its **antecedent** would be true, and that would provide a **contradiction**. But if the conditional is true, then so is its antecedent. Thus, by **modus ponens**, the **consequent** is true as well, and Santa Claus exists.

This general pattern of reasoning can be used to prove any statement A merely by considering the statement:

> If this conditional is true, then A.

Moreover, the **Liar paradox** can be seen to be merely a special case of the Curry paradox, since the **Liar sentence**:

> This sentence is false.

is **equivalent** to:

> If this statement is true, then ⊥.

where "⊥" is **falsum**, or any **contradiction**.

See also: **Open Pair, Semantically Closed Language, Truth-Teller, Yablo Paradox**

CURRY'S PARADOX see **Curry Paradox**

CUT   Cut is the following **structural rule**. If we have two **sequents** of the following forms:

> $\Delta \Rightarrow A$
>
> $\Gamma, A \Rightarrow B$

then we can write down a sequent of the form:

> $\Delta, \Gamma \Rightarrow B$

"cutting" A out of the **argument**.

The cut rule is a generalized version of **hypothetical syllogism**.

See also: **Contraction, Cut Elimination, Permutation, Substructural Logic, Transitivity, Weakening**

CUT ELIMINATION A cut elimination **proof** (or **haupsatz**, or **hauptsatz**) for a particular **formal system** formulated in the **sequence calculus** is a **demonstration** that anything that can be **proven** within that system can also be proven without recourse to the **cut** rule. Cut elimination theorems are of central importance to many of the interesting results obtainable using the sequent calculus, including Gerhard Gentzen's proof of the **consistency** of **arithmetic**.

See also: **Admissible Rule, Derivable Rule, Sequent, Substructural Logic**

D D is the **normal modal logic** whose sole additional **axiom** is:

D: $\Box P \rightarrow \Diamond P$

In **possible worlds semantics**, the modal logic D is **valid** on any **frame** in which the **accessibility relation** is **serial**.

D also refers to the **axiom** that is characteristic of the modal logic D. The axiom D is satisfied on any frame in which the accessibility relation is serial.

See also: **Deontic Modal Logic, Kripke Semantics, Kripke Structure, Modality**

DAGGER The dagger (or **joint denial**, or **Peirce dagger**, or **Sheffer dagger**) is the **binary connective** represented by "↓" whose **truth table** is:

P	Q	P↓Q
T	T	F
T	F	F
F	T	F
F	F	T

Intuitively, "P ↓ Q" can be read as "neither P nor Q," and is known as the **NOR** operation in computer science and **Boolean algebra**.

The dagger is an **expressively complete** connective – that is, every truth table in **propositional logic** can be represented by an expression containing only **propositional letters, punctuation,** and the dagger. For example, the **disjunction** of P and Q (i.e. "P ∨ Q") can be represented as:

(P ↓ Q) ↓ (P ↓ Q)

and the **negation** of P (i.e. "~ P") can be represented as:

(P ↓ P)

See also: **Boolean Operator, Sheffer Stroke**

DECIDABLE see **Recursive Function Theory**

DECIDABLE RELATION see **Recursive Relation**

DECIDABLE SET see **Recursive Set**

DECIDABLE THEORY   A **theory** is decidable if and only if the **set** of **Gödel numbers** of **theorems** of that theory is a **recursive set**.

See also: **Church's Theorem, Finitely Axiomatizable Theory, Semi-Decidable Theory**

DECISION PROCEDURE   A decision procedure is an **algorithm** that is guaranteed to **compute** the answer to a particular problem in a **finite** number of computational steps. Typically, the question at hand will be one whose answer is of a "yes" or "no" form (or, equivalently, of a "0" or "1" form).

See also: **Church's Theorem, Entscheidungsproblem, Recursive Function Theory, Recursively Axiomatizable Theory, Semi-Decidable Theory**

DEDEKIND FINITE see **Dedekind Infinite**

DEDEKIND INFINITE   A **set** A is Dedekind infinite if and only if there is some **subset** B of A such that there is a **one-to-one onto function** mapping B to A. A set is **Dedekind finite** if and only if it is not Dedekind infinite.

The notion of a set being Dedekind infinite should be contrasted with the notion of a set being **simply infinite**, since the two are **equivalent** only if one assumes the **axiom of choice**.

See also: **Absolute Infinite, Cofinite, Complete Infinity, Countably Infinite, Hereditarily Finite Set**

DEDEKIND-PEANO ARITHMETIC see **Peano Arithmetic**

DE DICTO   A **statement** is de dicto (from the Latin, "of the word") with respect to a **referring** expression if the statement is interpreted as being, in some sense, about that referring expression. For example, if:

> The number of planets is necessarily 9.

is interpreted as asserting that there could not have been fewer planets, or more planets, than there actually are, then the statement is de dicto (with respect to the phrase "number of planets"). If, however, the statement is interpreted as asserting that the object that is the number of planets (i.e. 9 itself) is necessarily identical to 9, then the statement is **de re**.

The de dicto/de re distinction typically arises in contexts where **modal language**, or another **referentially opaque** language, is being used.

See also: **Denotation, Scope, Semantic Value**

DEDUCTION see **Derivation**

DEDUCTION THEOREM   The deduction theorem holds for a **logic** L (containing a **conditional** "→") if and only if, for any formulas Φ and Ψ, and set of formulas Δ, we have that there is a **proof** of Ψ from Φ and Δ:

$$\Delta, \Phi \vdash \Psi$$

if and only if there is a proof of $\Phi \rightarrow \Psi$ from Δ:

$$\Delta \vdash \Phi \rightarrow \Psi$$

See also: **Conditional Proof, Conditionalization, Deductive Implication, Metatheorem, Proof Theory**

DEDUCTIVE ARGUMENT   A deductive argument is an **argument** where it is intended that it be **impossible** for the **premises** to be **true** and the **conclusion false**.

See also: **Abduction, Deductive Validity, Derivation, Inductive Argument, Sound Deductive Argument**

DEDUCTIVE CLOSURE see **Transitive Closure**

DEDUCTIVE CONSEQUENCE   A **statement** Φ is a deductive consequence (or **proof-theoretic consequence**, or **syntactic consequence**) of a **set** of statements Δ, relative to a **formal system**, if and only if there is a **derivation** in that formal system whose last line is Φ and all of whose undischarged assumptions are in Δ.

See also: **Consequence Relation, Formal Consequence, Inference, Logical Consequence, Material Consequence, Single Turnstile**

DEDUCTIVE EQUIVALENCE see **Deductively Equivalent**

DEDUCTIVE IMPLICATION   Deductive implication (or **proof-theoretic implication**, or **syntactic implication**) is the **relation** that holds between A and B if:

$$A \to B$$

is a **theorem**. The formula:

$$A \to B$$

is also said to be a deductive implication if the relation of deductive implication holds between A and B (in that order).

See also: **Conditionalization, Deductive Consequence, Logical Implication, Material Implication, Strict Implication**

DEDUCTIVE SYSTEM see **Formal System**

DEDUCTIVE VALIDITY   An **argument** is deductively valid (or **proof-theoretically valid**, or **syntactically valid**) relative to a **formal system** if and only if there is a **derivation** within the system whose only assumptions are the **premises** of the argument and which terminates with the **conclusion** of the argument.

See also: **Deductive Argument, Deductive Consequence, Deductive Implication, Logical Validity, Single Turnstile**

DEDUCTIVELY EQUIVALENT   Two **formulas** A and B are deductively equivalent (or **proof-theoretically equivalent**, or **syntactically equivalent**) if and only if they are interderivable (i.e. one can **prove** A using only B as a **premise**, and one can derive B using only A as premise). In other words, A and B are deductively equivalent if and only if:

A ↔ B

is a **theorem**. The **formula**:

A ↔ B

is said to be a **deductive equivalence**, if A and B are deductively equivalent.

See also: **Deductive Consequence, Deductive Implication, Deductive Validity, Logically Equivalent, Materially Equivalent**

DEDUCTIVISM Deductivism is the view that all **arguments** appearing in **natural language** are best analyzed as **deductive arguments**. Deductivism typically proceeds by "identifying" additional **premises** that are implicit in a particular informal, apparently **inductive argument**, but not explicitly stated. These additional premises render the argument a deductive one.

See also: **Consequence Relation, Derivation, Formal Language, Formal Proof, Natural Deduction**

DEFINABILISM see **Combinatorialism**

DEFINABLE SET A **set** of objects A is definable in a **language** L if and only if there is some **formula** Φ in L (with one **free variable**) such that Φ is **satisfied** by all and only the objects in A. A particular object o is definable in L if and only if its **singleton** {o} is definable in L in the manner described.

See also: **Axiom of Constructibility, Combinatorialism, Constructible Hierarchy, Constructible Sets, Definition, Recursive Definition**

DEFINIENDUM The definiendum of a **definition** is the expression whose meaning is being provided by the definition.

See also: **Definiens, Explicit Definition, Impredicative Definition, Intensional Definition, Ostensive Definition, Stipulative Definition**

DEFINIENS The definiens of a **definition** is the expression used to provide the meaning of the expression being defined.

See also: **Definiendum, Explicit Definition, Impredicative**

Definition, Intensional Definition, Ostensive Definition, Stipulative Definition

DEFINITE DESCRIPTION   A definite description is a **description** of the form "the Φ" where Φ is a **predicate**. Bertrand Russell famously analyzed definite descriptions in terms of **quantificational** constructions in order to eliminate puzzles involving expressions that fail to **refer**. For example, the **logical form** of a **statement** of the form:

"The Φ is Ψ"

according to Russell is:

$$(\exists x)(\Phi(x) \land (\forall y)(\Phi(y) \to y = x) \land \Psi(x))$$

In other words, "the Φ is Ψ" amounts to the **existentially quantified** expression asserting that (1) there is a Φ, (2) there is at most one Φ, and (3) the thing that is a Φ is also a Ψ.

See also: **Free Logic, Indefinite Description, Plato's Beard**

DEFINITION   A definition is an expression intended to provide the meaning of a word.

See also: **Explicit Definition, Implicit Definition, Impredicative Definition, Ostensive Definition, Stipulative Definition**

DEFLATIONISM   Deflationism is a family of views about **truth**, all of which share the thesis that truth is not a substantial **concept** and that an assertion that predicates truth to a **statement** does not ascribe any property to that statement. Deflationism comes in many varieties, including **disquotationalism**, the **redundancy theory of truth**, and **minimalism** about truth.

See also: **Coherence Theory of Truth, Compositionality, Correspondence Theory of Truth, Prosentential Theory of Truth, Revision Theory of Truth, Truthmaker**

DEGREE see **Adicity**

DEGREE-OF-TRUTH see **Verity**

DEGREE-THEORETIC SEMANTICS   Degree-theoretic semantics

(or **fuzzy logic**) is a type of **non-standard logic** that assigns each **statement** in a **language** a **real number** between 0 and 1 (that statement's **verity**). An assignment of 1 to a statement represents that the statement in question is completely **true**, an assignment of 0 to a statement represents that the statement in question is completely **false**, and assignments of values strictly less than 1 but strictly greater than 0 represent that the statements in question are partially true.

There are a number of different ways in which an assignment of degrees of truth to **atomic statements** can be extended to the entire language. The simplest manner is to assign each **conjunction** the minimum value of the two **conjuncts**:

$$v(\Phi \wedge \Psi) \quad = \quad min(v(\Phi), v(\Psi))$$

and to assign each **disjunction** the maximum value of the two **disjuncts**:

$$v(\Phi \vee \Psi) \quad = \quad max(v(\Phi), v(\Psi))$$

(with analogous rules for the **universal** and **existential quantifiers**, respectively). While this method is a natural extension of the rules for **classical semantics**, other methods for evaluating **compound expressions**, loosely based on the rules for the **probability calculus**, have been explored.

See also: **Conditional Probability, Probability Theory, Sorites Paradox, Sorites Series, Vagueness**

DEMONSTRATION see **Proof**

DEMONSTRATIVE A demonstrative is a context-dependent expression whose **referent** depends on the speaker's actions or intentions. Examples of demonstratives include "this," "that," "him," "her," and "they." It should be noted that not all occurrences of these expressions function as demonstratives, however. Each of these expressions can also figure in **anaphora**.

Demonstratives should be distinguished from **indexicals**, whose reference is context-dependent but does not depend on the actions or intentions of the speaker.

See also: **Anaphora, Contextualism, Indexical, Pragmatics, Semantics**

DEMORGAN DUALITY see **DeMorgan's Rules**

DEMORGAN NEGATION   DeMorgan negation is the **negation operator semantically** characterized by the following rules:

~ A is **true** if and only if A is false.

~ A is **false** if and only if A is true.

DeMorgan negation is **equivalent** to other versions of negation (such as **Boolean negation**) in **classical semantics**, but these accounts of negation are non-equivalent in **many-valued logics** such as **First-Degree Entailment**.

See also: **Bottom, Choice Negation, Exclusion Negation, Falsum, Tilde**

DEMORGAN'S DUALS see **DeMorgan's Rules**

DEMORGAN'S LAWS see **DeMorgan's Rules**

DEMORGAN'S RULES   Within propositional logic, DeMorgan's rules (or **DeMorgan's laws**) are the **rules of replacement** that allow the reasoner to replace:

~ (P ∨ Q)

with:

(~ P ∧ ~ Q)

(and vice versa), and to replace:

~ (P ∧ Q)

with:

(~ P ∨ ~ Q)

(and vice versa). The members of each of the equivalent pairs are the **duals** (or **DeMorgan's duals**) of each other.

See also: **Conjunction, Disjunction, Negation**

DENOTATION   Denotation is the **relation** that holds between a **description** and the object picked out by that description, if any. The object so picked out is also known as the denotation of the description.

See also: **Co-Referential, Definite Description, Indefinite Description, Reference, Semantic Value**

DENSE A **relation** R is dense if and only if, for any a and b if:

Rab

then there is a c such that:

Rac

and:

Rcb

See also: **Continuum, Discrete, Rational Numbers, Real Numbers**

DENUMERABLE see **Countable**

DENUMERABLY INFINITE see **Countably Infinite**

DENYING THE ANTECEDENT Denying the antecedent is the **formal fallacy** that occurs when one moves from a **conditional**, and the **negation** of the **antecedent** of that conditional, to the negation of the **consequent** of that conditional. In symbols we have:

$$\frac{\begin{array}{l} P \to Q \\ \sim P \end{array}}{\sim Q}$$

See also: **Affirming the Consequent, Conditional Proof, Hypothetical Syllogism, Modus Ponens, Modus Tollens**

DENYING THE CONSEQUENT see **Modus Tollens**

DEONTIC LOGIC see **Deontic Modal Logic**

DEONTIC MODAL LOGIC Deontic modal logic (or **deontic logic**) is the branch of **modal logic** that studies the **unary modal operators** "it is obligatory that Φ," "it is permissible that Φ," and "it is forbidden that Φ." The notions are typically **formalized** as "O Φ," "P Φ," and "F Φ" respectively.

See also: **D, Kripke Semantics, Kripke Structure, Ross's Paradox**

DEPENDENT CHOICE see **Axiom of Dependent Choice**

DE RE see **De Dicto**

DERIVABLE RULE   Within a particular **deductive system**, a **rule of inference** is a derivable rule if and only if a **schema** can be provided which **demonstrates** how to obtain the **conclusion** of the derivable rule from the **premises** of the rule. For example, in any deductive system that contains both **disjunctive syllogism**:

$$\frac{\begin{array}{l} P \lor Q \\ \sim P \end{array}}{Q}$$

and **addition**:

$$\frac{P}{P \lor Q}$$

ex falso quodlibet is a derivable rule, as the following schema demonstrates:

(1) P

(2) ~ P

(3) P ∨ Q   From (1), Addition

(4) Q   From (2) and (3), Disjunctive Syllogism

Every derivable rule is also an **admissible rule**, but not vice versa.

See also: **Cut, Cut Elimination, Derivation, Sequent Calculus, Valid**

DERIVATION   A derivation (or **deduction**) is a **finite sequence** of **statements** within a **formal system** where each statement in the sequence is either an **axiom**, an **assumption**, or the result of applying a **rule of inference** to one or more preceding statements. The final statement is the **conclusion** of the **argument** that has been derived, and each assumption is a **premise** of the argument derived.

See also: **Deductive Validity, Formal Proof, Natural Deduction, Proof Theory, Sequent Calculus, Single Turnstile**

DESCRIPTION see **Definite Description, Indefinite Description**

DESCRIPTIVE SET THEORY   Descriptive set theory is the branch of **set theory** dealing with certain types of "well-behaved" **sets** of **real numbers,** such as the **definable** sets, the Borel sets, the analytic sets, and the projective sets.

See also: **Combinatorial Set Theory, Constructible Set, Continuum, Continuum Hypothesis, Continuum Many, Generalized Continuum Hypothesis**

DESIGNATED VALUE   In **classical** or **many-valued logics,** the designated value or values of the **logic** are those **truth values** whose preservation is central to the **consequence relation** of the logic in question. In other words, in classical or many-valued logics, if Δ is a set of **statements** and Φ is a statement, then **logical consequence** is (typically) defined as:

> Φ is a logical consequence of Δ if and only if, whenever all members of Δ receive designated values, Φ receives a designated value as well.

In classical logic the only designated value is the **true.** In the **logic of paradox** the designated values are true and the **truth value glut** "both true and false," and in **analethic logic** the designated values are true and the **truth value gap** "neither true nor false."

See also: **Bivalence, Law of Non-Contradiction, Non-Standard Logic, Paraconsistent Logic**

DESTRUCTIVE DILEMMA   Destructive dilemma is the **rule of inference** which, given two **conditionals** and the **disjunction** of the **negations** of the **consequents** of those conditionals, allows one to infer the disjunction of the negations of the **antecedents** of those conditionals. In symbols we have:

$$\sim C \vee \sim D$$
$$A \to C$$
$$\underline{B \to D}$$
$$\sim A \vee \sim B$$

See also: **Classical Dilemma, Constructive Dilemma, Hypothetical Syllogism, Modus Ponens, Modus Tollens**

DETERMINATENESS see Axiom of Extensionality

DETERMINER   A determiner is an expression that, when attached to a noun or other **referring** expression, determines the type of reference which the noun in question has. Determiners include articles such as "a" and "the," **quantifiers** such as "all," "some," "none," and "most," possessives such as "my," "your," "their," and **demonstratives** such as "this," "that," and "those."

See also: **Definite Description, Existential Quantifier, Indefinite Description, Indexical, Universal Quantifier**

DETERMINISTIC POLYNOMIAL TIME   A **function** is **computable** in deterministic polynomial time (or is of **complexity class P**) if there is a polynomial equation which takes the length of an **argument** as input and provides the number of computational steps necessary for a **deterministic Turing machine** to obtain the value of the function on that argument as output.

Although deterministic Turing machines can compute any function that **non-deterministic Turing machines** can compute (and vice versa), it is not known whether every function that can be computed in **non-deterministic polynomial time** can be computed in deterministic polynomial time – in other words, even though both types of Turing machine can compute the same functions, it might take much longer to compute some functions on a deterministic Turing machine than on a non-deterministic Turing machine. Settling this issue is perhaps the most important outstanding problem of **complexity theory**.

See also: **Automaton, Church-Turing Thesis, NP, NP-Complete, Recursive Function Theory**

DETERMINISTIC TURING MACHINE   A deterministic Turing machine is a machine (usually conceived abstractly) which consists of (a) an **infinitely** long tape containing cells, each of which contains a symbol from some **finite** list (including a special symbol called the blank symbol), (b) a head that can read, write, and erase symbols in the cell at which it is located, and that can also move from a cell to either adjacent cell, (c) a state register which keeps track of the particular state the machine is in at any time, and (d) a table of instructions (the **action table**) that, given a particular state and the symbol on the cell inhabited by the head, tells the machine (d1) either to modify the symbol on the tape or to move the head one cell left or right, and (d2) the new state that the machine is in (which need not be different from the previous state). It is important to note that a deterministic Turing machine specifies a unique action for each state/cell content combination, as this is what differentiates deterministic Turing machines from **non-deterministic Turing machines**.

Functions which can be computed using deterministic Turing machines are **Turing computable**. Deterministic Turing machines are equivalent – that is, can compute exactly the same functions, or solve exactly the same problems – to a number of other formal models of computation, including non-deterministic Turing machines and **register machines**.

Typically, if the phrase "Turing machine" is used without qualification, then deterministic Turing machine is what is intended.

See also: **Automaton, Effectively Computable, NP, NP-Complete, P**

DEVIANT LOGIC   A deviant logic is a **logic** that shares a **language** with some system of **classical logic**, but which differs from that classical logic in its class of **theorems** or **logical consequences**. Thus, all deviant logics are **non-standard logics**, although not all non-standard logics are deviant.

See also: **Dialethic Logic, Intermediate Logic, Intuitionistic Logic, Many-Valued Logic, Paraconsistent Logic, Relevant Logic**

DIAGONAL ARGUMENT see **Diagonalization**

DIAGONALIZATION   Given a (possibly **infinite**) list of (possibly infinitely long or infinitely complex) entries, the method of diagonalization (or **diagonal argument**) allows one to construct an object (usually a number, sequence, or set) which is of the same type as the objects on the list, but which is guaranteed not to occur anywhere on the list. Diagonalization accomplishes this by making the first value of the constructed entity different from the first value of the first entry in the list, then making the second value of the constructed entity different from the second value of the second entry in the list, then making the third value of the constructed entity different from the third value of the third entry on the list, and so on. Intuitively, the construction proceeds by running through the "diagonal" of the list, and constructing an entity that disagrees with each value on this "diagonal." For example, if we are presented with a list of **real numbers** strictly between 0 and 1 (which can be thought of as infinite **sequences** of digits between 0 and 9):

0.	2	3	7	8	6	4	8	...
0.	8	6	9	6	8	5	8	...
0.	3	7	5	3	8	4	8	...
0.	4	8	6	5	8	9	5	...

etc.

(note that the 'diagonal' values are underlined) then we might adopt the following rule for constructing our diagonal real number:

The nth value in our construction = 5 if the nth value of the nth entry in the list is not 5

= 6 if the nth value of the nth entry in the list is 5

Then the first few digits of our constructed real number are:

    0.   5   5   6   6   ...

Diagonal methods are immensely important in **recursive function theory** and **set theory**, allowing for the proof of **Gödel's incompleteness theorems** in the former and the proof of **Cantor's theorem** in the latter.

See also: **Arithmetization, Diagonalization Lemma, Fixed Point, Gödel Sentence, Indefinite Extensibility, Russell's Paradox**

DIAGONALIZATION LEMMA   The diagonalization lemma states that, in any sufficiently strong system of arithmetic (such as **Peano arithmetic** or **Robinson arithmetic**), given any **predicate** $\Phi(x)$, we can find a sentence Ψ such that:

$$\Psi \leftrightarrow \Phi(<\Psi>)$$

is a **theorem** of that system of arithmetic (where $<\Psi>$ is the **Gödel number** of the sentence Ψ).

See also: **Arithmetization, Diagonalization, Fixed Point, Knower's Paradox, Liar Paradox, Tarski's Indefinability Theorem**

DIALETHEISM   Dialetheism is the view that some **statements** can be both **true** and **false**, and thus that some **contradictions** can be true. Dialetheism most often arises in discussions of **paradoxes** such as the **Liar paradox** or the various **set theoretic paradoxes**, where the dialetheist will claim that the **argument** to **contradiction** generated by such paradoxes is in fact **valid**, and as a result the paradoxical statement in question is both true and false.

The dialetheist typically needs to adopt a **paraconsistent logic**, that is, one that does not validate the **rule of inference ex falso quodlibet**:

$$\frac{P}{Q}$$

Otherwise, dialetheism would collapse into **triviality**.

See also: **Dialethic Logic, First-Degree Entailment, Inconsistent Arithmetic, Logic of Paradox, Truth Value Glut**

DIALETHIC LOGIC   A dialethic logic is any **many-valued logic** that allows sentences to be both **true** and **false** at the same time – in other words, dialethic logics allow statements to have the **truth value glut** as semantic value. Examples of dialetheist logics include the **logic of paradox** and the four-valued logic **first-degree entailment**.

See also: **Designated Value, Dialetheism, Ex Falso Quodlibet, Paraconsistent Logic, Triviality**

DIFFERENCE see **Relative Complement**

DILEMMA₁   Generally, a dilemma is a situation involving two choices, or a problem which offers two possible solutions, called the **horns** of the dilemma (usually with both solutions being inadequate in some manner).

See also: **False Dilemma**

DILEMMA₂   Within **formal logic**, dilemmas are either **disjunctions**, or the term is being used to indicate that disjunction (or something equivalent) is at the heart of the issue at hand.

See also: **Addition, Classical Dilemma, Constructive Dilemma, Destructive Dilemma, Disjunctive Syllogism**

DILUTION see **Weakening**

DIRECTED A **relation** R is directed if and only if, for any x, y, and z, if:

Rxy

and:

Rxz

then there is a w such that:

Ryw

and:

Rzw

See also: **Euclidean, Partial Ordering**

DISCHARGE Some **rules of inference** allow one to discharge an assumption, so that the **derivation,** after application of the rule in question, no longer depends on the assumption.

See also: **Classical Dilemma, Classical Reductio ad Absurdum, Conditional Proof, Reductio ad Absurdum**

DISCRETE A **set** S is discrete, relative to an **ordering** R, if and only if every **member** of the set, other than the largest and smallest, if there are such endpoints, has a unique **predecessor** and **successor** relative to the ordering R. Thus, on their standard orderings, the set of **natural numbers** is discrete while the set of **real numbers** is not.

See also: **Dense, Integers, Rational Numbers**

DISJOINT Two **sets** are disjoint when they have no **members** in common, that is, when there is no object that is a member of both sets.

See also: **Axiom of Choice, Pairwise Disjoint, Partition, Relative Complement, Symmetric Difference**

DISJUNCT The disjuncts of a **disjunction** are the **subsentences** of that **disjunction** that occur to either side of the "or" (or to either side of the formal language counterpart to "or," e.g. "∨").

See also: **Classical Dilemma, Constructive Dilemma, Destructive Dilemma, Dilemma, Disjunctive Syllogism, Vel**

DISJUNCTION   A disjunction is a **statement** of the form:

A or B

Within **propositional logic**, conjunctions are usually represented as:

A ∨ B

The term "disjunction" is also used to **denote**, not the entire **statement**:

A ∨ B

but rather the **logical operator** represented by "∨."

Sometimes the term disjunction is also used to designate a **sequence** of formulas linked together by the conjunction **operator**, such as:

P ∨ Q ∨ R ∨ S

There are two different readings of disjunction. The first, **inclusive disjunction**, takes:

A or B

to be **true** when one or the other or both of A and B are true, while the second, **exclusive disjunction**, takes the disjunction as being true when one or the other, but not both, of A and B are true. Typically, unless otherwise noted, disjunction is understood in the inclusive sense.

Within **classical logic** (on the inclusive understanding) disjunction has the following **truth table**:

P	Q	P ∨ Q
T	T	T
T	F	T
F	T	T
F	F	F

See also: **Disjunction Property, Disjunctive Normal Form, Disjunctive Syllogism, Excluded Middle, False Dichotomy, Vel**

DISJUNCTION ELIMINATION see **Disjunctive Syllogism**

DISJUNCTION INTRODUCTION see **Addition**

DISJUNCTION PROPERTY   A **logic** has the disjunction property if and only if, whenever a **disjunction** is a **theorem**, then one or the other of the **disjuncts** is also a theorem. In other words, if:

$$\vdash A \vee B$$

then either:

$$\vdash A$$

or:

$$\vdash B$$

See also: **Classical Logic, Excluded Middle, Intuitionistic Logic, Kreisel-Putnam Logic, Scott Logic, Weak Excluded Middle**

DISJUNCTIVE NORMAL FORM   A **formula** is in disjunctive normal form if and only if it is a **disjunction** of **conjunctions**, where each **conjunct** of each conjunction is either an **atomic formula** or the **negation** of an atomic formula. For example, if A, B, and C are atomic formulas, then:

$$(\sim A \wedge \sim B \wedge C) \vee (B \wedge \sim C) \vee (A \wedge \sim C)$$

is in disjunctive normal form.

In **classical propositional logic**, every **formula** is **logically equivalent** to one in disjunctive normal form.

See also: **Conjunctive Normal Form, Negation Normal Form, Prenex Normal Form, Skolem Normal Form**

DISJUNCTIVE SYLLOGISM   Disjunctive syllogism (or **disjunction elimination**, or **or elimination**) is the **rule of inference** which, given a **disjunction** and the **negation** of one of the **disjuncts**, allows the reasoner to **infer** the other **disjunct**. In symbols we have:

$$\frac{\begin{array}{l} A \vee B \\ \sim A \end{array}}{B}$$

or:

$$\frac{\begin{array}{l} A \vee B \\ \sim B \end{array}}{A}$$

See also: **Classical Dilemma, Constructive Dilemma, Destructive Dilemma**

DISQUOTATIONALISM Disquotationalism is the view of **truth** which asserts that the **truth predicate** is nothing more than a device for disquotation, allowing us to make claims about **statements** without the need for **mentioning** those statements explicitly.

There is no doubting that the truth predicate is useful as a tool that allows us to say things like:

> The first thing Betty says on Wednesday will be true.

when we do not yet know what Betty will say that day. Disquotationalists take this insight one step further, insisting that the only purpose of the truth predicate is to allow for roundabout **reference** to statements of this sort.

As a result, disquotationalists deny that there is a substantial **property** called "truth" that attaches to statements, and thus the view is a species of **deflationism**.

See also: **Coherence Theory of Truth, Correspondence Theory of Truth, Minimalism, Prosentential Theory of Truth, Redundancy Theory of Truth, Truthmaker**

DISTRIBUTION A **term** is distributed within a **categorical proposition** if and only if that **proposition** says something about all objects instantiating that term. Thus the **universal** categorical propositions – that is, **A-propositions** and **E-propositions** – distribute their **subject terms**, while the **negative** categorical propositions – that is, **E-propositions** and **O-propositions**, distribute their **predicate terms**.

See also: **Categorical Logic, Quality, Quantity, Term Logic**

DISTRIBUTION AXIOM The distribution axiom (or K) is the following principle of modal logic:

$$\Box(A \rightarrow B) \rightarrow (\Box A \rightarrow \Box B)$$

Modal logics that satisfy both the distribution axiom and the **necessitation rule** are **normal modal logics**.

See also: **Alethic Modal Logic, Kripke Semantics, Kripke Structure, Possible World**

DISTRIBUTIVE LAWS see **Distributivity**

DISTRIBUTIVE PREDICATION   A **predicate** is applied to a group of objects distributively if the **predicate** applies not only to the objects as a group, but also to each of the objects individually. An example of a distributive predication is:

> The children ate.

since, in order for the children, as a group, to eat, it must be the case that each individual child eats. A predicate that is applied to a group of objects, but that does not apply to each of the objects individually, is applied **collectively**. An example of a **collective predication** is:

> The children are numerous.

since the predicate "is numerous" applies to the group of children, but not to any individual child.

See also: **Fallacy of Composition, Fallacy of Division, Mereology, Part**

DISTRIBUTIVITY₁   Two **functions** f and g are distributive if the following holds for any a, b, and c:

> $f(a, g(b, c)) = g(f(a, b), f(a, c))$

> $g(a, f(b, c)) = f(g(a, b), g(a, c))$

Any pair of functions that satisfy the above formula are said to satisfy the **distributive laws**.

See also: **Absorbsion, Associativity, Boolean Algebra, Commutativity, Complement, Join, Lattice, Meet**

DISTRIBUTIVITY₂   Within **propositional logic**, distributivity is the **rule of replacement** that allows one to replace a **formula** of the form:

> $(A \land (B \lor C))$

with:

> $((A \land B) \lor (A \land C))$

(or vice versa), and allows one to replace a formula of the form:

> $(A \lor (B \land C))$

with:

$((A \lor B) \land (A \lor C))$

(or vice versa).

See also: **Absorbsion, Quantum Logic**

DIVISION see **Fallacy of Division**

DOMAIN₁ The domain (or **left field**) of a **function** is the **set** of objects that serve as **arguments** (inputs) of the function. In other words, the domain of a function f is the set A of objects such that f is defined on A.

See also: **Field, Fixed Point, Image, Range, Signature**

DOMAIN₂ The domain (or the **domain of discourse**, or **the universe of discourse**) of a **first-order theory** is the **set** of objects over which the **variables** of the **language** range. The domain of a theory can also be thought of as the set of objects that may serve as **referents** of the **constants** in the language or as **arguments** of **functions** and **relations** in the language.

See also: **Element, Finite Model Theory, Inclusive First-order Logic, Individual, Objectual Quantifier, Substitutional Quantifier**

DOMAIN OF DISCOURSE see **Domain**

DOMINANT CONNECTIVE In **propositional logic**, the dominant connective (or **dominant operator**, or **main connective**, or **main operator**) of a **formula** is the **connective** in the formula with the largest **scope**. Equivalently, the dominant connective is that connective which, in forming the formula according to the **formation rules** for the language, was added last. Parentheses are often used to disambiguate formulas in order to indicate clearly which is the dominant connective (and which connectives fall within the scope of which other connectives more generally). For example, in:

$A \land (B \lor C)$

the dominant connective is the **conjunction**, since the **disjunction** falls under the scope of the conjunction, as indicated by the parentheses.

See also: **Elimination Rule, Introduction Rule**

DOMINANT OPERATOR see **Dominant Connective**

DOUBLE NEGATION   Double negation refers to the result of prefixing a **formula** Φ with two instances of the **negation operator**, resulting in $\sim\,\sim\Phi$.

See also: **Boolean Negation, Choice Negation, DeMorgan Negation, Exclusion Negation, Glivenko's Theorem**

DOUBLE NEGATION ELIMINATION   Double negation elimination (or **negation elimination**) is the **rule of inference** that allows one to **infer** a **formula** from the result of attaching a pair of **negations** to that formula. In symbols we have:

$$\frac{\sim\,\sim A}{A}$$

See also: **Classical Dilemma, Classical Reductio ad Absurdum, Double Negation Introduction, Excluded Middle, Intuitionistic Logic, Reductio ad Absurdum**

DOUBLE NEGATION INTRODUCTION   Double negation introduction (or **negation introduction**) is the **rule of inference** that allows one to **infer** the result of attaching a pair of **negations** to a **formula** from the formula itself. In symbols we have:

$$\frac{P}{\sim\,\sim P}$$

See also: **Classical Dilemma, Classical Reductio ad Absurdum, Double Negation Elimination, Excluded Middle, Reductioad Absurdum**

DOUBLE TURNSTILE   The double turnstile symbol $\vDash$ is used to represent the **logical consequence relation**. If Δ is a set of **formulas**, and Φ a single **formula**, we write:

$$\Delta \vDash \Phi$$

if Φ is a logical consequence of Δ.

See also: **Consequence Relation, Deductive Consequence, Single Turnstile**

DOWNWARD LOWENHEIM-SKOLEM THEOREM The downward Lowenheim-Skolem theorem states that, given any **first-order theory** T and **model** M of T, where σ is the **cardinality** of the **set** of primitive **non-logical expressions** in the **language** of T, κ is the cardinality of the **domain** of M, and κ is **infinite**, then for any infinite cardinal number δ such that σ is less than or equal to δ, which is less than or equal to κ, there is a model of T whose domain is of cardinality δ.

If we restrict our attention to first-order theories with a **countable** number of primitive non-logical expressions, then the **theorem** can be stated more simply. If such a first-order theory T has an infinite domain whose cardinality is κ, then T has models whose domains are of any infinite cardinality less than κ.

The downward Lowenheim-Skolem theorem is one half of what is generally called the **Lowenheim-Skolem theorem** (the other half is the **upward Lowenheim-Skolem theorem**).

See also: **Categorical, Intended Interpretation, Limitation Result, Non-Standard Analysis, Non-Standard Arithmetic, Non-Standard Model, Skolem's Paradox**

DOXASTIC LOGIC see **Doxastic Modal Logic**

DOXASTIC MODAL LOGIC Doxastic modal logic is the branch of **modal logic** that studies the **unary modal operator** "it is believed that ...," which is usually **formalized** as "B Φ."

See also: **Epistemic Modal Logic, Provability Logic**

DUAL The dual of a **formula** in a **propositional language** containing only **conjunction, disjunction,** and **negation** is the result of replacing each conjunction with a disjunction, and each disjunction with a conjunction. Given two **logically equivalent** formulas in such a language, their duals will be logically equivalent as well.

See also: **DeMorgan's Laws**

DYADIC FUNCTION see **Binary Function**

DYADIC RELATION see **Binary Predicate**

DYNAMIC LOGIC see **Dynamic Modal Logic**

DYNAMIC MODAL LOGIC   Dynamic modal logic is a branch of **modal logic** that studies the **unary modal operators** "once a is performed, it is **necessarily** the case that ..." and "after performing a, it is **possible** that ..." (where a is any action). These are usually formulated as "a" and " ⓐ" respectively. Since there typically will be more than one action that can be performed, there typically will be more than one operator of the form a (and similarly for ⓐ). Thus, dynamic logic is a **multi-modal logic**.

See also: **Alethic Modal Logic, Causal Modal Logic, Counterfactual Logic**

E see 5

EFFECTIVE METHOD see **Effective Procedure**

EFFECTIVE PROCEDURE   An effective procedure (or **effective method**, or **algorithm**) is a **finite** list of instructions or rules for carrying out some **computation** or other procedure. Various informal notions of interest within **computability theory** are formulated in terms of the existence, or non-existence, of such effective procedures, and much of the formal work with computability theory revolves around developing and studying various **formal models** of effective procedures. For example, the **Church-Turing thesis** states that any effective procedure in **arithmetic** can be carried out by an appropriately programmed **Turing machine**, or is **equivalent** to some **recursive function**.

See also: **Automaton, Complexity Theory, Deterministic Turing Machine, Non-Deterministic Turing Machine, Recursive Function Theory, Register Machine**

EFFECTIVELY COMPUTABLE FUNCTION   A **function** f is effectively computable if and only if there is an **effective procedure** which will, if given an appropriate **argument** or **sequence** of arguments, allow us to **compute**, in a **finite** amount of time, the value of that function on that argument or arguments.

See also: **Automaton, Complexity Theory, Computation, Recursive Function Theory, Register Computable, Turing Computable Function**

EFFECTIVELY DECIDABLE RELATION A **relation** R is effectively decidable if and only if there is an **effective procedure** for determining, of any appropriate **sequence** of objects, whether it **satisfies** the relation.

See also: **Characteristic Function, Effectively Decidable Set, Primitive Recursive Relation, Recursive Function Theory**

EFFECTIVELY DECIDABLE SET A **set** A is effectively decidable if and only if there is an **effective procedure** for determining, of any object, whether or not it is a **member** of the set.

See also: **Characteristic Function, Effectively Decidable Relation, Primitive Recursive Set, Recursive Function Theory**

EFFECTIVELY DECIDABLE THEORY A **theory** is effectively decidable if and only if there is an **effective procedure** for determining, of any **formula**, whether or not it is a theorem of that theory.

See also: **Characteristic Function, Decidable Theory, Effectively Decidable Set, Recursive Function Theory**

EFFECTIVELY ENUMERABLE SET A **set** A is effectively enumerable if and only if there is an **effective procedure** for placing the **set** in a **one-to-one onto** correspondence with the **natural numbers,** or with some initial segment of the natural numbers.

See also: **Arithmetic, Computation, Enumeration, Recursive Function Theory**

ELEMENT An element of a collection or **structure** is an object that is contained in that collection or in the **domain** of that structure. If the collection is a **set**, then the object in question is a **member** of that set. The term "element," however, is also used more broadly for objects that are members of collections that are not sets, such as **proper classes, multisets,** and **sequences**.

See also: **Boolean Algebra, Individual, Ordered Pair, Ordered N-Tuple**

ELEMENTARY EQUIVALENCE   Two **models** are elementarily equivalent if and only if, for any **first-order formula** Φ, Φ is **true** in one if and only if Φ is true in the other. The **compactness** and **Lowenheim-Skolem theorems** guarantee the existence of distinct but elementarily equivalent models.

See also: **Categorical, Downward Lowenheim-Skolem Theorem, Intended Interpretation, κ-Categorical, Non-Standard Model, Upward Lowenheim-Skolem Theorem**.

ELIMINATION OF QUANTIFIERS   Elimination of quantifiers (or **quantifier elimination**) is a technique used within **mathematical logic** where one demonstrates that each **formula** within a **theory** is equivalent to a formula containing no **quantifiers**. The technique is useful since in many contexts it is easier to **prove** that quantifier-free formulas have some desirable **property** than it is to prove directly that all formulas have the property in question.

See also: **Existential Quantifier, Limitation Result, Metalogic, Metamathematics, Universal Quantifier**

ELIMINATION RULE   An elimination rule for a particular **logical connective** is a **rule of inference** that allows one to **infer** a **statement** not containing a dominant occurrence of a particular connective from statements that do contain that connective as a **dominant operator**.

See also: **Conditional Proof, Conjunction Elimination, Disjunctive Syllogism, Double Negation Elimination, Ex Falso Quodlibet, Introduction Rule**

EMPTY CONCEPT   The empty concept is the **concept** that holds of no objects – that is, the concept corresponding to the **predicate** "$x \neq x$."

See also: **Aristotelian Comprehension Schema, Aristotelian Second-order Logic, Empty Set, Inclusive First-order Logic**

EMPTY SET   The empty set (or **null set**) is that **set** which contains no **members**. It is typically **denoted** using the symbol "∅." The empty set is a **subset** of any **set**, including itself, and is thus a **member** of the **powerset** of any **set**.

See also: **Axiom of Empty Set, Empty Concept, Zermelo Fraenkel Set Theory**

EMPTY SET AXIOM see **Axiom of Empty Set**

ENDOMORPHISM   An endomorphism is a **homomorphism** between a **structure** and itself.

See also: **Automorphism, Epimorphism, Isomorphism, Monomorphism**

ENTAILMENT see **Logical Consequence**

ENTHYMEME   An enthymeme is an **argument** where one or more of the **premises** is not stated explicitly. For example, the argument:

> All men are mortal.
> Socrates is mortal.

is an enthymeme, since its **validity** depends on the missing premise:

> Socrates is a man.

See also: **Informal Fallacy, Red Herring**

ENTIRE see **Seriality**

ENTSCHEIDUNGSPROBLEM   The Entscheidungsproblem is the problem of finding a **decision procedure** for **first-order logic** – that is, of finding a **recursive function** which, when applied to an arbitrary **formula** of first-order logic, outputs 1 if the formula is a **logical truth** in **classical logic** and outputs 0 otherwise. **Church's Theorem** shows that there is no such decision procedure.

See also: **Busy Beaver Problem, Effective Procedure, Halting Problem, Limitation Theorem, Recursive Function Theory, Semi-Decidable Theory**

ENUMERABLE SET   A **set** A is enumerable if it can be put in a **one-to-one onto** correspondence with the **natural numbers,** or with some initial segment of the natural numbers. Thus, a set is enumerable if and only if it is **countable**.

See also: **Arithmetic, Church-Turing Thesis, Effectively Enumerable, Enumeration Recursively Enumerable**

ENUMERATION   An enumeration of a **set** is the **sequence** generated by a particular **function** used to show that a set is an **enumerable**

set. In other words, if a set A is enumerable, then there is a function f that maps **natural numbers onto** members of A. The enumeration of A is then the sequence <f(0), f(1), f(2), ... >

See also: **Arithmetic, Church-Turing Thesis, Effectively Enumerable, Recursively Enumerable**

EPIMENIDES PARADOX see **Liar Paradox**

EPIMORPHISM   An epimorphism is a **homomorphism** between two **structures** that is also **surjective**, or **onto**.

See also: **Automorphism, Endomorphism, Isomorphism, Monomorphism**

EPISTEMIC CONSTRAINT   Epistemic constraint (or **verification constraint**) is the principle stating that all **truths** must be in principle knowable. The principle of epistemic constraint figures centrally in many **arguments** for **intuitionistic logic.**

See also: **BHK-Interpretation, Bivalence, Constructive Logic, Excluded Middle, Fitch's Paradox, Logical Antirealism**

EPISTEMIC LOGIC see **Epistemic Modal Logic**

EPISTEMIC MODAL LOGIC   Epistemic modal logic is that branch of **modal logic** that studies the **unary modal operators** "it is known that Φ" and "it is knowable that Φ." Both of these notions are typically **formalized** as "K Φ."

See also: **Alethic Modal Logic, Doxastic Modal Logic, Provability Logic**

EPISTEMIC PARADOX   An epistemic paradox is a **paradox** that arises from basic intuitions regarding knowledge, belief, or related epistemic notions. Examples of epistemic paradoxes include **Fitch's paradox** and the **knower's paradox.**

See also: **Factivity, Insolubilia, Liar Paradox, Semantic Paradox**

EPISTEMICISM   Epistemicism is the view that **vagueness** is not caused by any imprecision in our predicates or in the world, but is instead a result of our incomplete knowledge about the world. In other words, an epistemicist believes that there is an exact number of grains of sand which marks the difference between a collection of grains being a heap and its failing to be a heap. Our intuition that there is no such sharp **borderline** is, for the epistemicist, caused by our in-principle inability to determine exactly what this number is.

See also: **Forced March Sorites, In Rebus Vagueness, Ontic Vagueness, Semantic Vagueness, Sorites Paradox, Sorites Series**

E-PROPOSITION Within **Aristotle's categorical logic,** an E-proposition is a **categorical proposition** asserting that all **objects** that are **members** of the **class designated** by the **subject term** are not members of the class designated by the **predicate term**. In other words, an E-proposition is a **proposition** whose **logical structure** is:

> All P are not Q.

Often, E-propositions are written in the following **equivalent** form:

> No P are Q.

The **quality** of an E-proposition is **negative** and its **quantity** is **universal**. An E-proposition **distributes** both its subject term and its predicate term.

See also: **A-Proposition, I-Proposition, O-Proposition, Square of Opposition**

EQUINUMEROUS Two **sets** A and B are equinumerous (or **equivalent**, or **equipollent**) if and only if they have the same **cardinal number** – that is, if there is a **one-to-one onto function** from A to B.

See also: **א, ב, Bijection, c, Co-extensive, Continuum Many**

EQUIPOLLENT see **Equinumerous**

EQUIVALENCE see **Deductively Equivalent, Logically Equivalent, Materially Equivalent**

EQUIVALENCE CLASS An equivalence class is any **set** of objects that are related to each other by an **equivalence relation**. Any **equivalence relation** separates the **domain** into one or more **disjoint** equivalence classes.

See also: **Exclusive, Exhaustive, Pairwise Disjoint, Partition**

EQUIVALENCE RELATION   An equivalence relation is any **relation** R such that R is:

> **Reflexive:** $(\forall x)(Rxx)$
>
> **Symmetric:** $(\forall x)(\forall y)(Rxy \rightarrow Ryx)$
>
> **Transitive:** $(\forall x)(\forall y)(\forall z)((Rxy \wedge Ryz) \rightarrow Rxz)$

An equivalence relation divides up the domain into one or more **disjoint equivalence classes** – that is, **sets** of **elements** – such that any two objects in the same equivalence class are related to each other by R, and no object in any equivalence class is related by R to any object not in that equivalence class.

See also: **Abstraction Principle, Exclusive, Exhaustive, Pairwise Disjoint, Partition**

EQUIVALENT₁ see **Deductively Equivalent, Logically Equivalent, Materially Equivalent**

EQUIVALENT₂ see **Equinumerous**

EQUIVOCATION   Equivocation is an **informal fallacy** which occurs when a word with more than one meaning is used within an **argument** twice, with each occurrence having a different meaning.

See also: **Ambiguity, Amphiboly**

EROTETIC LOGIC   Erotetic logic (or the **logic of questions and answers,** or **interrogative logic**) is the **logic** of reasoning about questions and answers. In particular, erotetic logic examines issues such as the distinction between answering a question incorrectly versus failing to answer the question at all and the presuppositions that underlie certain sorts of questions.

See also: **Imperative, Interrogative, Statement**

EUBULIDES PARADOX see **Liar Paradox**

EUCLIDEAN   A **relation** R is euclidean if and only if, for any objects x, y, and z, if:

> Rxy

and:

Rxz

then:

Ryz

See also: **Directed, 5, S5**

EXCHANGE see **Permutation**

EXCLUDED MIDDLE   Excluded middle (or the **law of excluded middle**, or the **principle of excluded middle**, or **tertium non datur**) is the following **formula** of **propositional logic**:

A ∨ ~ A

See also: **Bivalence, Classical Logic, Intermediate Logic, Intuitionistic Logic, Law of Non-Contradiction, Weak Excluded Middle**

EXCLUSION NEGATION   Within **three valued logic**, exclusion negation (or **external negation**) is the **unary logical operator** whose associated **truth function** outputs **true** if the sentence being **negated** is **false**, outputs false if the sentence being negated is true, and also outputs true whenever the sentence being negated takes the third value (whatever that is, for example, the **truth value gap** or **truth value glut**). Thus, the **truth table** for exclusion negation (where N is the third value) is:

A	~ A
T	F
N	T
F	T

See also: **Boolean Negation, Choice Negation, DeMorgan Negation, Double Negation, Tilde**

EXCLUSIVE   Two **sets** A and B are exclusive if no object is a **member** of both A and B. More generally, two **properties** are exclusive if no object is an instance of both properties.

See also: **Disjoint, Exhaustive, Intersection, Overlap, Pairwise Disjoint, Partition**

EXCLUSIVE DISJUNCTION   Exclusive disjunction is the interpretation of "**or**" where a **disjunction** of the form:

A or B

is taken to be **true** when exactly one of the **disjuncts** A and B is true. Exclusive disjunction would, within **classical logic**, have the following **truth table**:

P	Q	P v Q
T	T	F
T	F	T
F	T	T
F	F	F

Typically, unless otherwise indicated, disjunctions in **logic** are not interpreted as exclusive disjunction, but are instead interpreted as **inclusive disjunction**.

See also: **Classical Dilemma, Constructive Dilemma, Destructive Dilemma, Disjunctive Syllogism, Vel**

EXCLUSIVE OR see **Exclusive Disjunction**

EX FALSO QUODLIBET   Ex falso quodlibet (or **explosion**, or the **absurdity rule**, or **negation elimination**) is the **rule of inference** that allows one to **infer** any **formula** whatsoever from a **contradiction** (that is, from a **formula** and its **negation**). In symbols we have:

$$\frac{P}{\sim P} \\ \overline{Q}$$

It is the distinctive feature of **paraconsistent logics** that ex falso quodlibet fails.

See also: **Dialetheism, Elimination Rule, Triviality**

EXHAUSTIVE   Two **sets** A and B are exhaustive relative to a **domain** D if and only if every **member** of D is a member of either A or B. More generally, two **properties** are exhaustive if every object is an **instance** of at least one of the properties.

See also: **Exclusive, Partition, Underlap, Union**

EXISTENCE PREDICATE An existence predicate is a **predicate** that attaches to a **constant** to signify that the constant has a **referent**. If c is a constant, then the claim that c has a referent (i.e. that c "exists") is typically formulated as:

E!c

Often, but not always, the existence predicate is a **defined** notion:

$$E!x \quad =_{df} \quad (\exists y)(y = x)$$

Existence predicates usually occur in **free logics**, since in standard non-free logics constants are assumed to always refer.

See also: **Denotation, Existential Import, Existential Quantifier, Reference**

EXISTENTIAL ELIMINATION see **Existential Instantiation**

EXISTENTIAL GENERALIZATION₁ An existential generalization is a **formula** of **first-order logic** where an **existential quantifier** is the **dominant operator** in the formula, and the existential quantifier in question is not a **vacuous quantifier**. Thus:

$(\exists x)\Phi x$

is an existential generalization, while:

$(\forall x)(\exists y)(Lxy)$

is not. Existential generalizations assert the existence of at least one object in the **domain** which satisfies the **predicate** occurring in the **scope** of the **quantifier**.

See also: **Bound Variable, First-order Logic, First-order Variable, Σ-Formula, Σ-Sentence, Universal Generalization**

EXISTENTIAL GENERALIZATION₂ Existential generalization (or **existential introduction**) is the **rule of inference** that allows one to move from a **particular statement** to an **existential generalization** of that statement. In symbols we have (where Φ is any formula, and $\Phi[a/x]$ is the result of replacing one or more occurrences in Φ of "a" with "x"):

$$\frac{(\Phi)}{(\exists x)\Phi[a/x]}$$

See also: **Existential Instantiation, First-order Logic,**

Introduction Rule, Universal Generalization

EXISTENTIAL IMPORT A universally quantified formula whose **logical form** is:

$$(\forall x)(F(x) \rightarrow G(x))$$

(i.e. All F's are G's) has existential import if it is interpreted as **entailing** the existence of at least one object that falls under the **subject term** (i.e. F). Aristotle, in his **categorical logic**, treated all **universally quantified** statements as having existential import, although the modern view is that such formulas are neutral with regard to the existence of instances of their subject terms.

See also: **A-Proposition, E-Proposition, Immediate Inference, Subalternation, Term Logic, Universal Proposition**

EXISTENTIAL INSTANTIATION Existential instantiation (or **existential elimination**) is the **rule of inference** that allows one to move from a **existential generalization** to an **instantiation** of that existential generalization. In symbols we have (where Φ is any formula, and $\Phi[x/a]$ is the result of replacing all occurrences of "x" with "a"):

$$\frac{(\exists x)(\Phi)}{\Phi[x/a]}$$

Existential generalization can be applied only if the new constant "a" does not occur either in $(\exists x)(\Phi)$ or in any assumption upon which $(\exists x)(\Phi)$ depends.

See also: **Elimination Rule, Existential Generalization, First-order Logic, Universal Instantiation**

EXISTENTIAL INTRODUCTION see **Existential Generalization₂**

EXISTENTIAL QUANTIFIER An existential quantifier is a **quantifier** that allows us to assert that a **predicate** is satisfied by at least one object. Existential quantifiers are typically denoted by $\exists$, followed by the **variable** that the quantifier binds. Thus, if Φ is a **unary predicate**, then:

$$(\exists x)\Phi x$$

states that some object is a Φ, or that some object satisfies Φ.

Existential quantifiers can be used to quantify over objects, in which case they are called **first-order quantifiers**. (The variables ranged over by first-order quantifiers are usually taken from the end of the alphabet and written in lower case.) Existential quantifiers can also be used to quantify over **concepts, relations, properties,** or other **higher-order** entities, in which case they are called **second-** or **higher-order existential quantifiers**. (The variable bound by such a higher-order quantifier is usually written in upper case, in order to distinguish it from first-order quantifiers and the variables they bind.)

See also: **Bound Variable, Existential Variable, Generalized Quantifier, Σ-Formula, Σ-Sentence, Universal Quantifier**

EXISTENTIAL VARIABLE   An existential variable is a **variable bound** by an **existential quantifier**.

See also: **Bound Variable, First-order Variable, Higher-order Variable, Universal Variable, Vacuous Quantifier**

EXPLANANDUM   The explanandum of an **explanation** is the expression being explained.

See also: **Definiendum, Definiens, Definition, Explanans**

EXPLANANS   The explanans of an **explanation** is the expression used to provide the explanation.

See also: **Definiendum, Definiens, Definition, Explanandum**

EXPLANATION   An explanation is a **sequence** of **statements** where all but one of the **statements** (the **explanans**) are intended to provide understanding of or insight into why the remaining statement (the **explanandum**) is **true**. Explanations should be carefully distinguished from **arguments** and **definitions**.

See also: **Definiendum, Definiens**

EXPLICIT DEFINITION   An explicit definition is a **definition** that provides a means for replacing each occurrence of the **definiendum** with an appropriate instance of the **definiens**. Explicit definitions typically are of the form:

$$\Phi \ =_{df} \ \Psi$$

Where Φ is the definiendum, and Ψ is the definiens. Explicit definitions should be contrasted with **implicit definitions**, which provide an analysis of the meaning of the expression to be defined by providing one or more principles containing occurrences of that expression which must be **true**, but which do not allow for uniform replacement of definiendum with definiens.

See also: **Impredicative Definition, Intensional Definition, Ostensive Definition, Recursive Definition, Stipulative Definition**

EXPLOSION see **Ex Falso Quodlibet**

EXPORTATION   Within **propositional logic**, exportation is the **rule of replacement** that allows one to replace a **formula** of the form:

$$(A \land B) \to C$$

with:

$$A \to (B \to C)$$

and vice versa.

See also: **Conditional, Conditionalization, Conjunction**

EXPRESSIVE COMPLETENESS   A set of **logical connectives** (and the set of associated **truth functions**) is expressively complete (or **functionally complete**) if and only if every truth function can be expressed using some combination of those connectives. Examples of expressively complete **sets** of connectives (relative to **classical truth tables**) include $\{\sim, \lor\}$, $\{\sim, \land\}$ and $\{\sim, \to\}$, while $\{\lor, \land, \to, \leftrightarrow\}$ and $\{\sim, \leftrightarrow\}$ are not expressively complete. Both the **Sheffer stroke** and the **dagger** are expressively complete by themselves.

See also: **Boolean Algebra, Metatheorem, Propositional Logic**

EXTENSION₁   The extension of a **predicate** is the **set** of objects which **satisfy** the predicate. Thus, the extension of "is red" is the set of red things. More generally, the extension of an n-ary **relation** is the set of **n-tuples** that satisfy the relation.

See also: **Anti-Extension, Co-extensive, Supervaluational Semantics**

EXTENSION₂   An extension of a **language** or **logic** is a language or logic that results from adding additional resources to that logic (for example, additional **operators** or **rules of inference**).

See also: **Conservative Extension, Sublanguage, Sublogic**

EXTENSIONAL LOGIC see **Intensional Logic**

EXTENSIONAL MEREOLOGY Extensional mereology is the **mereological** theory obtained by assuming that the **parthood relation** is a **partial ordering** (where P is the **binary** parthood relation):

Reflexive:	$(\forall x)(Pxx)$
Transitive:	$(\forall x)(\forall y)(\forall z)((Pxy \wedge Pyz) \rightarrow Pxz)$
Antisymmetric:	$(\forall x)(\forall y)((Pxy \wedge Pyx) \rightarrow x = y)$

and that the **strong supplementation principle**:

$$(\forall x)(\forall y)(\sim Pyx \rightarrow (\exists z)(Pzy \wedge \sim (\exists w)(Pwx \wedge Pwz)))$$

holds.

See also: **Composition, General Extensional Mereology, Gunk, Mereological Extensionality, Weak Supplementation Principle**

EXTENSIONALITY see **Mereological Extensionality**

EXTENSIONALITY AXIOM see **Axiom of Extensionality**

EXTERNAL NEGATION see **Exclusion Negation**

FACTIVITY A **predicate** or **operator** which applies to **statements** is factive if and only if its holding of a statement guarantees that that statement is **true**. Thus, both the **truth predicate** and the epistemic **modal operator** for knowledge are factive, although a predicate holding of a statement if and only if it is believed is not factive.

See also: **Epistemic Paradox, Provability Predicate, Semantic Paradox, Semantically Closed Language, Tarski's Indefinability Theorem**

FALLACY   A fallacy is a flaw in an **argument** that prevents the argument from being either **valid** (if the argument is a **deductive argument**) or **strong** (if the argument is an **inductive argument**). Fallacies are typically divided into **formal fallacies** and **informal fallacies**.

See also: **Counterexample, Countermodel, Refutation**

FALLACY OF COMPOSITION   The fallacy of composition is the **informal fallacy** that occurs when the reasoner illicitly moves from a **premise** asserting that the **parts** of an object individually have a certain **property** to the **conclusion** that the object as a whole has that same property

See also: **Composition, Fallacy of Division, Mereology, Proper Parthood**

FALLACY OF DIVISION   The fallacy of division is the **informal fallacy** that occurs when the reasoner illicitly moves from a **premise** asserting that some object, as a whole, has a certain **property**, to the **conclusion** that the **parts** of the object have same property individually.

See also: **Composition, Fallacy of Composition, Mereology, Proper Parthood**

FALLACY OF FOUR TERMS   The fallacy of four terms is the **formal fallacy** that occurs when a **categorical syllogism** involves four **terms**. Typically, the fallacy occurs because of an **equivocation**, where a word is used twice with two distinct meanings, producing the illusion that the **argument** involves only three terms.

See also: **Major Premise, Major Term, Middle Term, Minor Premise, Minor Term**

FALSE DICHOTOMY   False dichotomy (or **false dilemma**) is the **informal fallacy** that occurs when the reasoner presents her audience with two choices, when in fact there are other, unconsidered options. Typically, a false dichotomy resembles a **valid disjunctive syllogism**, and the fallacy results from the mistaken assumption that the **disjunction** involved in the **argument** is **true**.

See also: **Dilemma, Horn**

FALSE DILEMMA see **False Dichotomy**

FALSEMAKER see **Truthmaker**

FALSITY see **Truth**

FALSUM   Falsum is a primitive, **necessarily false statement** often denoted by "⊥." Typically, falsum is introduced in order to define **negation** as:

$$\sim A \quad =_{df} \quad (A \rightarrow \bot)$$

See also: **Bottom, Top, Verum**

FDE see **First-Degree Entailment**

"FIDO"-FIDO PRINCIPLE   The "Fido"-Fido principle is the assumption that the meaning of an expression is the object that that expression **refers** to.

See also: **Denotation, Gödel's Slingshot Argument, Referential Opacity, Semantic Value, Slingshot Argument**

FIELD   The field of a **function** is the **union** of the **domain** and **range** of that function.

See also: **Fixed Point, Image, Signature**

FIGURE see **Syllogistic Figure**

FINITARY   A **structure** is finitary if and only if it does not involve **infinitely** large collections or **sets**, infinitely many operations, etc. For example, finitary logics prohibit **proofs** which are infinitely long or **rules of inference** whose application involves infinitely many **premises**. A structure that is not finitary is **infinitary**.

See also: **Absolute Infinite, Ad Infinitum, Cofinite, Complete Infinity, Dedekind Infinite, Simply Infinite**

FINITARY ARITHMETIC   Finitary arithmetic is the sub–system of **Peano arithmetic**, which David Hilbert hoped to use to prove that Peano arithmetic was **consistent**. Although characterized informally by Hilbert, finitary arithmetic contains **primitive recursive functions** and **relations** as well as statements containing **bounded**

quantifiers. Hilbert believed that finitary arithmetic could be interpreted in terms of operations on concrete **numerals,** and thus did not involve the introduction of **abstract objects** or **concepts**. As a result, finitary arithmetic was, according to Hilbert, epistemologically secure in a sense in which Peano arithmetic was not.

See also: **Finitary, Finitism, Infinitary Logic, ω-Rule, Robinson Arithmetic**

FINITARY FORMAL SYSTEM   A finitary formal system (or **finitary logic**) is a **formal system** where the vocabulary of the language is either **finite** or **countably infinite,** the **well-formed formulas** are finite in length, and all **rules of inference** are finite (that is, they allow only a finite number of **premises** and finitely many **conclusions**). A formal system that is not finitary is an **infinitary formal system,** or **infinitary logic.**

See also: **Finitary Arithmetic, Finitism**

FINITARY LOGIC see **Finitary Formal System**

FINITE see **Dedekind Infinite, Simply Infinite**

FINITE CHARACTER   A **property** has finite character if and only if the property holds of a **set** S if and only if it holds of all the **finite subsets** of S.

See also: **Hereditary Property**

FINITE MODEL THEORY   Finite model theory is the study of **formal languages** and **formal systems** when their **interpretations** are restricted to **models** with **finite domains.** Many of the standard theorems and **limitation results** regarding **first-order logic,** such as the **compactness theorem,** fail when attention is restricted to finite models.

See also: **Finitary, Finitary Formal System, Model Theory, Formal Semantics**

FINITELY AXIOMATIZABLE   A **theory** is finitely axiomatizable if and only if there is some **finite** list of principles such that every **formula** in the theory can be **derived** from these principles.

See also: **Recursively Axiomatizable Theory, Semi-Decidable Theory**

FINITISM   Finitism is the view that only **finitely** many objects exist, and that we can only perform operations on collections or **sets** that are finite. Thus, the finitist will, like the **intuitionistic mathematician** or **logician**, reject **actual infinite** collections but, unlike the intuitionist, the finitist rejects **potentially infinite** collections as well.

See also: **Dedekind Infinite, Finitary, Simply Infinite**

FIRST-DEGREE ENTAILMENT   First–degree entailment (or **FDE**) is a **non-standard, paraconsistent logic** with four **truth values**: **true** (T), **false** (F), both true and false (B, the **truth value glut**) and neither true nor false (N, the **truth value gap**). The logic has two **designated values**: true and both. One can obtain the **logic of paradox** from first–degree entailment by requiring that no **statement** is assigned N, and one obtains standard **classical propositional logic** from first–degree entailment by requiring that no statement is assigned either B or N.

See also: **Analethic Logic, Designated Value, Dialethic Logic, Ex Falso Quodlibet, Strong Paraconsistency, Weak Paraconsistency**

FIRST-ORDER LOGIC   First–order logic (or **quantificational logic**, or **predicate logic**) is the **formal logic** obtained by **extending propositional logic** through the addition of **variables** and the **universal** and **existential quantifiers** that bind them. The explosion in logical studies that occurred at the beginning of the twentieth century was due in large part to the discovery of first–order logic (and higher–order logic) by Gottlob Frege. Although Aristotle's **categorical logic** already contained quantifiers for "all" and "some," it was only through Frege's systematic development of quantificational theory that the true power of these expressions could be harnessed. For example, categorical logic is not able to handle either **relations** or quantifiers that occur in the **scope** of other quantifiers. Part of the reason for this second shortcoming is that earlier logicians had no notion of variable, and thus there was no means for keeping track of which quantifiers governed which **argument** places in **compound formulas** with more than one quantifier. Thus, neither of:

Everyone loves someone.   Someone loves everyone.

could be dealt with adequately using the resources of categorical logic. Within first-order logic, however, these can be represented as:

$$(\forall x)(\exists y)Lxy \qquad\qquad (\exists x)(\forall y)Lxy$$

These formulas make the differing **logical forms** of the two English statements apparent and also illustrate the power of first-order logical methods for studying the behavior of quantifiers within **natural language**.

See also: **First-order Theory, Free Logic, Inclusive First-order Logic, Monadic First-order Logic, Pure First-order Logic, Quantified Modal Logic**

FIRST-ORDER MODAL LOGIC see **Quantified Modal Logic**

FIRST-ORDER THEORY   A first-order theory is a **set** of **statements** in the **language** of **first-order logic** that is **closed** under the **logical consequence relation**. In other words, a first-order theory is any set Σ of first-order formulas where, if Δ is a **subset** of Σ, and Φ is a first-order formula that is a logical consequence of Δ, then Φ is a **member** of Σ. Every first-order theory contains **infinitely** many members, since every **logical truth** is a member of every first-order theory.

See also: **Finitely Axiomatizable Theory, Recursively Axiomatizable Theory, Semi-Decidable Theory, Transitive Closure**

FIRST-ORDER VARIABLE   A first-order variable is a **variable** whose value ranges over the objects in the **domain** of the **model** in question. First-order variables are typically represented by lower-case letters from the end of the alphabet ("x," "y," "z"), and they occur in both **first-order** and **higher-order logics**.

See also: **Bound Variable, First-order Logic, First-order Theory, Higher-order Variable, Vacuous Quantifier**

FITCH PARADOX   The Fitch paradox (or **Fitch's Paradox**, or the **knowability paradox**, or the **paradox of knowability**) refers to the fact that we can derive the patently **false** claim that all **true statements** are known from the apparently much weaker, and less implausible, claim that all true statements are knowable. This latter principle is the principle of **epistemic constraint**. The **derivation**, somewhat informally, goes as follows. Assume, for **reductio ad**

absurdum, that there is a statement S such that S is true but not known to be true. Then the claim:

> S, and no one knows that S

is true. So, since we are assuming that all truths can be known, it follows that:

> It is **possible** that someone knows that (S and no one knows that S).

Since knowing a **conjunction** is equivalent to knowing each of its **conjuncts,** we obtain:

> It is possible that (someone knows S and knows that no one knows S)

Knowledge is **factive** – that is, if a claim is known, then it is true – so it follows that:

> It is possible that (someone knows S and no one knows S).

But the contents of the parentheses is a **contradiction,** and thus is not possible.

The Fitch paradox is particularly troubling to defenders of **intuitionistic logic** or **constructive logic** (and **intuitionistic mathematics** or **constructive mathematics**), who often motivated their rejection of **classical logic** in terms of their acceptance of the view that all truths are in principle able to be known.

See also: **BHK-Interpretation, Bivalence, Constructive Proof, Excluded Middle, Intuitionism, Logical Antirealism**

FITCH'S PARADOX see **Fitch Paradox**

5 Axiom 5 (or **E**) is the following principle of modal logic:

> 5: $\Diamond A \rightarrow \Box \Diamond A$

In **possible worlds semantics,** axiom 5 is satisfied on any **frame** in which the **accessibility relation** is **euclidean.**

See also: **Kripke Semantics, Kripke Structure, Modality, S5**

FIXED POINT₁ In mathematics, a fixed point of a **function** f is an object a such that:

> $f(a) = a$

See also: **Domain, Field, Image, Range, Signature**

FIXED POINT$_2$ In **logic**, a fixed point of a **predicate** Φ is a **statement** G such that:

$$G \leftrightarrow \Phi(<G>)$$

is a **theorem** (where <G> is the **Gödel code**, or some other appropriate name, of the statement G).

See also: **Gödel Sentence, Gödel's First Incompleteness Theorem, Gödel's Second Incompleteness Theorem, Liar Paradox, Liar Sentence**

FORCED MARCH SORITES   A forced march Sorites is a variant of the **Sorites paradox**. Given a **vague predicate** such as "is bald," the forced march Sorites asks us to imagine a competent user of the predicate who is forced to travel down a **Sorites series** of men ranging from a clear case of "is bald" to a clear case of "is not bald," where each adjacent pair of men differ in the amount of their hair by some marginal amount. The competent user of the predicate is forced, for each man in the series, to answer the question "Is this man bald?" Even if we allow any answer whatsoever, including "sort of," "maybe," "not sure," etc., there will be a first instance where the competent user fails to say "yes," suggesting that vague predicates might admit of sharp borders after all.

See also: **Borderline Case, Higher-order Vagueness, In Rebus Vagueness, Ontic Vagueness, Semantic Vagueness**

FORCING   Forcing is a **set-theoretic** technique which, given a particular **model** of **set theory**, provides a new model containing **sets** not contained in the original model (in contrast to the method of constructing **inner models**). When using the method of forcing, one obtains the new model by finding a **subset** G of the **domain** of the original model where G does not form a set in the original model, and where G is a generic partial filter on the model. One then constructs a new model in terms of G. Forcing is **equivalent** to the technique of Boolean-valued models, although the latter, while easier to understand, is usually harder to carry out in practice.

See also: **Boolean Algebra, Continuum Hypothesis, Generalized Continuum Hypothesis, Independence Result, Large Cardinal, Reflection Principle**

FORM see **Logical Form**

FORMAL CALCULUS see **Formal System**

FORMAL CONSEQUENCE   A formal consequence is an **argument** where the **premises** follow **necessarily** from the **conclusion**, and this fact holds merely in terms of the formal structure of the **statements** involved. Formal consequence is contrasted with the weaker notion of **material consequence**, where a conclusion follows necessarily from the premises of an argument, but this fact depends not only on the form, but also on the content of the **statements** involved.

See also: **Consequence Relation, Deductive Consequence, Inference, Logical Consequence**

FORMAL FALLACY   A formal fallacy is a flaw in an **argument** that depends on the **logical form** or grammatical form of that argument, and not on the meanings of the **non-logical** expressions contained in the argument. As a result, if an argument commits a formal fallacy, then any argument of that same form will commit the same fallacy.

See also: **Counterexample, Countermodel, Deductive Argument, Deductive Validity, Fallacy, Informal Fallacy**

FORMAL LANGUAGE   A formal language is a basic vocabulary plus a **finite** list of **formation rules** specifying which **sequences** of basic symbols are **well-formed formulas** of the system. For example, the **language** of **first-order logic** is a formal language. Among its basic vocabulary are the symbols for **conjunction** ($\wedge$), **disjunction** ($\vee$), **negation** ($\sim$), and the **existential** and **universal quantifiers** ($\exists$, $\forall$), and a typical formation rule might look like:

If Φ and Ψ are well-formed formulas, then ($\Phi \wedge \Psi$) is a well-formed formula.

See also: **Formal Logic, Formal Proof, Formal Semantics, Formal System, Mathematical Logic**

FORMAL LOGIC   A formal logic is a **formal language** supplemented with a **consequence relation** – that is, a **binary relation** holding between **formulas** and **sets** of formulas such that the relation holds if and only if the formula is a consequence of the set of formulas (according to that logic). The consequence relation of a formal logic can be either a **deductive** or **logical** (that is, **semantic**) notion. Thus, all **formal systems** are formal logics, but not vice versa.

See also: **Deductive Consequence, Logical Consequence, Model Theory, Natural Deduction, Sequent Calculus**

FORMAL PROOF   A formal proof is the codification of a (possibly informal) **proof** within a particular **formal system**.

See also: **Deductive Consequence, Derivation, Formal Logic**

FORMAL SEMANTICS   A formal semantics is an **interpretation** of a **formal language**. Thus, **truth value assignments** to **statements** of **propositional logic** are a formal semantics for the **language** of propositional logic, and **model theory** provides a formal semantics for the language of **first-order logic**.

See also: **Double Turnstile, Logical Consequence, Logical Truth, Logical Validity, Semantics**

FORMAL SYSTEM   A formal system (or **calculus**, or **deductive system**, or **formal calculus**, or **logistic system**, or **syntactic system**) is a **formal language** supplemented with a set of **axioms** and/or **rules of inference** specifying which **sequences** of **formulas** from the language are to count as **derivations**.

See also: **Deductive Consequence, Formal Proof, Natural Deduction, Proof Theory, Sequent Calculus, Single Turnstile**

FORMATION RULES   A formation rule is a rule that, given one or more **well-formed formulas** of a particular **language**, states that some combination of those formulas and primitive vocabulary (such as **connectives**, **quantifiers**, and **parentheses**) is also a well-formed formula. For example, a typical formation rule for **conjunction** might state that:

> If Φ and Ψ are well-formed formulas, then $(\Phi \wedge \Psi)$ is a well-formed formula.

See also: **Atomic Formula, Compound Formula, Propositional Letter, Singular Proposition, Subformula, Syntax**

FORMULA   A formula is any **sequence** of symbols from the basic vocabulary of a **formal language**. A formula need not conform to the **formation rules of the language**. If it does, then it is a **well-formed formula**.

See also: **Atomic Formula, Compound Formula, Open Formula, Propositional Letter, Subformula**

FOUNDATION see **Axiom of Foundation**

FOUNDATION AXIOM see **Axiom of Foundation**

4   Axiom 4 is the following principle of **modal logic**:

   4:   $\Box A \rightarrow \Box \Box A$

In **possible worlds semantics**, axiom 4 is **satisfied** on any **frame** in which the **accessibility relation** is **transitive**.

See also: **Kripke Semantics, Kripke Structure, Modality, S4**

FRAME   In **modal logic**, a frame is an **ordered pair** $<W, R>$ consisting of a **set** W, the set of **possible worlds** of the frame, and a **relation** R on W × W – the **accessibility relation** on W. A frame is turned into a **model** by the addition of a **valuation** providing **interpretations** of the **non-logical** vocabulary.

See also: **Kripke Semantics, Kripke Structure, Ternary Semantics**

FRAME SEMANTICS see **Kripke Semantics**

FREE CHOICE SEQUENCE   In **intuitionistic** and **constructivist mathematics**, the **real numbers** are defined by free choice sequences (or **choice sequences**). As in **classical mathematics**, the intuitionistic **real numbers** can be represented by Cauchy **sequences** of **rational numbers**. Unlike in the classical setting, however, where Cauchy sequences are pre-existing, arbitrary sequences, a real number in the intuitionistic setting is a sequence of free choices, subject to some Cauchy-style restriction.

See also: **Bivalence, Excluded Middle, Logical Antirealism, Strong Counterexample, Weak Counterexample**

FREE LOGIC   A free logic is a modification of **first-** or **higher-order logic** where **constants** in the language (i.e. names) need not **refer** to any object. Free logics are usually supplemented with an **existence predicate** "E!," so that:

E!r

means that r exists (i.e. that the constant r refers).

See also: **Constant, Existential Import, Existential Instantiation, Existential Variable, Singular Term**

FREE VARIABLE see **Bound Variable**

FREGE'S THEOREM   Frege's theorem states that all of the **second-order Peano axioms** for **arithmetic** can be **derived** from **Hume's Principle**:

$$(\forall P)(\forall Q)(\text{NUM}(P) = \text{NUM}(Q) \leftrightarrow P \approx Q)$$

A **proof** of Frege's theorem was sketched by Gottlob Frege in his *Grundlagen der Arithmetik* and *Grundgesetze der Arithmetik*, although the details were provided by later logicians. Frege's theorem is the central logical result underlying **mathematical abstractionism**.

See also: **Abstraction Principle, Bad Company Objection, Basic Law V, Caesar Problem**

FULL PREDICATE LOGIC see **Polyadic First-order Logic**

FUNCTION   A function is a mathematical entity that takes objects, or **sequences** of objects, as input (the **arguments** of the function) and provides a unique object (the **image** of the argument or arguments) as output. Intuitively, functions are mappings from the **domain** of the function (the set of permissible arguments) to the **range** of the function (the set of permissible outputs of the function).

See also: **Adicity, Composition, Field, One-to-One, Onto, Ordered Pair, Partial Function**

FUNCTIONAL COMPLETENESS see **Expressive Completeness**

FUSION see **Mereological Fusion**

FUZZY LOGIC see **Degree-Theoretic Semantics**

G

GAMBLER'S FALLACY   The gambler's fallacy is an **informal fallacy** which occurs when one draws faulty **conclusions** regarding the **probability** of a future event based on a series of past outcomes, all of which are **independent** of each other. The fallacy occurs when the reasoner concludes that a particular outcome is more likely because that outcome has not occurred recently, or has occurred less frequently than other outcomes in the past. For example, when tossing a fair coin, one is committing the gambler's fallacy if one concludes that "tails" is highly likely after flipping "heads" ten times in a row.

See also: **Bayes' Theorem, Conditional Probability, Probability Calculus, Probability Theory**

GAME-THEORETIC SEMANTICS   Game-theoretic semantics is a method of assigning **semantic values** to **formulas** in terms of idealized games played between a "verifier" and a "falsifier." **Atomic sentences** are assigned **truth values** as usual, and then a **compound formula** receives a truth value based on playing games with respect to the formula in question. We define game play as follows. At each "move" in the game, a formula Φ is in play:

If Φ is **atomic**, then the verifier wins if Φ is **true**, and the falsifier wins if Φ is **false**.

If Φ is a **conjunction** $\Psi \wedge \Sigma$, then the falsifier picks one of Ψ or Σ and play continues on the selected formula.

If Φ is a **disjunction** $\Psi \vee \Sigma$, then the verifier picks one of Ψ or Σ and play continues on the selected formula.

If Φ is a **negation** $\sim \Psi$, then the verifier and falsifier switch roles and play continues on Ψ.

If Φ is a **universally quantified formula** $(\forall x)\Psi x$, then the falsifier picks a member of the **domain** b and play continues on Ψb.

If Φ is a **existentially quantified formula** $(\exists x)\Psi x$, then the verifier picks a member of the domain b and play continues on Ψb.

A compound formula is true if and only if there is a winning strategy for the verifier on that formula – that is, there is a set of moves such that the verifier can guarantee that he will win the game on that formula no matter what the falsifier does. Similarly, a formula is false if and only if there is a winning strategy for the falsifier.

See also: **Independence-Friendly Logic**

GAP see **Truth Value Gap**

GEACH-KAPLAN SENTENCE   The Geach-Kaplan sentence is the **statement**:

Some critics admire only one another.

This statement has no adequate paraphrase within **first-order logic** – in order to capture its import, it must be formalized using **set theory**, **branching quantifiers**, or **higher-order quantifiers**. Since set theory does not seem to be involved in the informal English version of the sentence, the Geach-Kaplan sentence, and sentences like it, are often used as **evidence** in favor of branching quantifiers or higher-order logics.

See also: **Independence-Friendly Logic, Many-Sorted Logic, Plural Quantification, Second-order Logic**

GENERAL EXTENSIONAL MEREOLOGy   General extensional mereology is the **mereological** theory obtained by assuming that the **parthood relation** is a **partial ordering** (where P is the **binary** parthood relation):

Reflexive: $(\forall x)(Pxx)$

Transitive: $(\forall x)(\forall y)(\forall z)((Pxy \wedge Pyz) \rightarrow Pxz)$

Antisymmetric: $(\forall x)(\forall y)((Pxy \wedge Pyx) \rightarrow x = y)$

and that the **strong supplementation** principle:

$$(\forall x)(\forall y)(\sim Pyx \rightarrow (\exists z)(Pzy \wedge \sim (\exists w)(Pwx \wedge Pwz)))$$

and the **unrestricted fusion** principle (where O is the defined **overlap** relation):

$$(\exists x)\Phi(x) \rightarrow (\exists y)(\forall z)(Ozy \rightarrow (\exists w)(\Phi(w) \wedge Ozw))$$

hold.

See also: **Classical Mereology, Composition, Extensional**

Mereology, Ground Mereology, Minimal Mereology, Weak Supplementation Principle

GENERAL MEREOLOGY see **Classical Mereology**

GENERALIZATION see **Existential Generalization, Universal Generalization**

GENERALIZED CONTINUUM HYPOTHESIS George Cantor proved that the **cardinality** of the **powerset** of any **set** is strictly greater than the cardinality of the set itself.

Since $\aleph_{a+1}$ represents the **infinite cardinal number** immediately after $\aleph_a$, that is, it is the cardinal number of an infinite **set** which is bigger than any set of size $\aleph_a$, but for which there is no set intermediate cardinal number between it and $\aleph_a$, Cantor's result can be stated as:

$$2^{\aleph_a} \geq \aleph_{a+1}$$

The generalized continuum hypothesis is the claim that the cardinal number of the powerset of any set is, in fact, the next largest cardinal number, that is:

$$2^{\aleph_a} = \aleph_{a+1}$$

Standard **set theories**, such as **Zermelo Fraenkel set theory (ZFC)**, do not settle the question of how much larger the powerset of X is relative to X. In other words, the generalized continuum hypothesis is **independent** of such systems – it can be neither **proven** nor disproved within them.

See also: **⊐, Constructible Universe, Forcing, Independence Result, Inner Model**

GENERALIZED QUANTIFIER Generalized quantifiers are generalizations of the standard **universal** and **existential quantifiers** arrived at by thinking of these quantifies as denoting **sets of subsets** of the **domain**. Thus, instead of understanding a universally quantified phrase:

$$(\forall x)\Phi x$$

as stating that every object has Φ, we can understand it as asserting that the **extension** of Φ (that is, the set of all objects that **satisfy** Φ) is a member of the set of sets denoted by the universal quantifier (which is the set containing the entire domain as its only **element**). Similarly, an existentially quantified statement can be understood as asserting that the extension of the **predicate** being quantified over is a member of the set of sets denoted by the existential quantifier (i.e. the set of all non-empty subsets of the domain).

Once we understand existential and universal quantifiers in this manner, it is easy to see that this method can be generalized, introducing new quantifiers in terms of the particular set of subsets of the domain that they denote. For example, we can have a **numerical quantifier** which, when applied to a predicate Φ, expresses that there are exactly five Φ's. Such a quantifier would denote the set of all subsets of the domain of **cardinality** five, and one can construct generalized quantifiers of this sort for any cardinality, including **infinite** quantifiers such as "there are infinitely many x's such that. ..."

See also: **Infinitary Logic, Permutation Invariant**

GL see **Provability Logic**

GLIVENKO'S THEOREM   Glivenko's theorem states that, for any **formula** Φ in the language of **propositional logic**, Φ is a **theorem** of **classical logic** if and only if $\sim \sim \Phi$ is a theorem of **intuitionistic logic**.

See also: **Constructive Logic, Constructive Proof, Disjunction Property, Double Negation, Idempotent, Logical Antirealism**

GLOBAL CHOICE   Global choice is a stronger variant of the **axiom of choice**. While the axiom of choice states that there is a **choice function** on any **set** of non-empty sets, global choice states that there is a choice function on any collection of non-empty sets, including **proper classes** of non-empty sets. Global choice is equivalent to **global well-ordering**.

See also: **Reflection Principle, Trichotomy Law, Well-Ordering, Well-Ordering Principle, Zorn's Lemma**

GLOBAL WELL-ORDERING   Global well-ordering is the **set-theoretic** principle stating that there is a **well-ordering** on the entire **set-theoretic universe**. Global well-ordering implies the **axiom of choice** (since the axiom of choice is **equivalent** to the claim that any **set** can be well-ordered) but not vice versa, and global well-ordering is **equivalent** to **global choice**.

See also: **Reflection Principle, Well-Ordering Principle, Zorn's Lemma**

GLUT see **Truth Value Glut**

GÖDEL CODING see **Gödel Numbering**

GÖDEL LOGIC see **Gödel-Dummett Logic**

GÖDEL NUMBERING   Gödel numbering (or **Gödel coding**) is a method of **arithmetization** by which each symbol, **sequence** of symbols (including **formulas**), and sequence of sequences of symbols (i.e. sequences of formulas, or potential **proofs**) in a **formal language** for **arithmetic** are assigned unique **natural numbers**. These numbers are the Gödel numbers of the expressions (or sequences of expressions). The methods used to assign such numbers vary, but the method must be **recursive**. As a result of assigning each expression a number, various claims about the **syntax**, **proof theory**, etc. of the arithmetical theory in question can be formulated and studied within that same theory by using the numbers assigned to expressions as proxies for the expressions themselves. The method was first used in Kurt Gödel's proofs of his **incompleteness theorems** for arithmetic, and has been a central tool in various areas of **mathematical logic** since.

See also: **Diagonalization Lemma, Gödel Sentence, Gödel's First Incompleteness Theorem, Gödel's Second Incompleteness Theorem, Peano Arithmetic, Recursive Function Theory**

GÖDEL SENTENCE   A Gödel sentence is a **statement** of **arithmetic** which can be shown, in the **metatheory**, to be neither **provable** nor **refutable** within arithmetic. Kurt Gödel constructed his Gödel sentence by formulating an arithmetic **provability predicate** "Bew" such that "Bew(x)" was true if and only if x was the **Gödel number** of a statement provable within **Peano arithmetic**. He then applied the **diagonalization lemma** to obtain a statement G such that:

$$G \leftrightarrow \sim Bew(<G>)$$

is provable in Peano arithmetic (where "<G>" denotes the Gödel code of G). Loosely put, G is **equivalent** to the claim that G is not provable, so, assuming that Peano arithmetic is **consistent**, G is **true** but not provable.

See also: **Arithmetization, Gödel's First Incompleteness Theorem, Peano Arithmetic, Robinson Arithmetic**

GÖDEL-DUMMETT LOGIC Gödel-Dummett logic (or **Gödel logic**) is the **intermediate logic** obtained by adding all instances of:

$$(A \rightarrow B) \vee (B \rightarrow A)$$

to **intuitionistic propositional logic**.

See also: **Constructive Logic, Disjunction Property, Excluded Middle, Kreisel-Putnam Logic, Logic of Weak Excluded Middle, Scott Logic**

GÖDEL'S FIRST INCOMPLETENESS THEOREM   Gödel's first incompleteness theorem states that any sufficiently strong **theory** of arithmetic (e.g. **Peano arithmetic** or **Robinson arithmetic**) that is **consistent** (or ω-**consistent**) is **incomplete**. That is, in any such system there will be a **statement** of arithmetic where neither it nor its **negation** is **provable** from the principles contained in the theory. In addition, the arithmetic theory will be ω-**incomplete**.

See also: **Arithmetization, Diagonalization Lemma, Gödel's Sentence, Gödel's Second Incompleteness Theorem, Limitation Result, Provability Predicate**

GÖDEL'S INCOMPLETENESS THEOREM see **Gödel's First Incompleteness Theorem, Gödel's Second Incompleteness Theorem**

GÖDEL'S SECOND INCOMPLETENESS THEOREM   Gödel's second incompleteness theorem states that any sufficiently strong **theory** of **arithmetic** (e.g. **Peano arithmetic** or **Robinson arithmetic**) that is **consistent** (or ω-**consistent**) cannot **prove** its own consistency. It is important to note that this is not an expressive limitation – the claim that "0 = 1" cannot be proven in the theory is expressible in the theory – it just cannot be proven using the theory itself.

See also: **Arithmetization, Diagonalization Lemma, Gödel's First Incompleteness Theorem, Limitation Result, ω-Completeness, Provability Predicate**

GÖDEL'S SLINGSHOT ARGUMENT Gödel's slingshot argument is an **argument** which purports to show that any two **true statements denote** the same object. The argument depends on four assumptions:

(a) If a constituent of a **compound formula** is replaced by another expression with the same **referent** as the constituent, then the denotation of the compound formula remains unchanged.

(b) Every true statement can be treated as being in subject/predicate (i.e. "Fa") form.

(c) The statements "F(a)" and "a = (ιx)(Fx ∧ x = a)" denote the same object.

(d) For any a and b, there is a predicate R such that Rab.

Given these assumptions, we can run Gödel's reasoning as follows. Let Φ and Ψ be the two formulas which we want to show to be co-referential, and Fa and Gb to be their subject/predicate form **equivalents** respectively. Then:

(1) Φ
(2) Fa   (by (b))
(3) a = (ιx)(Fx ∧ x = a)   (by (c))
(4) a = (ιx)(Rxb ∧ x = a)   (by (a), (d))
(5) Rab   (by (c))
(6) b = (ιx)(Rax ∧ x = b)   (by (c))
(7) b = (ιx)(Gx ∧ x = a)   (by (a), (d))
(8) Gb   (by (c))
(9) Ψ

It is critical that one notes that (1)–(9) above is not meant to be an argument. The move from each line to the next is stronger, since each line is guaranteed, by one or more of (a) through (d), to denote the same object as the line which proceeds it.

See also: **Co-Referential, Denotation, Reference, Referential Opacity, Semantic Value, Slingshot Argument**

GREATEST LOWER BOUND Given a **partial ordering** ≤ on a **set** S, if x is a **member** of S and A is a **subset** of S, then x is the greatest lower bound (or **infimum**) of A if and only if x ≤ y for all y in A, and, for any z in S such that z ≤ y for all y in A, z ≤ x. In other words, the greatest lower bound of A is the **element** (if any) that is less than or equal to all of the members of A and is the greatest such element of S. Greatest lower bounds, if they exist, are unique.

See also: **Join, Least Upper Bound, Lower Bound, Meet, Upper Bound**

GRELLING PARADOX   The Grelling paradox (or the **Grelling-Nelson paradox**, or **Grelling's paradox**, or the **heterological paradox**) concerns **predicates** that apply to themselves. For example, "short" is short, but "long" is not long. Call those predicates that apply to themselves **autological**, and those that do not **heterological**. "Heterological" is itself a predicate, so we can ask if it applies to itself – in other words, is "heterological" heterological? A moment's reflection shows that, given the **definition** above, "heterological" is heterological if and only if "heterological" is not heterological.

See also: **Liar Paradox, Liar Sentence, Russell Paradox, Russell Set, Self-Reference**

GRELLING-NELSON PARADOX see **Grelling Paradox**

GRELLING'S PARADOX see **Grelling Paradox**

GROUND MEREOLOGY   Ground mereology is the **mereological** theory obtained by assuming that the **parthood relation** is a **partial ordering**:

Reflexive:	$(\forall x)(Pxx)$
Transitive:	$(\forall x)(\forall y)(\forall z)((Pxy \wedge Pyz) \rightarrow Pxz)$
Antisymmetric:	$(\forall x)(\forall y)((Pxy \wedge Pyx) \rightarrow x = y)$

See also: **Classical Mereology, Extensional Mereology, General Extensional Mereology, Minimal Mereology**

GUNK   In **mereology**, gunk (or **atomless gunk**) **refers** to objects that have **proper parts**, but which have no **atoms** as **proper parts**. In other words, all of the parts of gunk have proper parts, and all of these have further proper parts, and so on. Formally, we can express the existence of gunk as (where "PP" is the defined proper parthood relation):

$$(\exists x)(\forall y)(Pyx \rightarrow (\exists z)(PPzy))$$

The stronger claim that all that exists is gunk can be expressed more simply as:

$(\forall x)(\exists y)(PPyx)$

See also: **Atom, Composition, Mereological Nihilism, Mereology, Unrestricted Fusion**

HALTING PROBLEM   The halting problem concerns whether one can describe a **Turing machine** that, if given as input the description of a Turing machine and an input for that machine, will determine whether the described Turing machine will eventually halt if given that input, or whether it will run forever. Alan Turing proved that no such Turing machine is possible – thus, the set of **ordered pairs** where each pair consists of the description of a Turing machine followed by an input on which it will halt is not a **recursive set**.

See also: **Automaton, Busy Beaver Problem, Deterministic Turing Machine, Non-Deterministic Turing Machine, Recursive Function Theory**

HARMONY   Harmony is a proposed constraint on **rules of inference** for the **logical connectives**. Given a particular connective * and an **introduction** and **elimination rule** for *, these rules are in harmony if and only if, given a set of **premises** Δ and **conclusion** Φ, we can obtain Φ from Δ by applying the introduction rule for * and immediately applying the elimination rule for * only if we can obtain Φ from Δ without such an introduction-then-elimination construction. Intuitively, the idea is that one should not be able to obtain more content from a *-elimination than was already present prior to the *-introduction.

See also: **Inferentialism, Natural Deduction, Proof Theory, Tonk**

HASTY GENERALIZATION   Hasty generalization (or **converse accident**) is the **informal fallacy** that occurs when one draws a general **conclusion** from a sample that is too small, **biased**, or otherwise unrepresentative.

See also: **Informal Fallacy, Universal Generalization**

HAUPSATZ see **Cut Elimination**

HAUPTSATZ see **Cut Elimination**

HENKIN QUANTIFIER see **Branching Quantifier**

HENKIN SEMANTICS Henkin semantics is a **non-standard semantics** for **second-order logic**. In Henkin semantics, a **model** is an **ordered triple** $<D, D_2, I>$, where D is the **domain** of objects (those entities the **first-order variables** range over), and I is an **interpretation function** assigning appropriate values to the **non-logical vocabulary**. D_2 is the domain of **concepts** or **properties**, and is a **subset** of the **powerset** of D. Intuitively, in Henkin models the **second-order quantifiers** need not range over all possible subsets of the domain of objects as they do in standard semantics for second-order logic. Instead, the second-order quantifiers range only over those subsets of the domain that are contained in D_2.

Unlike second-order logic with standard semantics, second-order logic with Henkin semantics is no more expressive than **first-order logic**, since on the Henkin semantics approach a second-order language is equivalent to a **many-sorted first-order language**.

See also: **Branching Quantifier, Comprehension Schema, Higher-order Quantifier, Model Theory, Plural Quantification**

HENKIN SENTENCE A **statement** P is a Henkin sentence for a **theory** T if and only if:

$$P \leftrightarrow Bew(<P>)$$

is **provable** in T, where "Bew" is the **provability predicate** for T, and "$<P>$" is the **Gödel code** of P.

See also: **Diagonalization, Gödel Sentence, Löb's Theorem**

HEREDITARILY FINITE SET A hereditarily finite set is a **set** A where there are only **finitely** many **members** of A, each of the members of A has only finitely many members, each of the members of the members of A has only finitely many members, and so on. More formally, a hereditarily finite set is a finite set where the property "has finitely many members" is a **hereditary property**

on the **membership relation** restricted to the **transitive closure** of A.

See also: **Ad Infinitum, Dedekind Infinite, Finitary, Simply Infinite**

HEREDITARY PROPERTY A **concept** F is hereditary relative to a **relation** R if and only if, whenever:

Fx

and:

Rxy

we have:

Fy

More formally, we can **define** the notion of a concept F being hereditary relative to a relation R as:

$$\text{Hered}(F, R) \quad = \quad (\forall x)(\forall y)(Rxy \to (Fx \to Fy))$$

See also: **Ancestral, Finite Character, Hereditarily Finite, Inductive Set**

HETEROLOGICAL see **Autological**

HETEROLOGICAL PARADOX see **Grelling Paradox**

HIERARCHY A hierarchy is any grouping of a **set** or **proper class** of objects into levels. Although the individual objects found in a hierarchy need not be ordered, the levels into which they are grouped typically are **linearly ordered**. Important hierarchies within philosophical logic and the philosophy of mathematics include the **arithmetic hierarchy**, the **cumulative hierarchy**, and **Tarski's hierarchy** of **metalanguages**.

See also: **Constructible Universe, Iterative Conception of Set, Rank**

HIGHER-ORDER LOGIC Higher-order logic is an **extension** of **first-order logic** which allows **quantifiers** to bind not only objectual **variables** (i.e. those variables that range over objects) but also to bind **predicate** variables. Thus, in higher-order logic we can not only infer:

$$(\exists x)(Px \wedge Qx)$$

(i.e. something is both P and Q) from:

$$Pa \wedge Qa$$

(a is P and a is Q), we can also infer:

$$(\exists X)(Xa \wedge Xb)$$

(a and b have something in common) from:

$$Pa \wedge Pb$$

(a is P and b is P). Typically, upper-case letters from the end of the alphabet (e.g. "X," "Y," "Z") are used for higher-order variables.

See also: **Aristotelian Second-order Logic, Comprehension Schema, Henkin Semantics, Higher-order Quantifier, Plural Quantification, Second-order Logic**

HIGHER-ORDER QUANTIFIER   A higher-order quantifier is a **quantifier** that binds a **higher-order variable** – that is, a **variable** that ranges over **concepts, relations,** or **functions**. Higher-order quantifiers, like **first-order quantifiers**, typically come in two varieties: **existential quantifiers** and **universal quantifiers**.

See also: **Comprehension Schema, Geach-Kaplan Sentence, Henkin Semantics, Plural Quantification, Second-order Logic**

HIGHER-ORDER VAGUENESS   A **predicate** exhibits higher-order vagueness if there are not only objects that are **borderline cases** for the predicate (i.e. objects that are neither definite instances of the predicate nor definite instances of the **negation** of the predicate), but there are also borderline cases of borderline cases – that is, there are objects that are neither definite cases of definite cases of the predicate, nor definite cases of failing to be definite cases of the predicate, and there are objects that are neither definite cases of definite cases of the negation of the predicate, nor definite cases of failing to be definite cases of the negation of the predicate.

See also: **Forced March Sorites, Hierarchy, In Rebus Vagueness, Semantic Vagueness, Sorites Paradox, Vagueness**

HIGHER-ORDER VARIABLE   A higher-order variable is a **variable** whose value ranges over **concepts, relations,** or **functions**. Concept and relation variables are typically represented using upper-case letters, while function variables are often lower-case letters from the middle of the alphabet ("f," "g," "h").

See also: **Comprehension Schema, Henkin Semantics, Higher-order Logic, Higher-order Quantifier, Plural Quantification, Second-order Logic**

HILBERT'S PROGRAM   Hilbert's Program was an attempt to secure the foundations of mathematics by demonstrating the **consistency** of mathematics (in particular, **arithmetic**) within a weak theory of arithmetic called **finitary arithmetic**. **Gödel's second incompleteness theorem** is usually taken to show that Hilbert's Program is doomed to failure.

See also: **Gödel's First Incompleteness Theorem, Logicism, Reverse Mathematics**

HOLISM   Holism is the view that the meaning of an expression is partly or wholly a function of the **semantic relations** that hold between that expression and some or all of the other expressions contained in the **language**.

See also: **Compositionality, Contextualism, Pragmatics, Semantics**

HOMOMORPHISM   A homomorphism between two **structures** is a **function** f from one structure to the other (plus a correlation between functions or **relations** on the first structure and functions and relations on the second structure) such that the function f is structure-preserving. In other words, if f is a homomorphism between two structures, then, for any relation R on the first structure, and the corresponding relation S on the second structure, we have:

$$R(x, y)$$

if and only if

$$S(f(x), f(y))$$

and, for any **binary function** g on the first structure and corresponding function h on the second structure, we have:

$$f(g(x, y)) = h(f(x), f(y))$$

See also: **Automorphism, Endomorphism, Epimorphism, Isomorphism, Monomorphism**

HORN A horn of a **dilemma** is one of the two (usually inadequate) options presented by a dilemma.

See also: **Disjunction, Disjunctive Syllogism, False Dilemma**

HUME'S PRINCIPLE Hume's Principle is the **abstraction principle**:

$$(\forall P)(\forall Q)(NUM(P) = NUM(Q) \leftrightarrow P \approx Q)$$

where "P $\approx$ Q" abbreviates the **second-order formula** asserting that there is a **one-to-one onto function** from P to Q. Hume's Principle states that every **concept** has a **cardinal number** associated with it, and two concepts receive the same cardinal number if and only if they have the same number of instances. According to **mathematical abstractionism**, Hume's Principle provides an **implicit definition** of the concept "cardinal number," and we can obtain **a priori knowledge** of the cardinal numbers merely by stipulating the **truth** of Hume's Principle and **deriving** the **Peano axioms** (and their consequences) from it.

See also: **Abstraction, Bad Company Objection, Basic Law V, Caesar Problem, Russell Paradox**

HYBRID LOGIC A hybrid logic is an **extension** of modal logic obtained by adding **nominals** or **satisfaction operators** to **modal logic**. A nominal is an atomic formula "a" which 'picks out' a world. "a" is **true** at a **possible world** ω, relative to an assignment of nominals to worlds, if and only if "a" is assigned to ω. A satisfaction operator is a **binary operator** ":" holding between a nominal and a **formula**, and is used to assert that the formula in question is true at the world picked our by the nominal. Thus, "a:Φ" is true in at a world ω, relative to an assignment of nominals to worlds, if and only if Φ is true at the world assigned to "a."

See also: **Alethic Modal Logic, Kripke Semantics, Kripke Structure**

HYPERSET see **Non-Well-Founded Set**

HYPOTHETICAL SYLLOGISM Hypothetical syllogism is the **rule of inference** that allows one to **infer** a **conditional** from two other conditionals as **premises**, where the **antecedent** of the **conclusion** is the antecedent of the first premise, the **consequent** of the conclusion is the consequent of the second conditional, and the consequent of the first premise is identical to the antecedent of the second premise. In symbols we have:

$$P \rightarrow Q$$
$$\frac{Q \rightarrow R}{P \rightarrow R}$$

See also: **Affirming the Consequent, Cut, Denying the Antecedent, Modus Ponens, Modus Tollens, Transitivity**

IDEMPOTENT₁ A **unary function** or **operation** is idempotent if and only if applying that function twice to an argument produces the same result as applying it once. In other words, a unary function f is idempotent if and only if, for all x, we have:

$$f(x) = f(f(x))$$

See also: **Fixed Point**

IDEMPOTENT₂ A **binary function** or **operation** is idempotent if and only if, when we apply it to two instances of the same argument, we receive that same argument. In other words, a binary function f is idempotent if and only if, for all x, we have:

$$x = f(x, x)$$

In **classical logic** and most **non-standard logics**, the **truth functions** corresponding to **conjunction** and **disjunction** are idempotent.

See also: **Constant Function, Fixed Point, Identity Function**

IDENTITY Identity is a **binary relation**, usually **denoted** by "=," which only holds between an object and itself. The identity relation is typically taken to be a **logical** constant within **first-** and **higher-order logics**. Identity is typically the only such primitive logical relation in first-order logic. Within higher-order logics identity need not be taken as primitive, since we can define identity in terms of **indiscernibility**:

$$x = y \quad =_{df} \quad (\forall Z)(Zx \leftrightarrow Zy)$$

See also: **Idempotent, Identity Function, Leibniz's Law, Indiscernibility of Identicals, Necessity of Identity**

IDENTITY FUNCTION₁   A **unary function** is an identity function if and only if, for any **argument**, the output is **identical** to that argument. In other words, an identity function maps each object to itself, or:

$$f(x) = x$$

See also: **Constant Function, Fixed Point, Idempotent**

IDENTITY FUNCTION₂   The **identity functions** (or **projection functions**) are basic functions of **recursive function theory**. Each identity function id_n^m takes m **arguments** as input, and gives the nth value as output. For example, if the arguments for id_2^3 are 1, 2, 3, then the output will be 2.

See also: **Composition, Minimization, Primitive Recursion, Successor Function, Zero Function**

IDENTITY OF INDISCERNIBLES see **Leibniz's Law**

IFF   "Iff" is a common abbreviation for "if and only if," that is, the **material biconditional**.

See also: **Biconditional**

IF-LOGIC see **Independence-Friendly Logic**

IGNORATIO ELENCHI see **Red Herring**

IMAGE₁   The image of a **function** is the **set** of objects that are values (outputs) of the function. In other words, the image of a function f is the **set** A of objects such that x is a **member** of A if and only if there is a y such that $f(y) = x$. Note that the image of a function can be a **proper subset** of the **range** of that function.

See also: **Domain, Field, Fixed Point, Signature**

IMAGE₂   The image of an object under a **function** is the value of that function given that object as **argument**. In other words, given an object x and function f, the image of x under f is y if and only if $f(x) = y$.

See also: **Domain, Field, Fixed Point, Range, Signature**

IMMEDIATE INFERENCE   An immediate inference is an **inference** from a **statement** to another statement which is **logically equivalent** to it. The notion of immediate inference most commonly occurs in discussions of **categorical logic**, where three types of immediate inference are identified: **conversion, obversion**, and **contraposition**.

See also: **Rule of Replacement, Square of Opposition, Subaltern, Subalternation, Superaltern**

IMPERATIVE   An imperative is an expression that expresses a desire that someone bring about some action or state of affairs. In other words, an imperative is a command, entreaty, or request.

See also: **Imperative Logic, Interrogative, Proposition, Statement**

IMPERATIVE LOGIC   Imperative logic is the logical study of **imperatives** – that is, commands of the form "Do P." Typically within imperative logic, a command to do P is represented as P̲. Note that P does not, in general, imply P̲, or vice versa.

See also: **Alethic Modal Logic, Modal Logic**

IMPLICATION see **Deductive Implication, Formal Implication, Logical Implication, Material Implication, Strict Implication**

IMPLICIT DEFINITION see **Explicit Definition**

IMPOSSIBILITY   A **statement** is impossible if it cannot be **true**. Impossible statements are contrasted with both **necessary** statements (which must be true) and **contingent** statements, which can be true, but which can also be **false**.
  Within **modal logic**, where **possibilities** are represented by **possible worlds**, an impossible statement is one where there is no **accessible** possible world in which it is true. This is represented in the **language** of modal logic as:

$$\sim \Diamond A$$

or:

$$\Box \sim A$$

See also: **Modality, Normal Modal Logic**

IMPOSSIBLE WORLD An impossible world (or **non-normal world**) is a world, within **possible worlds semantics** for **modal logic**, where either the standard laws of **logic** fail to hold or where **contradictions** are **true**. Impossible worlds are not considered in standard semantics for **normal modal logics**, but some logicians have suggested semantics which include impossible worlds in order to deal with various paradoxes including the **Liar paradox** and the **Curry paradox**, as well as for dealing with **counternecessary statements**.

See also: **Accessibility Relation, Actual World, Paraconsistent Logic, Ternary Semantics**

IMPREDICATIVE DEFINITION An impredicative definition is a **definition** which **quantifies** over (or otherwise presupposes) the very thing it is defining. For example, the following definition is impredicative:

x is the smallest number in S $=_{df}$ for any y in S, x ≤ y

since x is one of the **members** of S which are quantified over in the right-hand side of the definition. A definition which does not quantify over or presuppose that which it is defining is a **predicative definition**.

See also: **Explicit Definition, Intensional Definition, Ostensive Definition, Stipulative Definition**

INACCESSIBLE CARDINAL see **Strongly Inaccessible Cardinal, Weakly Inaccessible Cardinal**

INCLUSIVE DISJUNCTION Inclusive disjunction is the **interpretation** of "or" where a **disjunction** of the form:

A or B

is taken to be **true** when one or the other or both of A and B are true. Inclusive disjunction, within **classical logic**, has the following **truth table**:

P	Q	P ∨ Q
T	T	T
T	F	T
F	T	T
F	F	F

Typically, unless otherwise indicated, disjunctions in logic are interpreted as inclusive disjunctions.

See also: **Classical Dilemma, Constructive Dilemma, Destructive Dilemma, Disjunctive Syllogism, Exclusive Disjunction, Vel**

INCLUSIVE FIRST-ORDER LOGIC   Inclusive first-order logic is the **logic** obtained by modifying the standard **semantics** for **first-order logic** by allowing models with empty **domains** (and making analogous modifications to the **deductive system**).

See also: **Free Logic, Monadic First-order Logic, Pure First-order Logic**

INCLUSIVE OR see **Exclusive Disjunction**

INCOMPLETENESS see **Expressive Completeness, Maximal Completeness, Negation Completeness, ω-Completeness, Strong Completeness, Weak Completeness**

INCOMPLETENESS THEOREM see **Gödel's First Incompleteness Theorem, Gödel's Second Incompleteness Theorem**

INCONSISTENCY see **Maximal Consistency, Negation Consistency, ω-Consistency, Post Consistency**

INCONSISTENT ARITHMETIC   An inconsistent arithmetic is a **formal system** of **arithmetic** within which there are **true contradictions**. For example, an inconsistent arithmetic might contain all of the standard **axioms** for arithmetic (e.g. the axioms of **Peano arithmetic**), but also contain:

$$(\exists x)(x = x + 1)$$

(i.e. there is a natural number that is its own **successor**) as an axiom. Inconsistent arithmetics are formulated within **paraconsistent**

logics in order to avoid **triviality**.

See also: **Dialetheism, Ex Falso Quodlibet, First-Degree Entailment, Non-Standard Arithmetic, Strong Para-consistency, Weak Paraconsistency**

INCONSISTENT TRIAD see **Antilogism**

INDEFINITE DESCRIPTION An indefinite description is a **description** of the form "a Φ" where Φ is a **predicate**. Indefinite descriptions can usually be formalized within **first-order logic** in a straightforward manner, using **existential quantifiers**. Thus:

A Φ is Ψ

can be formalized as:

$(\exists x)(\Phi x \wedge \Psi x)$

Indefinite descriptions should be carefully distinguished from **definite descriptions** – that is, expressions of the form "the Φ" – which are more difficult to analyze.

See also: **Free Logic, Plato's Beard**

INDEFINITE EXTENSIBILITY A **concept** is indefinitely ex-tensible if and only if, whenever we are given a definite collection (or **set**) of objects falling under the concept, there is an operation that we can perform on that collection which will provide an object falling under the concept which is not in the collection. Concepts which are often taken to be examples of indefinite extensibility include set, **ordinal number**, and **cardinal number**. For example, given any definite collection of ordinal numbers – that is, any set of ordinal numbers – we can consider the **successor** of the **least upper bound** of that set, which will be an ordinal number which is not in the set.

See also: **Absolute Infinite, Set-Theoretic Paradox, Universal Set, Vicious Circle Principle**

INDEPENDENCE RESULT An independence result is a **metatheoretical proof** that a certain principle which is expressible in the **language** of some **theory** is **independent** of that theory, that is, that the theory is sufficient neither to **prove** nor to **refute** the principle in question. Important independence results include the proofs that the **continuum hypothesis** and the **axiom of choice**

are independent of **Zermelo Fraenkel set theory**, and **Gödel's first** and **second incompleteness theorems**.

See also: **Forcing, Inner Model, Limitation Result**

INDEPENDENCE-FRIENDLY LOGIC Independence-friendly logic (or **IF logic**) is an **extension** of **first-order logic** which contains **quantifiers** equivalent in expressive power to **branching quantifiers**. Instead of the two–dimensional branching notation, however, independence-friendly quantifiers are written in a **linear** notation which explicitly notes which **variables** are dependent on which other variables. For example, the **branching quantifier**:

$$\left.\begin{matrix}(\forall x)(\exists y)\\(\forall z)(\exists w)\end{matrix}\right] \Phi$$

is represented within independence-friendly logic as:

$$(\forall x)(\forall z)(\exists y/\forall z)(\exists w/\forall x)\Phi$$

where "$(\exists y/\forall z)$" indicates that the **existential variable** y is independent of the **universal variable** z (and likewise for "$(\exists y/\forall z)$").

Independence-friendly logic is usually provided with a **game-theoretic semantics**.

See also: **Geach-Kaplan Sentence, Henkin Semantics, Higher-order Logic, Plural Quantification, Second-order Logic**

INDEPENDENT₁ A **statement** A is independent of a **set** of statements S if and only if neither A nor ~ A is a **logical consequence** of S.

See also: **Axiom of Choice, Continuum Hypothesis, Independence Result, ZFC**

INDEPENDENT₂ A **set** of **statements** S is independent if and only if there is no **statement** Φ in S such that Φ is a **logical consequence** of the remaining statements in S. In other words, S is independent if and only if there is no Φ such that

$$S - \Phi \models \Phi$$

See also: **Axiomatization, Independence Result**

INDETERMINACY OF TRANSLATION The thesis of the in-determinacy of translation states that divergent **translation** manuals could be set up which provide translations of **statements** of a **language** L_1 into statements of another language L_2 where: (1) both manuals are compatible with all empirical evidence, but where (2) the two manuals translate statements of L_1 as completely different, and incompatible, statements of L_2.

See also: **Natural Language, Referential Opacity**

INDEXICAL An indexical is a context-dependent expression whose **referent** does not depend on the speaker's actions or intentions. Examples of indexicals include "I," "today," "actual," and possibly "here" and "now." It should be noted that not all occurrences of these expressions function as indexicals, however.

Indexicals should be distinguished from **demonstratives**, whose referents are not only context-dependent but depend on the actions or intentions of the speaker. Sometimes, however, the term "indexical" is used more broadly to encompass both indexicals as understood here and demonstratives.

See also: **Anaphora, Contextualism, Demonstrative, Pragmatics, Semantics**

INDICATIVE CONDITIONAL An indicative conditional is a **statement** of the form:

If A then B

which can be understood along the lines of:

If A is the case, then B is the case.

Indicative conditionals are distinguished from **subjunctive** or **counterfactual conditionals** of the form:

If A were the case, then B would have been the case.

or:

If A had been the case, then B would have been the case.

respectively. It is important to note that the indicative conditional is a notion arising with respect to "if … then …" statements in **natural language,** and that there is no general consensus regarding which formal apparatus (e.g. the **material conditional**, conditionals in **relevance logics**, etc.) best represents the indicative conditional.

See also: **Conditional, Conditional Logic, Counterfactual Logic, Strict Conditional**

INDIRECT PROOF see **Reductio ad Absurdum**

INDISCERNIBILITY   Two objects x and y are indiscernible if and only if exactly the same **concepts** or properties hold of the two objects. In other words, x and y are indiscernible if and only if:

$$(\forall X)(Xa \leftrightarrow Xb)$$

See also: **Indiscernibility of Identicals, Leibniz's Law, Necessity of Identity, Second-order Logic**

INDISCERNIBILITY OF IDENTICALS   The indiscernibility of identicals is the principle asserting that **identical** objects have the same **properties**. The principle can be formulated within **second-order logic** as:

$$x = y \rightarrow (\forall Z)(Zx \leftrightarrow Zy)$$

The indiscernibility of identicals is a **theorem** of standard **second-order logic** (unless identity is **defined** in terms of **indiscernibility**, in which case it is **true** by **definition**).

See also: **Leibniz's Law, Necessity of Identity**

INDISPENSABILITY ARGUMENT   The indispensability argument (or **Quine-Putnam indispensability argument**), is an argument for the existence of mathematical objects. According to the indispensability argument, **quantification** over mathematical entities is indispensable to our best scientific **theories**. Furthermore, we should believe in those entities that our best scientific theories are committed to. As a result, we should believe in mathematical entities such as **natural numbers, real numbers**, and **sets**, since our best scientific theories are committed to these entities.

See also: **Abduction, Platonism, Quine's Dictum, Set-Theoretic Realism**

INDIVIDUAL   An individual is any object that is taken to fall in the range of the **quantifiers** of a **first-order theory**.

See also: **Existential Quantifier, Free Logic, Quine's Dictum**

INDUCTION see **Inductive Argument, Induction on Well-Formed Formulas, Mathematical Induction, Strong Mathematical Induction, Transfinite Induction, Weak Mathematical Induction**

INDUCTION ON WELL-FORMED FORMULAS   Induction on well-formed formulas (or **induction on wffs**) is a form of **proof** by **induction** where one **proves** that a certain **property** holds of all **well-formed formulas** in some **formal language**. Induction on well-formed formulas comes in one of two forms. In either case, the **basis** step amounts to proving that the property in question holds of all **atomic formulas** or **propositional letters**. The **inductive step** then consists in proving either:

> If P holds of all well-formed formulas of length less than n, then P holds of all well-formed formulas of length n.

or:

> If P holds of arbitrary well-formed formulas Φ and Ψ, then P holds of all formulas that can be obtained from Φ and Ψ through one application of a **formation rule** (typically, that P holds of $\Phi \wedge \Psi$, $\Phi \vee \Psi$, $\Phi \rightarrow \Psi$, $\sim \Phi$, and $\sim \Psi$ if the language in question is **propositional**, and that P holds of those as well as $(\forall x)\Phi$, and $(\exists x)\Phi$ if the language in question is **first-order**.)

See also: **Inductive Hypothesis, Inductive Set, Mathematical Induction, Transfinite Induction**

INDUCTION ON WFFs see **Induction on Well-Formed Formulas**

INDUCTION SCHEMA see **Mathematical Induction**

INDUCTIVE ARGUMENT$_1$ An inductive argument is an **argument** where it is intended that it be improbable (but **possible**) for the **premises** to be **true** and the **conclusion false**.

See also: **Abduction, Cogent Inductive Argument, Deductive Argument, Informal Fallacy, Strong Induction Argument**

INDUCTIVE ARGUMENT$_2$ see **Induction Over Well-Formed Formulas, Mathematical Induction, Strong Mathematical Induction, Transfinite Induction, Weak Mathematical Induction**

INDUCTIVE DEFINITION see **Recursive Definition**

INDUCTIVE HYPOTHESIS   In a **proof by induction**, the inductive hypothesis is the **antecedent** of the **conditional** proved in the **induction step** of the **proof**. Thus, if the proof is a **weak mathematical induction**, and the inductive step involves proving that if P holds of n, then P holds of n+1, then the inductive hypothesis is the claim that P holds of n.

See also: **Basis, Induction on Well-Formed Formulas, Mathematical Induction, Strong Mathematical Induction, Transfinite Induction**

INDUCTIVE PROOF see **Inductive Argument, Induction on Well-Formed Formulas, Mathematical Induction, Strong Mathematical Induction, Transfinite Induction, Weak Mathematical Induction**

INDUCTIVE SET   An inductive set is any **set** X such that, for any y where y is a **member** of X, the **successor** of y is also a member of X. The simplest example of an inductive set is the set of **natural numbers**.

See also: **Cardinal Successor, Hereditary Property, Ordinal Successor, Strong Mathematical Induction, Transfinite Induction, Weak Mathematical Induction**

INDUCTIVE STEP   In a **proof by induction**, the inductive step is the step in the **proof** where one shows that if the **property** in question holds of previous cases, then the property in question holds of the next case. For example, if the proof is a **mathematical induction**, then one shows that if the property holds of n, then it holds of n+1 (if the proof is a **weak mathematical induction**), or one shows that if the property holds of all **natural numbers** less than n, then it holds of n (if the proof is a **strong mathematical induction**).

See also: **Basis, Inductive Hypothesis, Inductive Set, Inductive Step, Transfinite Induction**

INFERENCE   An inference is an action whereby the reasoner moves from belief in the **premises** of an **argument** to belief in the **conclusion** of the argument.

See also: **Consequence Relation, Fallacy, Formal Fallacy, Informal Fallacy**

INFERENCE RULE see **Rule of Inference**

INFERENCE TO THE BEST EXPLANATION see **Abduction**

INFERENTIALISM   Inferentialism is the view that the meaning of expressions in our **language** is constituted by the rules that govern their use. Within **logic**, inferentialism amounts to the thesis that the meaning of the **logical connectives** and **quantifiers** are given by **rules of inference** and not by **semantics** or **model theory**. Inferentialists regarding logic often ascribe particular importance to pairs of rules for each connective or quantifier, their **introduction** and **elimination rules**.

See also: **BHK-Interpretation, Compositionality, Contextualism, Harmony, Proof Theory, Tonk**

INFINITARY see **Finitary**

INFINITARY FORMAL SYSTEM see **Finitary Formal System**

INFINITARY LOGIC see **Finitary Formal System**

INFINITE see **Dedekind Infinite, Simply Infinite**

INFINITESIMAL   An infinitesimal is a number greater than 0, but less than any positive **rational number**. Loosely speaking, an infinitesimal is an **infinitely** small positive number. **Non-standard analysis** involves the addition of infinitesimals to the standard **real numbers**.

See also: **Non-Standard Arithmetic, Non-Standard Model**

INFINITY AXIOM   An infinity axiom is any **axiom** that entails that there are **infinitely** many objects in the **domain**. An infinity axiom should be clearly distinguished from the **axiom of infinity** in set theory, which asserts the existence of a **set** with infinitely many **members**. An infinity axiom can be true in a **model** where the set theoretic axiom of infinity fails, since there might be infinitely many **finite** sets, and nothing else.

See also: **Axiom of Zermelo Infinity, Dedekind Infinite, Pairing Function, Simply Infinite**

INFIX NOTATION   A **function** symbol, **relation** symbol, or **logical constant** is an instance of infix notation if it occurs between two or more of its **arguments**. For example, the addition function is typically represented in infix notation, since we denote the sum of x and y as x + y, and **conjunction** is typically represented in infix notation, since we denote the conjunction of A and B as A ∧ B.

See also: **Polish Notation, Prefix Notation, Suffix Notation**

INFORMAL FALLACY   An informal fallacy is a flaw in an **argument** that does not depend on the **logical form** of that argument, and is instead traceable to the meanings of the non–logical expressions contained in the argument. As a result, an argument can commit an informal fallacy while other arguments of that same general form might not be fallacious.

See also: **Formal Fallacy, Inductive Argument**

INJECTION   An injection is an **injective**, or **one-to-one**, **function**.

See also: **Bijection, Surjection**

INJECTIVE see **One-to-One**

INNER MODEL   An inner model of a **theory** is a **model** that is obtained by taking a **substructure** of another **model**. Often, the term "inner model" is used more narrowly, to refer to Kurt Gödel's method of constructing models of **set theory** using the **hierarchy** of **constructible sets**.

See also: **Axiom of Choice, Constructible Universe, Continuum Hypothesis, Forcing, Generalized Continuum Hypothesis, Independence Results**

IN REBUS VAGUENESS   **Vagueness** is *in rebus* if and only if it is a result of indeterminacy in the world, and not due to any inadequacy in the **language** we use to describe the world. For example, on might think that the **predicate** "is six feet tall" is vague, not because there is any imprecision or 'fuzziness' in the predicate "is six feet tall," but rather because the physical structure of the world is such that there is no precise fact of the matter regarding the heights of objects.

See also: **Borderline Case, Forced March Sorites, Higher-order Vagueness, Ontic Vagueness, Semantic Vagueness**

INSOLUBILIA   During the medieval period a number of **paradoxes** and puzzles similar to the **Liar paradox** were collected together under the heading of insolubilia. These include the Liar paradox itself:

This sentence is false.

as well as other variations, including:

Every sentence is false.

which is paradoxical if it is the only **statement** ever uttered.

See also: **Open Pair, Semantic Paradox, Semantically Closed Language, Truth-Teller, Yablo Paradox**

INSTANTIATION   Instantiation is the process of replacing **variables** with **constants** (and also eliminating **quantifiers** that **bound** the variables being eliminated). Thus:

Fa

is an instantiation of:

$(\forall x)Fx$

and:

Gb

is an instantiation of:

$(\exists y)Gy$

See also: **Bound Variable, Existential Generalization, Substitution, Substitution Instance, Universal Generalization, Vacuous Quantifier**

INTEGERS   The integers are the **natural numbers** and their negatives, that is $\{0, 1, -1, 2, -2, 3, -3, \ldots\}$

See also: **Discrete, Rational Numbers, Real Numbers**

INTENDED INTERPRETATION   The intended interpretation of a **formal system** is the **structure** which the formal system is meant to describe. For example, **first-order Peano arithmetic** is meant to describe the structure of the **natural numbers** – that is, the structure which contains exactly the **finite cardinal numbers**, and on which addition, subtraction, exponentiation, etc. are defined as usual. **Limitation results** such as the **Lowenheim-Skolem theorems** show that, for the vast majority of formal systems whose intended interpretations have an **infinite domain**, there are additional, non-**isomorphic** (and thus unintended) structures that will satisfy them. Such structures are **non-standard models**.

See also: **Categorical, Downward Lowenheim-Skolem Theorem, κ-Categorical, Non-Standard Analysis, Non-Standard Arithmetic, Upward Lowenheim-Skolem Theorem**

INTENSION   The intension of an expression is the meaning of that expression and should be distinguished from that which it **refers** to or **denotes**. Importantly, two expressions can refer to or denote the same entity without having the same intension. For example, the expressions "the morning star" and "the evening star" have different intensions, but pick out the same object.

See also: **Extension, "Fido"-Fido Principle, Intensional Logic, Sense**

INTENSIONAL DEFINITION   An intensional definition provides the meaning of an expression by specifying **necessary** and **sufficient conditions** for correct application of the expression. An intensional definition should be distinguished from an **extensional definition**, which merely provides a list of those instances in which the expression being defined is applicable. For example, we might provide an intensional definition of "bachelor" by specifying that bachelors are unmarried men. An extensional definition of bachelor, on the other hand, would consist merely of a list of those men.

See also: **Explicit Definition, Impredicative Definition, Ostensive Definition, Persuasive Definition, Recursive Definition, Stipulative Definition**

INTENSIONAL LOGIC   Intensional logics are **non-standard logics** that contain the resources for distinguishing between two expressions which have different meanings even though they have the same **semantic value**. For example, an intensional logic might allow us to **quantify** over **concepts** where concepts C_1 and C_2 can be distinct even though every object in the domain that is an instance of C_1 is also an instance of C_2. Logics that are not intensional are **extensional logics**.

See also: **Extension, Intension, Reference, Sense**

INTERMEDIATE LOGIC An intermediate logic (or **super-intuitionistic logic**) is any **propositional logic** intermediate in strength between **classical** and **intuitionistic propositional logic**. In other words, an intermediate logic is any propositional logic (other than classical propositional logic and intuitionistic propositional logic themselves) where every proof which is **valid** in intuitionistic logic is also valid in the intermediate logic, and every proof valid in the intermediate logic is also valid in classical logic. There are **continuum-many** distinct intermediate propositional logics.

See also: **Disjunction Property, Gödel-Dummett Logic, Kreisel-Putnam Logic, Logic of Weak Excluded Middle, Scott Logic**

INTERNAL NEGATION see **Choice Negation**

INTERPOLATION THEOREM The interpolation theorem (or **Craig's interpolation theorem**) states that, if a **conditional** $A \rightarrow B$ is a **theorem** of **propositional logic**, and if A and B share at least one **propositional letter** in common, then there is a **formula** C, containing only propositional letters occurring in both A and B, such that $A \rightarrow C$ and $C \rightarrow B$ are theorems.

See also: **Deduction Theorem, Metatheorem, Proof Theory**

INTERPRETATION An interpretation is any mathematical construction used to assign **semantic values** to the **formulas** of a **theory** in a **formal language**. Thus, **truth value assignments** are interpretations of theories in **propositional logic**, and **models** are interpretations of theories in **first-order logic**.

See also: **Intended Interpretation, Model, Model Theory, Structure, Truth Table, Valuation**

INTERROGATIVE An interrogative is an expression that expresses a desire that someone supply information of some sort. In other words, an interrogative is a question.

See also: **Erotetic Logic, Imperative, Proposition, Statement**

INTERROGATIVE LOGIC see **Erotetic Logic**

INTERSECTION₁ The intersection of **two** sets A and B, written "A ∩ B," is the set whose **members** are exactly the objects that are members of both A and B.

See also: **Relative Complement, Symmetric Difference, Union**

INTERSECTION₂ The intersection of a **set** A, written "∩A," is the set whose **members** are exactly those objects that are members of every member of A.

See also: **Relative Complement, Symmetric Difference, Union**

INTRODUCTION RULE An introduction rule for a particular **logical connective** is a **rule of inference** that allows one to **infer** a **statement** containing a dominant occurrence of that connective from statements that do not contain that connective as a **dominant operator**.

See also: **Addition, Conditional Proof, Conjunction Introduction, Double Negation Introduction, Elimination Rule, Reductio ad Absurdum**

INTUITIONISM Intuitionism is a view in the philosophy of **logic** and the philosophy of mathematics that is motivated by the belief that there is an **epistemic constraint** on **truth**. In other words, intuitionists believe that any statement that is true can, at least in principle, be known to be true, and any **structure** about which we can utter true claims is a structure which we can, in principle, construct. As a result, intuitionism can be distinguished from other views regarding logic and mathematics in terms of both the logic accepted as correct and in terms of the nature of mathematical reality: intuitionists accept **intuitionistic logic**, where many **classically valid theorems** such as **excluded middle** are **invalid**. In addition, intuitionists typically believe that mathematical structures are mental constructions, and, as a result, reject those structures, such as the classical **real numbers**, which cannot be viewed as the result of an idealized mental construction.

See also: **BHK-Interpretation, Constructive Proof, Double Negation, Free Choice Sequence, Intuitionistic Mathematics, Logical Antirealism**

INTUITIONISTIC LOGIC   Intuitionistic logic is a **non-standard constructive logic** which does not contain either:

$$P \vee \sim P$$

or:

$$\sim \sim P \to P$$

as **theorems**. In addition, within intuitionistic logic, if a **disjunction** A ∨ B is **provable**, then one or the other of the **disjuncts** is provable.

Intuitionistic logic is typically motivated by arguing that a statement can only be **true** if it is knowable or **provable** – this is the principle of **epistemic constraint** – and then pointing out that non-intuitionistic principles, such as those above, are implausible on this understanding of truth.

See also: **BHK-Interpretation, Bivalence, Disjunction Property, Double Negation, Excluded Middle, Logical Antirealism**

INTUITIONISTIC MATHEMATICS   Intuitionistic mathematics is the version of **constructive mathematics** obtained by requiring, first, that only **intuitionistic logic** be used in **derivations**, and second, that the mathematical **structures** being investigated be constructible. This latter requirement, for the intuitionist, amounts roughly to the claim that the only acceptable mathematical structures are **finite** or **potentially infinite** ones.

The collection of **theorems** in intuitionistic **arithmetic** is a subcollection of the theorems of classical arithmetic. Within **analysis**, however, there are intuitionistic theorems which are not theorems of classical analysis, and in fact are **false** in classical analysis.

See also: **Bivalence, Excluded Middle, Free Choice Sequence, Markov's Principle, Strong Counterexample, Weak Counterexample**

INVALID see **Valid**

INVALID DEDUCTIVE ARGUMENT see **Valid Deductive Argument**

INVERSE   The inverse (or **converse**) of a **relation** R is the relation R^{-1}

such that, for any x and y:

Rxy

if and only if:

$R^{-1}yx$

See also: **Composition, Converse-Well-Founded**

INVOLUTION   A **unary function** or **operation** is an involution if and only if, when we apply it to an **argument** and then apply it again to the result, we regain the original argument. In other words, a unary function f is an involution if and only if, for all x, we have:

$x = f(f(x))$

The debate between **intuitionistic logic** and **classical logic** can be viewed, at least in part, in terms of whether one believes the **truth function** corresponding to the **negation** operator is an involution – that is, whether the **truth value** of:

Φ

is **identical** to that of

~ ~ Φ

See also: **Double Negation, Double Negation Elimination, Double Negation Introduction, Fixed Point, Glivenko's Theorem, Idempotent**

I-PROPOSITION   An I-proposition is a **categorical proposition** asserting that there is at least one object which is a **member** of the **class designated** by the **subject term** and which is also a member of the class designated by the **predicate term**. In other words, an I-proposition is a **proposition** whose **logical form** is:

Some P are Q.

The **quality** of an I-proposition is **affirmative**, and its **quantity** is **particular**. An I-proposition **distributes** neither its subject term nor its predicate term.

See also: **A-Proposition, E-Proposition, O-Proposition, Square of Opposition**

IRRATIONAL NUMBERS see **Rational Numbers**

IRREFLEXIVITY   A **binary relation** R is irreflexive if and only if, for any object x, we have:

> ~ Rxx

In other words, an irreflexive relation is nowhere **reflexive**.

See also: **Coreflexivity, T**

"IS" OF IDENTITY   The "is" of identity is the use of the word "is" to assert that two objects are, in fact, the same. Thus:

> Gottlob Frege is the author of the *Grundgesetze der Arithmetik*.

is an example of the "is" of identity, while:

> Gottlob Frege is German.

is not.

See also: **Identity, Indiscernibility of Identicals, "Is" of Predication, Leibniz's Law, Necessity of Identity**

"IS" OF PREDICATION   The "is" of predication (or **copula**) is the use of the word "is" to assert that that a **concept** holds of some object. Thus:

> Bertrand Russell is British.

is an example of the "is" of predication, while:

> Bertrand Russell is a co-author of the *Principia Mathematica*.

is not.

See also: **"Is" of Identity, Predicate**

ISLAND OF KNIGHTS AND KNAVES   The Island of Knights and Knaves is a fictional island inhabited by two tribes, the **knights** and the **knaves**. Knights, as a matter of **necessity**, can never lie, while knaves can never tell the **truth** (i.e. only utter falsehoods). Furthermore, the inhabitants of the island are forbidden to allow themselves into situations which would force them to break these rules.

The island has been used by Raymond Smullyan and others to formulate **logical** puzzles which illuminate various logical principles. A simple example of such a puzzle is:

> Confronted with an inhabitant of the island, what "yes" or "no"

question can you ask him such that, after he answers, you will know to which tribe he belongs?

See also: **Diagonalization, Knower's Paradox, Liar Paradox, Liar Sentence, Semantic Paradox**

ISOMORPHISM   An isomorphism is a **homomorphism** between two **structures** that is also **bijective**. In other words, if there is an isomorphism between two structures, then they have exactly the same formal features.

See also: **Automorphism, Endomorphism, Epimorphism, Monomorphism**

ITERATION   Iteration is the act of repeating. Thus, within **logic**, iteration refers to any construction where one applies some **function** or **operation** to a starting point, and then applies the function or operation again to the result of the first application, and then applies the function or operation again to the result of the second application, and so on **ad infinitum**.

See also: **Arithmetic Successor, Cardinal Successor, Cumulative Hierarchy, Iterative Conception of Set, Ordinal Successor, Successor Function**

ITERATION THEOREM see **S-M-N Theorem**

ITERATIVE CONCEPTION OF SET   The iterative conception of **set** is a conception of set where sets are "formed" at **ranks**. At the first rank we form, into sets, all possible collections of non–sets or **urelements** (if there are no urelements, then the only set formed at this rank is the **empty set**). At the second rank, we form, into sets, all possible collections of objects formed as the first rank. At the third rank we form, into sets, all possible collections of objects formed in the previous two ranks. And so on. After all of the finite ranks there is an infinite rank, rank ω, where we form, as sets, all possible collections of objects formed at one of the finite ranks. Next, there is rank $\omega + 1$, where we form, as sets, all possible collections of objects formed at any previous rank. And so on, **ad infinitum**. On the iterative conception of set, a collection must be formed at some rank in order to be a set. Thus, there is, on this conception, no **universal set**. Collections which are not "formed" into sets at any rank are **proper classes**.

The iterative conception of set is motivated by the desire to eliminate any circles or **infinite** descending chains in the **set-theoretic membership relation**. In other words, when forming sets according to the iterative conception, we will never encounter any sequence of sets x_1, x_2, x_3, ... x_{n-1}, x_n such that x_1 is a member of x_2, x_2 is a member of x_3, ... x_{n-1} is a member of x_n and x_n is a member of x_1. Since the **Russell paradox** and other **set-theoretic paradoxes** involve such circular, or **non-well-founded** collections, this conception of set is thought to avoid the paradoxes.

See also: **Burali-Forti Paradox, Limitation-of-Size Conception of Set, Reflection Principle, Zermelo Fraenkel Set Theory**

JOIN   In **Boolean algebra** or the **theory** of **lattices**, the join of two **elements** is the **least upper bound** of those elements. The join of A and B is usually denoted by "A ∪ B."

See also: **Greatest Lower Bound, Lower Bound, Meet, Upper Bound**

JOINT DENIAL see **Dagger**

K   The **modal logic** K is the minimal **normal modal logic**. In other words, K contains the **distributive axiom**:

K: $\Box (A \to B) \to (\Box A \to \Box B)$

And the **necessitation rule**:

If:

$\vdash A$

Then:

$\vdash \Box A$

In **possible worlds semantics,** the modal logic K is **valid** on any **frame**.

K also refers to the **axiom** that is characteristic of the modal logic K – that is, the **distributive axiom**. The axiom K is satisfied on any frame. Modal logics which satisfy both the K axiom and the necessitation rule are normal modal logics.

See also: **Kripke Semantics, Kripke Structure, Modality**

κ-CATEGORICAL   A **theory** is κ-categorical (or **categorical in** κ) if and only if all of its **models** of **cardinality** κ are **isomorphic**.

See also: **Categorical, Downward Lowenheim-Skolem Theorem, Non-Standard Model, Upward Lowenheim-Skolem Theorem**

KELLEY-MORSE SET THEORY see **Morse-Kelley Set Theory**

KLEENE CONNECTIVES see **Strong Kleene Connectives, Weak Kleene Connectives**

KLEENE HIERARCHY see **Arithmetical Hierarchy**

KM see **Morse-Kelley Set Theory**

KNAVES   On the **Island of Knights and Knaves,** Knaves are a tribe of island natives who, as a matter of **necessity,** can only utter **falsehoods**.

See also: **Knights, Knower's Paradox, Liar Paradox**

KNIGHTS   On the **Island of Knights and Knaves,** Knights are a tribe of island natives who, as a matter of **necessity,** can only utter **truths**.

See also: **Knaves, Knower's Paradox, Liar Paradox**

KNOWABILITY PARADOX see **Fitch Paradox**

KNOWER'S PARADOX   The knower's paradox (or **paradox of the knower**) is a **paradox** that can be constructed within **arithmetic** supplemented with a **unary predicate** "K" which applies to (the **Gödel numbers** of) exactly those **statements** that are known.

Utilizing the **diagonalization lemma** we can find a **statement** Φ such that:

$$\Phi \leftrightarrow \sim K(<\Phi>)$$

(where $<\Phi>$ is the Gödel number of Φ) is a **theorem**. We need only assume that that knowledge is **factive**, and that theorems are known, in order to derive a **contradiction** from this statement.

See also: **Epistemic Paradox, Fitch Paradox, Liar Paradox, Semantic Paradox**

KÖNIG PARADOX   The König paradox is the **paradox of denotation** that arises from consideration of the expression:

> The smallest **ordinal number** that cannot be specified uniquely.

Since our **language** has a **finite** (or, perhaps, **countably infinite**) vocabulary, there are no more than a countable infinity of expressions that **denote** ordinal numbers. Thus, there must be a first ordinal number that is not denoted by such an expression. Call that ordinal number α. Thus, the offset expression above denotes α. But then there is an expression that uniquely specifies α. **Contradiction**.

See also: **Berry Paradox, Richard Paradox**

KÖNIG'S LEMMA$_1$ König's lemma is a **statement** in graph theory which asserts that if one has a graph containing no cycles where each node is connected to **finitely** many other nodes, then if there are **infinitely** many nodes in the graph, then there is an infinite path in the graph – that is, an infinite sequence of nodes n_1, n_2, n_3 ... where each of these nodes is connected to the next.

König's lemma is **equivalent** to a version of the **axiom of choice** called the **axiom of dependent choice**.

See also: **Zorn's Lemma**

KÖNIG'S LEMMA$_2$ König's lemma is a **theorem** in **set theory** regarding adding and multiplying (possibly **infinite**) collections of (possibly **infinite**) **cardinal numbers**. If we have two **sequences** of cardinal numbers m_1, m_2, m_3 ... and n_1, n_2, n_3 ... (where these sequences can be **transfinite**, but are of the same length), and, for each i, $m_i < n_i$, then the sum of the m's is less than the product of the n's. The proof of König's lemma requires the **axiom of choice**.

See also: **Arithmetic, Cardinal Arithmetic, Ordinal Arithmetic**

KÖNIG'S PARADOX see **König Paradox**

KREISEL-PUTNAM LOGIC Kreisel–Putnam logic is the **intermediate logic** obtained by adding all instances of:

$$(\sim A \to (B \vee C)) \to ((\sim A \to B) \vee (\sim A \to C))$$

to **intuitionistic propositional logic**. Kreisel–Putnam logic (along with **Scott logic**) is one of the few intermediate logics known to satisfy the **disjunction property**.

See also: **Constructive Logic, Gödel–Dummett Logic, Logic of Weak Excluded Middle**

KRIPKE SEMANTICS Kripke semantics (or **relational semantics**, or **frame semantics**, or **possible worlds semantics**) is a method of **formal semantics** which has been used to provide semantics for both **modal logics** and **non-standard propositional logics**. In Kripke semantics a **model** is an ordered triple <W, I, R, A> (a **Kripke structure**) where W is the set of nodes of the model, I is a **subset** of W (the distinguished, or initial, nodes), R is the **relation** between nodes, and A is a **function** from node/**atomic formula** pairs to **truth values** (intuitively, A assigns each atomic formula a truth value at each node). Truth values are then assigned to **compound formulas** at each node.

If the language contains **modal vocabulary**, then the **connectives** are typically treated in the standard way on each node, "□P" is true at a node n if and only if "P" is true at every node related to n by R, and "◇P" is true at a node n if and only if "P" is true at some node related to n by R.

If, on the other hand, Kripke semantics is used to interpret a non-standard propositional logic, then different clauses will be used to assign truth values to **compound statements** at a node. For example, in the Kripke semantics for **intuitionistic logic** a **conditional** "A → B" is true at a node n if and only if "B" is true at every node related to n by R where "A" is true, and a **negation** "∼ A" is true at a node n if and only if "A" fails to be true at every node related to n by R.

See also: **Accessibility Relation, Constructive Logic, Frame, Ternary Semantics**

KRIPKE STRUCTURE   A Kripke structure is an ordered triple $<W, I, R, A>$ where W is a set of nodes, I is a **subset** of W (the distinguished, or initial nodes), R is a **relation** between nodes, and A is a function from node/**atomic formula** pairs **to truth values.** Kripke structures are used extensively in providing the **semantics** for **modal logic** and a number of systems of **non-standard logic.**

See also: **Accessibility Relation, Frame, Kripke Semantics, Ternary Semantics**

KRIPKE-PLATEK SET THEORY   Kripke–Platek set theory is a **formal set theory** which contains the following standard set-theoretic axioms:

Axiom of Extensionality: $(\forall x)(\forall y)(x = y \leftrightarrow (\forall z)(z \in x \leftrightarrow z \in y))$

Axiom of Empty Set: $(\exists x)(\forall y)(y \notin x)$

Axiom of Union: $(\forall x)(\exists y)(\forall z)(z \in y \leftrightarrow (\exists w)(z \in w \wedge w \in x))$

Axiom of **Induction:** For any **predicate** P, if, for any set y, P holding of the **members** of y implies that P holds of y, then P holds of all sets.

Axiom of Σ_0 **Separation:** Given any set x and any **unary predicate** P where all **quantifiers** in P are **bounded**, there is a set containing exactly the members of x such that P holds of them.

Axiom of Σ_0 **Collection:** Given any **binary predicate** P, if, for every set z, there is a set w such that Pzw, then for any set u there is a set v such that, for any member r of u, there is a member s of v, such that Prs.

Kripke–Platek set theory differs from **Zermelo Fraenkel set theory** in that the **axiom of powerset,** the **axiom of infinity,** and the **axiom of choice** all fail.

See also: **Morse-Kelley Set Theory, New Foundations, Positive**

Set Theory, Von Neumann Bernays Gödel Set Theory, Zermelo Fraenkel Set Theory

K₃   K₃ (or **Strong Kleene Logic**) is a **three-valued logic** where the third **semantic value** is the **truth value gap** "neither **true** nor **false**" (typically denoted "N"), and the sole **designated value** is the true. **Compound sentences** are assigned truth values based on the **truth tables** for the **strong Kleene connectives**.

See also: **Analethic Logic, Deviant Logic, Logic of Paradox, Many-Valued Logic, Non-Standard Logic**

KURATOWSKI ORDERED PAIR see **Ordered Pair**

KURATOWSKI-ZORN LEMMA see **Zorn's Lemma**

κ-VALIDITY   A **statement** is κ-valid (or **valid in** κ) if and only if it is **true** on any **interpretation** where the **cardinality** of the **domain** is κ.

See also: **Deductive Validity, κ-Categorical, Semantic Validity**

L   L denotes the **proper class** of **constructible sets**.

See also: **Constructible Universe, Cumulative Hierarchy, Independence Results, Inner Model**

LAMBDA-CALCULUS see **λ-Calculus**

LAMBEK CALCULUS   The Lambek calculus was the first **non-commutative logic** and has become an important tool in computational linguistics.

See also: **Sequent Calculus, Structural Rule, Substructural Logic**

LANGUAGE   A language is a system of symbols used to communicate. Typically, in order to count as a language, the system of symbols in question must be, for the most part, arbitrary – that is, there is no requirement that there be some "special" relationship between a symbol and what it symbolizes – and there must be grammatical rules that distinguish between meaningful and meaningless combinations of such symbols. Typically, but not always, these rules will imply that the language contains **infinitely** many distinct meaningful expressions.

See also: **Formal Language, Metalanguage, Natural Language, Object Language, Sublanguage, Translation**

LARGE CARDINAL   A large cardinal is a **cardinal number** whose existence is not guaranteed by **Zermelo Fraenkel set theory**. **Axioms** that assert the existence of various sorts of large cardinal are of central importance to a number of areas of **set theory**, including the search for extensions of set theory which might settle outstanding questions such as the **continuum hypothesis**. Varieties of large cardinal include **inaccessible cardinals, compact cardinals, Mahlo cardinals**, and **measurable cardinals**.

See also: **Forcing, Large Cardinal Axiom, Reflection Principle, Strongly Inaccessible Cardinal, Weakly Inaccessible Cardinal**

LARGE CARDINAL AXIOM   A large cardinal axiom is a **set-theoretic** principle that asserts the existence of one or more **large cardinals**.

See also: **Compact Cardinal, Mahlo Cardinal, Measurable Cardinal, Strongly Inaccessible Cardinal, Weakly Inaccessible Cardinal**

LATTICE   A lattice is any **partially ordered set** $(A, \leq)$ where any two **elements** x and y have both a **least upper bound** and a **greatest lower bound**. Equivalently, a lattice is any **set of objects** A and **binary functions** on A (typically represented by $\cap$ and $\cup$) which **satisfy** the following **axioms**:

Associativity:	$A \cap (B \cap C) = (A \cap B) \cap C$
	$A \cup (B \cup C) = (A \cup B) \cup C$
Commutativity:	$A \cap B = B \cap A$
	$A \cup B = B \cup A$
Absorbsion:	$A \cap (A \cup B) = A$
	$A \cup (A \cap B) = A$

To prove the **equivalence** of these two **definitions**, we need merely note that ∪ and ∩ are least upper bound and greatest lower bound respectively, and that as a result we have:

x ≤ y if and only if x = x ∪ y

and:

x ≤ y if and only if y = y ∩ x

The **function** ∩ is **meet**, and the **function** ∪ is **join**.
    Boolean algebras are an important type of lattice.

See also: **Complement, Distributivity**

LAW OF BIVALENCE see **Bivalence**

LAW OF CONTRADICTION see **Law of Non-Contradiction**

LAW OF EXCLUDED MIDDLE see **Excluded Middle**

LAW OF NON-CONTRADICTION₁   The law of non-contradiction (or the **law of contradiction**, or the **principle of non-contradiction**) is the **metatheoretic** claim that no **statement** is both **true** and **false**. It can be expressed in the metatheory as:

$$(\forall P) \sim (T(P) \wedge T(\sim P))$$

(assuming we read "T(~P)," that is, "the **negation** of P is true," as **equivalent** to "P is false").

See also: **Bivalence, Dialetheism, Semantically Closed Language, Truth Value, Truth Value Gap, Truth Value Glut**

LAW OF NON-CONTRADICTION₂   The law of non-contradiction (or the **law of contradiction**) is the following **formula** of **propositional logic**:

$$\sim (A \wedge \sim A)$$

See also: **Bivalence, Dialethic Logic, Impossible World, Logic of Paradox, Paraconsistent Logic**

λ-CALCULUS   The λ-calculus (or **lambda calculus**) is a **formal system** used to investigate the manner in which **functions** are **defined** and applied. λ-calculus was developed in part in an attempt to found mathematics on functions instead of **sets**, although its mathematical and philosophical interest has long since outstripped this initial motivation.

Within the κ-calculus every expression is a **unary function**. For example:

$$(\lambda x)(x+1)$$

is the name of the function that adds two to its **argument**. Application of a function to an argument (which will also be a unary function) is symbolized by writing the function name before the argument. Thus:

$$(\lambda x)(x+1)\ 2$$

represents the application of the "plus 1" function to two, which yields 3.

The λ-calculus has become an important tool in **recursive function theory** and **complexity theory**, and is also of central importance in certain areas of computer science.

See also: **Church–Turing Thesis, Recursive Function Theory**

LEAST UPPER BOUND   Given a **partial ordering** ≤ on a **set** S, if x is a member of S and A is a **subset** of S, then x is the least upper bound (or **supremum**) of A if and only if y ≤ x for all y in A, and, for any z such that y ≤ z for all y in A, x ≤ z. In other words, the least upper bound of A is the **element** (if any) that is greater than or equal to all of the members of A, and is the least such element of S. Least upper bounds, if they exist, are unique.

See also: **Greatest Lower Bound, Join, Lower Bound, Meet, Upper Bound**

LEFT FIELD see **Domain**

LEIBNIZ'S LAW   Leibniz's law (or the **identity of indiscernibles**) is the principle asserting that any two objects with the exact same **properties** are identical. A more intuitive way of putting this is that there cannot be two distinct objects with exactly the same properties. The principle can be formulated within **second-order logic** as:

$$(\forall Z)(Zx \leftrightarrow Zy) \rightarrow x = y$$

Leibniz's law is a **theorem** of standard second-order logic (unless **identity** is defined in terms of **indiscernibility**, in which case it is **true** by **definition**).

The term "Leibniz's law" is also sometimes used to **refer** to the **conjunction** of the identity of indiscernibles and the **indiscernibility of identicals**.

See also: **Higher-order Logic, Necessity of Identity**

LEMMA A lemma is a **theorem** which holds little independent interest on its own, and is **proved** primarily for the sake of a later theorem whose **proof** requires the lemma.

See also: **Corollary**

LIAR PARADOX The Liar paradox (or **Epimenides paradox**, or **Eubulides paradox**, or **paradox of the liar**) results from consideration of the **Liar sentence**:

> This statement is false.

or, more formally:

> L: Statement L is false.

The Liar sentence immediately **implies**:

$$L \leftrightarrow \sim T<L>$$

(where "T" is the **truth predicate**, and assuming that falsity is the **negation** of **truth**). As a result, if we assume the instance of the **T-schema** applied to L:

> L if and only if T<L>

then we can conclude that:

$$T<L> \leftrightarrow \sim T<L>$$

a **contradiction**.

See also: **Curry Paradox, Open Pair, Semantic Paradox, Semantically Closed Language, Truth-Teller, Yablo Paradox**

LIAR SENTENCE The liar sentence is the following **statement**:

> This statement is false.

or, more formally:

> L: Statement L is false.

The liar sentence, along with other plausible principles regarding **truth**, such as the **T-schema**, leads to the **Liar paradox**.

See also: **Antinomy, Bivalence, Insolubilia, Law of Non-Contradiction, Semantic Paradox**

LIMIT CARDINAL   A **cardinal number** κ is a limit cardinal if and only if there is some cardinal number γ less than κ and, for all such γ less than κ, the **cardinal successor** of γ is also less than κ. Loosely put, a limit cardinal is a cardinal number other than 0 which cannot be reached from smaller cardinals by successive application of the cardinal successor operation.

See also: **Cardinal Arithmetic, Limit Ordinal, Regular Cardinal**

LIMIT ORDINAL   An **ordinal number** α is a limit ordinal if and only if there is some ordinal number β less than α and, for all such β less than α, the **ordinal successor** of β is less than α. Loosely put, a limit ordinal is an ordinal other than 0 which cannot be reached from smaller ordinals by successive application of the ordinal successor operation.

See also: **Limit Cardinal, ω, Ordinal Arithmetic, Regular Ordinal**

LIMITATION-OF-SIZE CONCEPTION OF SET   The limitation-of-size conception of set is a conception of **set** where sets are "formed" only if the collection of objects is not too "large." Largeness here can be understood in a number of ways, including there being as many objects in the collection as there are **ordinal numbers**, there being as many objects in the collection as there are sets, or there being as many objects in the collection as there are objects in the universe. Each of these corresponds to a different variant of the limitation-of-size conception of set. Collections which are too large to be "formed" into sets are **proper classes**.

The limitation-of-size conception of set is motivated by the desire to eliminate sets that are too large and thus somehow "badly behaved." Since the **Russell paradox** and other **set-theoretic paradoxes** – in particular, the **Burali-Forti paradox** – involve collections which are at least as large as the collection of ordinals, this conception of set is thought to avoid the paradoxes.

See also: **Cumulative Hierarchy, Iterative Conception of Set, Vicious Circle Principle, Zermelo Fraenkel Set Theory**

LIMITATION RESULT A limitation result is a **metatheoretical proof** that a certain **formal system** or other logical **structure** cannot, in principle, have certain (usually desirable) properties. Important limitation results include the **upward** and **downward Lowenheim-Skolem Theorems** and **Gödel's first** and **second incompleteness theorems**.

See also: **Church's Theorem, Compactness, Tarski's Indefinability Theorem**

LINEAR LOGICS Linear logics are **substructural logics** within which the **structural rules weakening**:

$$\frac{\Delta \Rightarrow \Gamma}{\Delta, A \Rightarrow \Gamma}$$

$$\frac{\Delta \Rightarrow \Gamma}{\Delta \Rightarrow \Gamma, A}$$

and **contraction**:

$$\frac{\Delta, A, A \Rightarrow B, \Gamma}{\Delta, A \Rightarrow B, \Gamma}$$

$$\frac{\Delta, A \Rightarrow B, B, \Gamma}{\Delta, A \Rightarrow B, \Gamma}$$

fail. Linear logic is motivated by the idea that a **premise** or **conclusion** is a consumable resource, and that each occurrence of a premise or conclusion must as a result be used exactly once in a **proof**.

See also: **Multiset, Sequent Calculus**

LINEAR ORDER see **Linear Ordering**

LINEAR ORDERING A linear ordering (or **linear order**, or **simple ordering**, or **total ordering**) is a binary relation R on a set of objects S which is:

Antisymmetric: $(\forall x)(\forall y)((Rxy \land Ryx) \rightarrow x = y)$

Transitive: $(\forall x)(\forall y)(\forall z)((Rxy \land Ryz) \rightarrow Rxz)$

Total: $(\forall x)(\forall y)(Rxy \lor Ryx)$

Given a linear ordering, one can define a **strict total ordering R*** as:

R*xy if and only if Rxy and x ≠ y.

See also: **Partial Ordering, Pre-Ordering, Strict Ordering, Well-Ordering**

LÖB PARADOX see **Curry Paradox**

LÖB'S THEOREM   Löb's theorem states that, in any **theory** containing **arithmetic**, if one can **prove**, for some **statement** A, that the provability of A **implies** A, then A itself is provable. In other words, where "**Bew**(x)" is the **provability predicate** and <A> is the **Gödel number** of the statement A, Löb's theorem states that if we can prove:

Bew<A> → A

then we can prove A.

See also: **Arithmetization, Diagonalization Lemma, Gödel's First Incompleteness Theorem, Gödel's Second Incompleteness Theorem**

LOGIC   Logic is the study of **arguments**, and the various methods of logic are used to investigate the structure of arguments and to classify them, in terms of their structure, into those that ought to be persuasive and those that ought not to be persuasive.

Although the primary purpose of logic is to evaluate real arguments in natural languages, the term has grown to encompass much more than this. The reason for this broadening of the application of the term "logic" is not hard to isolate. Over the past century powerful mathematical tools have been developed for studying the structure of arguments, leading to the development of the field of **mathematical logic**. These tools, however, have proven to be useful in areas other than their original domain – in particular, in computer science and in the foundations of mathematics.

See also: **Consequence Relation, Fallacy, Logical Form, Philosophical Logic, Philosophy of Logic**

LOGIC GATE   A logic gate is a mechanical or electronic device, or an abstract representation of such a device, whose patterns of input and output mirror one of the **truth functions**. For example, an AND gate might be an electronic device with two circuits as inputs and one circuit as output, where the device is designed in such a way that the output circuit has positive voltage if and only if both of the input circuits have positive voltage.

See also: **Boolean Algebra, Dagger, Logical Connective, Sheffer Stroke**

LOGIC OF ATTRIBUTES see **Monadic First-Order Logic**

LOGIC OF CONDITIONALS see **Conditional Logic**

LOGIC OF PARADOX The logic of paradox (or **LP**) is a **three-valued logic** where the third **truth value** is the **truth value glut** "both **true** nor **false**" (typically denoted "B"), and the **designated values** are "true" and "both true nor false." **Compound sentences** are assigned truth values based on the **truth tables** for the **strong Kleene connectives**. The logic of paradox is usually used to provide **dialethic** solutions to various paradoxes including the **Sorites paradox** and **semantics paradoxes** such as the **Liar paradox**.

See also: **Ex Falso Quodlibet, Paraconsistent Logic, Strong Paraconsistency, Triviality, Weak Paraconsistency**

LOGIC OF QUESTIONS AND ANSWERS see **Erotetic Logic**

LOGIC OF RELATIONS see **Polyadic First-Order Logic**

LOGIC OF WEAK EXCLUDED MIDDLE The logic of weak excluded middle is the **intermediate logic** obtained by adding all instances of **weak excluded middle**:

$\sim A \vee \sim \sim A$

to **intuitionistic propositional logic**.

See also: **Double Negation, Excluded Middle, Gödel-Dummett Logic, Kreisel-Putnam Logic, Scott Logic**

LOGICAL ANTIREALISM Logical antirealism is the view that rejects the **identification** of **truth** with correspondence to some external reality, and instead insists on the equation of truth and in-principle verifiability – this type of restriction is known as **epistemic constraint**. As a result, logical anti-realists reject **logical laws**, such as the **law of excluded middle**:

$P \vee \sim P$

whose truth amounts, on their interpretation, to implausible claims about our epistemic powers. Thus, logical antirealism is associated with the rejection of **classical logic** in favor of a **non-standard logic**, often **intuitionistic logic**.

See also: **Bivalence, Constructive Logic, Intuitionism, Intuitionistic Mathematics**

LOGICAL CONNECTIVE   A logical connective (or **propositional connective**) is a symbol that joins one or more **statements** to form a **compound statement**. Simply put, the logical connectives are the subcollection of the **logical constants** that occur within **propositional logic**. The logical connectives are typically taken to include **conjunction** (∧), **disjunction** (∨), **negation** (~), the **conditional** (→), and the **biconditional** (↔), although other connectives, including the **Sheffer stroke** (|) and the **dagger** (↓), have been studied.

See also: **Boolean Operator, Compound Formula, Permutation Invariance, Truth Function, Truth Table**

LOGICAL CONSEQUENCE   A **statement** Φ is a logical consequence (or **model-theoretic consequence**, or **semantic consequence**) of a **set** of statements Δ (or Φ is **entailed** by Δ) if and only if there is no interpretation that makes all of the statements in Δ true while making Φ false.

See also: **Consequence Relation, Deductive Consequence, Double Turnstile, Formal Consequence, Material Consequence, Semantics**

LOGICAL CONSTANT   A logical constant (or **logical operator**, or **operator**, or **logical operation**, or **operation**) is an expression which contributes to the **logical form** of a larger expression. There is widespread agreement that the logical constants include the **logical connectives** (**conjunction, disjunction, negation**, the **material conditional**, the **material biconditional**, etc.) the **quantifiers** (both **universal** and **existential**) and the **identity predicate** "=." There is no general agreement, however, on what criteria separate the logical constants from **non-logical vocabulary**, although numerous criteria have been proposed (including that the logical constants are those expressions that require a **recursive** clause in the **meaning theory** for a **language**; those expressions that are **topic neutral**; and those expressions that are invariant under **permutations** of the **domain** of objects in a **model**).

See also: **Boolean Operator, Compound Formula, Compound Statement, Generalized Quantifiers, Permutation Invariant**

LOGICAL EQUIVALENCE see **Logically Equivalent**

LOGICAL FALSEHOOD A logical falsehood is a **formula** for which there is no **interpretation** that makes it **true**. In other words, a logical falsehood is a formula that must be false, no matter what the **semantic values** its constituent expressions receive. All **substitution instances** of logical falsehoods are also logical falsehoods.

See also: **Contradiction, Logical Truth, Theorem, Truth-in-a-Model, Valid**

LOGICAL FORM The logical form (or **logical structure**) of a **statement** (or **sequence** of statements, such as an **argument**) is the underlying structure of the statement (or sequence). Typically, two expressions are said to have the same logical form if they have the same syntactic or grammatical form and they contain the same **logical constants** (i.e. **connectives, quantifiers**, etc.) playing the same roles.

For example, consider:

(1) John is bad and Robert is good.

(2) John is bad and Mary is fair.

(3) John is bad or Robert is good.

Here, statement (1) and (2) have the same logical form, since they have the same syntactic structure (i.e. <**term, predicate, binary connective**, term, predicate>), and the **logical connective** (**conjunction** in this case) is the same. (1) and (3), however, although of the same syntactic structure, have different connectives joining the two component statements.

See also: **Consequence Relation, Formal Fallacy, Formal Logic, Syllogistic Figure, Syllogistic Mood**

LOGICAL IMPLICATION Logical implication is the **relation** that holds between A and B if the material conditional:

A → B

is a **logical truth**. The **formula**:

A → B

is also said to be a logical implication if the relation of logical implication holds between A and B (in that order).

See also: **Deductive Implication, Inference, Material Implication, Strict Implication**

LOGICAL MONISM   Logical monism is the view that there is a single **logic** that correctly codifies the **consequence relation**. Logical monism is contrasted with **logical pluralism** – the view that there is more than one logic that correctly, or best, codifies the consequence relation.

See also: **Formal Logic, Logic, Mathematical Logic**

LOGICAL OPERATOR see **Logical Constant**

LOGICAL PARADOX see **Semantic Paradox**

LOGICAL PLURALISM see **Logical Monism**

LOGICAL STRUCTURE see **Logical Form**

LOGICAL THEOREM see **Logical Truth, Theorem**

LOGICAL TRUTH   A logical truth is a **formula** of that which is **true** on all **interpretations**. In other words, a logical truth is a formula that must be true, no matter what the **semantic values** its constituent expressions receive. All **substitution instances** of logical truths are also logical truths.

See also: **Logical Falsehood, Tautology, Theorem, Truth-in-a-Model, Valid**

LOGICAL VALIDITY An **argument** is logically valid (or **semantically valid**) if and only if every **interpretation** which **satisfies** the **premises** of the argument is also an interpretation which satisfies the **conclusion** of the argument.

See also: **Double Turnstile, Logical Consequence, Valid**

LOGICALLY EQUIVALENT   Two formulas A and B are logically equivalent (or **semantically equivalent**) when they are **true** in exactly the same **interpretations**. In other words, A and B are logically equivalent if the **material biconditional**:

A ↔ B

is a **logical truth**. The **formula**:

A ↔ B

is said to be a **logical equivalence** if A and B are logically equivalent.

See also: **Deductively Equivalent, Materially Equivalent**

LOGICISM   Logicism is the thesis that mathematics (and, in particular, **arithmetic**) can be reduced to **logic**. Logicism thus consists of two theses. First, that the central **concepts** of mathematics can be **defined** in terms of logical vocabulary. Second, that the **truths** of mathematics will turn out, given their **translation** into logical vocabulary, to be **logical truths**. The fact that contemporary logic has no existential commitments, while mathematics has infinitely many existential commitments, is taken by many to doom logicism to failure.

See also: **Abstraction Principle, Basic Law V, Hume's Principle, Mathematical Abstractionism, Russell Paradox**

LOWENHEIM-SKOLEM THEOREM see **Downward Lowenheim-Skolem Theorem, Upward Lowenheim-Skolem Theorem**

LOWER BOUND   Given a **partial ordering** ≤ on a set S, if x is a **member** of S and A is a **subset** of S, then x is a lower bound of A if and only if x ≤ y for all y in A.

See also: **Greatest Lower Bound, Join, Least Upper Bound, Meet, Upper Bound**

LP see **Logic of Paradox**

M

MAHLO CARDINAL   A Mahlo cardinal is a type of **large cardinal number**.

See also: **Large Cardinal Axiom, Strongly Inaccessible Cardinal, Weakly Inaccessible Cardinal**

MAIN CONNECTIVE see **Dominant Connective**

MAIN OPERATOR see **Dominant Connective**

MAJOR PREMISE   The major premise of a **categorical syllogism** is the **premise** that contains the **major term** – that is, the premise that contains the **predicate term** of the **conclusion**.

See also: **Middle Term, Minor Premise, Minor Term, Subject Term**

MAJOR TERM   In **categorical logic**, the major term of a **categorical syllogism** is the **predicate term** of the **conclusion**.

See also: **Major Premise, Middle Term, Minor Premise, Minor Term, Subject Term**

MANY-SORTED LOGIC   A many-sorted logic is a **first-order logic** where the **domain** of a **model** is separated into two or more distinct "universes." **Quantifiers** are typically restricted to one of these "universes" in one of two ways. First, distinct sorts of **variable** might be used to range over the two "universes." Along these lines, we can reinterpret **second-order logic** as a many-sorted first-order logic, where the lower-case variables range over one universe (the universe of **concrete objects**), and the upper-case variables range over a second universe (the universe of **concepts**, conceived of as a special sort of object, on this understanding). Second, we might use only one sort of variable, but introduce a special **predicate** for each "universe" in order to distinguish between the two subcollections of the domain.

See also: **Henkin Semantics, Higher-Order Logic, Plural Quantification, Second-Order Logic**

MANY-VALUED LOGIC   A many-valued logic (or **multivalent**

logic) is a **non-standard logic** where **statements** can be assigned **semantic values** other than the traditional two values **true** and **false**. Common many-valued logics include **truth value gap** logics (where statements can be neither true nor false), **truth value glut** logics (where statements can be both true and false), and **degree-theoretic semantics** (where statements can receive any value between 1, representing complete truth, and 0, representing complete falsity).

See also: **Analethic Logic, Designated Value, First-Degree Entailment, K₃**

MARKOV'S PRINCIPLE Markov's principle (or the **principle of constructive choices**, or **constructive choices**) is a **logical truth** within **classical first-order logic** that is not **valid** within **intuitionistic first-order logic**. Markov's principle states that, for any **decidable predicate** Φ, that:

$$\sim \sim (\exists x)\Phi x \rightarrow (\exists x)\Phi x$$

It has been argued that Markov's principle is justifiable on **constructive** grounds. If we can **refute** the claim that no object has Φ, then we can "run through" all objects until we find one that has Φ.

See also: **Constructive Mathematics, Double Negation, Effective Procedure, Epistemic Constraint, Primitive Recursive Relation, Recursive Relation**

MATERIAL BICONDITIONAL A material biconditional is a **statement** of the form:

A if and only if B

which is **true** if and only if A and B have the same **truth value**. Within **classical logic** the material biconditional has the following **truth table**:

P	Q	P ↔ Q
T	T	T
T	F	F
F	T	F
F	F	T

Within **propositional logic**, material biconditionals are usually represented as:

A ↔ B

Or as:

A ≡ B

The term "material biconditional" is also used to **denote**, not the entire statement:

A ↔ B

but rather the **logical connective** represented by "↔."

See also: **Conditional, Iff**

MATERIAL CONDITIONAL   A material conditional (or **Philonian conditional**) is a **statement** of the form:

If A then B

which is **true** if and only if either A is **false** or B is true. Thus, it should be distinguished from **subjunctive** or **counterfactual conditionals**, whose **truth values** depend on a connection between **antecedent** and **consequent**. Within **classical logic** the material conditional has the following **truth table**:

P	Q	P → Q
T	T	T
T	F	F
F	T	T
F	F	T

Within **propositional logic**, material conditionals are usually represented as:

A → B

Or as:

A ⊃ B

The term "material conditional" is also used to **denote**, not the entire **statement**:

A → B

but rather the **logical connective** represented by "→."

See also: **Conditionalization, Counternecessary Conditional, Indicative Conditional, Strict Conditional**

MATERIAL CONSEQUENCE A material consequence is an **argument** where the **premises** follow **necessarily** from the **conclusion**, but this fact does not hold merely in terms of the **logical form** of the **statements** involved. Thus, a material consequence is not an instance of **logical consequence** (which must also be formal). An example of a material consequence is:

> Bill is the father of Alice.
> _____
> Thus, Alice is the child of Bill.

While this conclusion cannot be **false** if the premise is **true**, this fact depends not only on the logical form of the premises and conclusion, but on their content as well.

See also: **Consequence Relation, Deductive Consequence, Formal Consequence**

MATERIAL EQUIVALENCE see **Materially Equivalent**

MATERIAL IMPLICATION Material implication is the **relation** that holds between A and B if

$$A \rightarrow B$$

is true, where the **conditional** in question is the **material conditional**. In other words, material implication is the relation that holds between two **statements** if and only if either the first is **false**, or the second is **true**. The **formula**:

$$A \rightarrow B$$

is also said to be a material implication, if the relation of material implication holds between A and B (in that order).

See also: **Deductive Implication, Logical Implication, Strict Implication**

MATERIALLY EQUIVALENT Two **formulas** A and B are materially equivalent when they have the same **truth value**. In other words, A and B are materially equivalent if the **material biconditional**:

$$A \leftrightarrow B$$

is **true**. The **formula**:

$$A \leftrightarrow B$$

is said to be a **material equivalence** if A and B are materially equivalent.

See also: **Deductively Equivalent, Elementary Equivalence, Logically Equivalent**

MATHEMATICAL ABSTRACTIONISM Mathematical abstractionism (or **abstractionism**, or **neo-fregeanism**, or **neologicism**) is the view that we can obtain **a priori** knowledge of the **truths** of mathematics by laying down various **abstraction principles** as **implicit definitions** of mathematical **concepts** – for example, the abstractionist claims that we can stipulate **Hume's Principle**:

$$(\forall P)(\forall Q)(NUM(P) = NUM(Q) \leftrightarrow P \approx Q)$$

as a definition of the concept **cardinal number**. Since the **axioms** of **second-order Peano arithmetic** follow from Hume's Principle, the abstractionist claims that we can know these axioms, and their consequences, a priori in virtue of the fact that we know the truth of Hume's Principle a priori.

See also: **Abstraction, Bad Company Objection, Basic Law V, Caesar Problem, Frege's Theorem**

MATHEMATICAL INDUCTION₁ Mathematical induction is a powerful method for **proving** that some property holds of all **elements** of an **infinite** collection. If the collection can be viewed as being the smallest **set** that contains some **basis** set and is closed under one or more **operations**, then we can prove that a **property** holds of every **member** of that set by proving that the property holds of the members of the basis set, and that the property is preserved by application of the various operations – that is, that if a number of objects have the property, then the result of applying the operation in question to those objects has the property as well.

See also: **Induction on Well-Formed Formulas, Strong Mathematical Induction, Transfinite Induction, Weak Mathematical Induction**

MATHEMATICAL INDUCTION₂ Mathematical induction (or the

induction schema, or the **mathematical induction schema**) is the following **axiom schema** of **arithmetic** (for any predicate Φ):

$$(\Phi(0) \wedge (\forall x)(\Phi(x) \rightarrow \Phi(S(x)))) \rightarrow (\forall x)\Phi(x)$$

(where S(x) is the **arithmetic successor function**). Mathematical induction is an axiom schema of **Peano arithmetic**, but not of many weaker systems, including **Robinson arithmetic**.

See also: **Inductive Set, Strong Mathematical Induction, Weak Mathematical Induction**

MATHEMATICAL INDUCTION SCHEMA see **Mathematical Induction**

MATHEMATICAL LOGIC   Mathematical logic is the mathematical study of **formal systems**.

See also: **Formal Language, Formal Logic, Formal Proof, Formal Semantics, Model Theory, Proof Theory**

MATRIX   The matrix of a **formula** in **prenex normal form** is the **quantifier**-free formula that results by removing the initial sequence of quantifiers.

See also: **Conjunctive Normal Form, Disjunctive Normal Form, Negation Normal Form, Skolem Normal Form**

MAXIMAL CONSISTENT SET   A maximal consistent set of **formulas** is a **set** of formulas S such that S is **consistent**, and there is no formula Φ in the **language** in question which is not a **member** of S, but for which S + Φ is consistent.

See also: **Negation Consistency, ω-Consistency, Post Consistency**

MEASURABLE CARDINAL   A measurable cardinal is type of **large cardinal number**.

See also: **Large Cardinal Axiom, Strongly Inaccessible Cardinal, Weakly Inaccessible Cardinal**

MEET   In Boolean algebra or the **theory** of **lattices**, the meet of two **elements** is the **greatest lower bound** of those **elements**. The meet of A and B is usually denoted by "A ∩ B."

See also: **Join, Least Upper Bound, Lower Bound, Upper Bound**

MEINONGIANISM   Meinongianism is the view that certain objects, such as mathematical objects and non-existent **possible** objects, do not exist, but rather subsist. In other words, there are some things, such as mathematical objects and non-existent possible objects, which do not exist, but which nevertheless in some sense are. As a result, according to Meinongianism, existence is a **property** which only applies to some of the things that are, while the remainder are said to merely subsist.

See also: **Mathematical Abstractionism, Nominalism, Platonism, Set-Theoretic Realism**

MEMBER   A member of a **set** is an object that is contained in that set.

See also: **Axiom of Extensionality, Element, Set Theory, Subset**

MEMBERSHIP   Membership is the **relation** that holds between a **set** and any of the objects contained in that **set**. Membership is usually denoted by "∈."

See also: **Axiom of Extensionality, Element, Set Theory, Subset**

MENTION see **Use**

MERE POSSIBILIA   Mere possibilia are entities which could **possibly** exist, but which do not, in fact, actually exist. The debate between **modal actualism** and **modal realism** concerns whether or not mere possibilia exist, and thus whether or not we can use mere possibilia in accounting for the **truth conditions** of **modal claims**.

See also: **Actual World, Contingency, Modal Agnosticism, Modal Fictionalism, Possible World**

MEREOLOGICAL EXTENSIONALITY   Mereological extensionality is the principle according to which, if two objects which have **proper parts** have exactly the same proper parts, then they are **identical**. This can be formulated as follows (where "PP" is the **defined** proper parthood **relation**):

$(\forall x)(\forall y)(((\exists z)(PPzx) \wedge (\exists z)(PPzy)) \rightarrow ((\forall z)(PPzx \leftrightarrow PPzy) \rightarrow x = y))$

Mereological extensionality is a **theorem** of **extensional mereology**, but not of **minimal mereology**.

See also: **Classical Mereology, Composition, General Extensional Mereology, Ground Mereology**

MEREOLOGICAL FUSION The mereological fusion (or **mereological sum**) of a **set** of objects is the unique object x such that any object has a **part** in common with x if and only if it has a part in common with at least one of the **members** of the set. More intuitively, the mereological fusion of a set of objects is the object one gets by mereologically "summing up" all of these objects into a single object.

Within formal mereology the mereological fusion of two objects x and y (if it exists) is usually denoted by:

$x + y$

and the fusion of all objects x such that $\Phi(x)$ (again, if it exists) is denoted by:

$\sigma x \Phi$

See also: **Composition, Overlap, Proper Parthood, Underlap, Unrestricted Fusion**

MEREOLOGICAL NIHILISM Mereological nihilism is the view that every object is an **atom** – that is, no object has any proper parts. Mereological nihilism can be formulated by adding the following principle to any **theory** with which it is **consistent** (where "PP" is the defined **proper parthood** relation):

$(\forall x) \sim (\exists y)(PPyx)$

Although mereological nihilism is compatible with many substantial **mereological** theses and theories (including **general extensional mereology**), it is both philosophically and formally uninteresting since the following is an immediate **corollary** (where "P" is the **parthood relation**):

$(\forall x)(\forall y)(Pxy \leftrightarrow x = y)$

In other words, according to mereological nihilism, the parthood relation is **co-extensive** with the **identity** relation.

See also: **Gunk, Mereological Fusion, Unrestricted Fusion**

MEREOLOGICAL SUM see **Mereological Fusion**

MEREOLOGY   Mereology is the formal study of the **relation** of **part** to whole. Mereology has been suggested as a replacement for traditional mathematics as part of a larger defense of **nominalism**, but it has obtained the bulk of its notoriety as a formal tool with which to study various metaphysical problems and puzzles.

See also: **Atom, Composition, Fallacy of Composition, Fallacy of Division, Gunk, Proper Parthood**

METALANGUAGE   A metalanguage is a **language** used when **proving theorems** about **formal systems**. The formal system being studied using the metalanguage is called the **object language**. Typically, the object language is taken to be contained in, or a **part** of, the metalanguage, although the metalanguage needs to be more expressively powerful than the object language. Thus, the metalanguage is the language of the metatheory.

See also: **Independence Results, Limitation Result, Metalogic, Metamathematics, Metatheorem, Metatheory, Tarskian Hierarchy**

METALOGIC   Metalogic is the mathematical study of **formal systems,** especially those that are intended to capture correct reasoning. Thus, metalogic can be captured, loosely, by the slogan "reasoning about reasoning."

See also: **Metalanguage, Metamathematics, Metatheorem, Metatheory, Tarskian Hierarchy**

METAMATHEMATICS   Metamathematics is the mathematical study of **formal systems** of mathematics. Thus, metamathematics is the use of mathematics itself to study mathematics, especially the foundations of mathematics.

See also: **Independence Results, Limitation Result, Metatheorem, Metatheory**

METATHEOREM   A metatheorem is a **theorem** about a **formal system** which is **proven** in the **metatheory**.

See also: **Independence Results, Limitation Result, Meta-mathematics**

METATHEORY The metatheory is the **theory** within which we **prove theorems** about **formal systems**. Thus, **metalogic** takes place in the **metatheory**. As a result of **Gödel's first and second incompleteness theorems**, the metatheory typically has to be stronger than the formal system being studied in order to obtain substantial results.

See also: **Independence Results, Limitation Result, Meta-language, Tarski's Indefinability Theorem**

MIDDLE TERM The minor term of a **categorical syllogism** is the **term** that occurs in both **premises** (and thus does not occur in the **conclusion**).

See also: **Major Premise, Major Term, Minor Premise, Minor Term, Predicate Term, Subject Term**

MINIMAL MEREOLOGY Minimal mereology is the **mereological** theory obtained by assuming that the **parthood relation** is a **partial ordering**:

>   **Reflexive:** $(\forall x)(Pxx)$
>
>   **Transitive:** $(\forall x)(\forall y)(\forall z)((Pxy \wedge Pyz) \rightarrow Pxz)$
>
>   **Antisymmetric:** $(\forall x)(\forall y)((Pxy \wedge Pyx) \rightarrow x = y)$

and that the **weak supplementation principle**:

$$(\forall x)(\forall y)((Pxy \wedge x \neq y) \rightarrow (\exists z)(Pzy \wedge \sim (\exists w)(Pwx \wedge Pwz)))$$

holds.

See also: **Mereological Extensionality, Proper Parthood, Strong Supplementation Principle, Unrestricted Fusion**

MINIMALISM Minimalism about **truth** is the view that all instances of **Tarski's T-schema**:

>   Where T is the **truth predicate**, A is any **statement**, and n is any **name** of A:
> $T(n) \leftrightarrow A$

are trivially true (or are true by **definition**, or are true **analytically**) and that there is nothing additional to say about truth.

As a result, minimalists deny that there is a substantial **property** called "truth" that attaches to statements, and thus the view is a species of **deflationism**.

See also: **Correspondence Theory of Truth, Disquotationalism, Prosentential Theory of Truth, Redundancy Theory of Truth**

MINIMIZATION   Minimization is one of the simple **function** building operations of **recursive function theory**. Given a **computable** n+1-ary function $f(x_1, x_2, \ldots x_n, y)$, the minimization of f is the n-ary function h such that:

h($x_1, x_2, \ldots x_n$) = the smallest y such that $f(x_1, x_2, \ldots x_n, y) = 0$, if such a y exists.

h($x_1, x_2, \ldots x_n$) is undefined if no such y exists.

Note that, unlike the other functions and function-building operations of recursive function theory, minimization can be applied to a **total function** and result in a **partial function**.

See also: **Composition, Identity Function, Primitive Recursion, Successor Function, Zero Function**

MINOR PREMISE   The minor premise of a **categorical syllogism** is the **premise** that contains the **minor term** – that is, the premise that contains the **subject term** of the **conclusion**.

See also: **Major Premise, Major Term, Middle Term, Predicate Term**

MINOR TERM   In **categorical logic**, the minor term of a **categorical syllogism** is the **subject term** of the **conclusion**.

See also: **Major Premise, Major Term, Middle Term, Minor Premise, Predicate Term**

MK see **Morse–Kelley set theory**

MODAL ACTUALISM   Modal actualism is the view that the only things that exist are actual things – in other words, there are no **mere possibilia**. As a result, modal actualists attempt to explain the **truth conditions** of **alethic modal claims** in terms of the characteristics of actually existing things (since those are all that exist). **Modal realism** is the view that actualism is wrong and that there are objects that exist **possibly** but not actually.

See also: **Actual World, Contingency, Modal Agnosticism, Modal Fictionalism, Possible World**

MODAL AGNOSTICISM   Modal agnosticism is the view where we retain the common-sense interpretation of **modal** talk in terms of the existence of **possible worlds**, but we are uncommitted regarding the existence of such worlds – in other words, we refuse to take a definite stand regarding whether there are **possible** but not actual objects, places, etc. According to the modal agnostic, this view has decided advantages in combining the best parts of **modal actualism** and **modal realism**. Like the modal actualist, we need not be committed to the existence of a multitude of worlds other than our own. We can retain many of our intuitions regarding modal claims, however, since many claims regarding the non-existence of particular possible worlds will remain true regardless of whether the modal actualist or modal realist turns out to be correct.

See also: **Actual World, Contingency, Modal Fictionalism**

MODAL COUNTERPART see **Counterpart Theory**

MODAL FICTIONALISM   Modal fictionalism involves, as a part, **modal actualism**: the view that there are no **possible worlds** – in other words, there are no **mere possibilia**. Modal fictionalists differ from traditional actualists, however, in that they nevertheless find talk of possible worlds indispensable in explaining the **truth conditions** of **alethic modal claims**. As a result, the fictionalist asserts that talk of possible worlds is a useful fiction, which is helpful in explaining our modal talk, but which need not be taken as literally **true**.

See also: **Actual World, Contingency, Modal Agnosticism, Modal Realism**

MODAL LOGIC   Modal logic is the study of **logics** that contain **modal operators**. Modal operators are sentential operators such as the **alethic modal operators necessarily** Φ ($\Box \, \Phi$ or $L \, \Phi$), **possibly** Φ ($\Diamond \, \Phi$ or $M \, \Phi$); the **deontic modal operators** obligatory Φ ($O \, \Phi$), it is permissible that Φ ($P \, \Phi$), it is forbidden that Φ ($F \, \Phi$); the **temporal modal operators** it will always be the case that Φ

(G Φ), it will be the case that Φ (F Φ), it has always been the case that Φ (H Φ), it was the case that Φ (P Φ); the **epistemic modal operators** it is known that Φ (K Φ), it is knowable that Φ (K Φ); and the **doxastic modal operator** it is believed that Φ (B Φ).

There are a number of important modal logics, including the **normal modal logics K, T, D, B, S4**, and **S5**, and **non-normal modal logics**. Modal logics are typically studied using **possible world semantics**.

See also: **Causal Modal Logic, Conditional Logic, Counterfactual Logic, Dynamic Logic, Provability Logic, Quantified Modal Logic**

MODAL OPERATOR see **Modal Logic**

MODAL POSSIBILISM see **Modal Realism**

MODAL REALISM   Modal realism (or **modal possibilism**) is the view that there are **possible** objects that are not actual objects (i.e. there are **mere possibilia**), and that there are **possible worlds** distinct from the **actual world**. As a result, modal realists attempt to explain the **truth conditions** of **alethic modal claims** in terms of the characteristics of these possible but non-actual objects. **Modal actualism** is the view that modal realism is wrong and that the only objects that possibly exist are the ones that actually exist.

See also: **Contingency, Modal Agnosticism, Modal Fictionalism**.

MODALITY   A modality is a **sequence** of "~"s, "□"s, and "◇"s prefixed to a **formula** in **modal logic**. Many modal logics have a **finite** number of distinct modalities. For example, in the modal logic **S4**, any formula consisting of Φ prefixed by a modality, of any length, is **equivalent** to one of:

$$Φ \quad ◇Φ \quad □Φ \quad ◇□Φ \quad □◇Φ \quad □◇□Φ \quad ◇□◇Φ$$
$$\sim\!Φ \quad \sim\!◇Φ \quad \sim\!□Φ \quad \sim\!◇□Φ \quad \sim\!□◇Φ \quad \sim\!□◇□Φ \quad \sim\!◇□◇Φ$$

See also: **Accessibility Relation, Contingency, Impossibility, Necessity, Possibility**

MODEL   A model (or **structure**, or **Tarskian model**) is a means of assigning **truth values** to sentences of **first-** or **higher-order languages**. A model consists of a **set** of objects (the **domain** of the model) plus an **assignment** of **semantic values** to the **non-logical vocabulary** of a first- or higher-order language (usually with an eye to making some particular **theory true** on the model). Thus, a model involves designating a domain of objects for the **first-order quantifiers** to range over (and for the **second-order quantifiers** to range over **subsets** of the domain, etc.), assigning a **member** of the domain to each non-logical **constant**, and assigning appropriate sets of **n-tuples** from the domain to each **predicate** and **relation** symbol.

See also: **Formal Semantics, Interpretation, Model Theory, Semantics**

MODEL THEORETIC CONSEQUENCE see Logical Consequence

MODEL THEORY Model theory is the branch of **mathematical logic** that studies the characteristics of **structures** (or **models**) that satisfy different **theories**. Important results in model theory include the **upward** and **downward Lowenheim-Skolem theorems** and the **compactness** theorem.

See also: **Categorical, Elementary Equivalence, Intended Interpretation, κ-Categorical, Non-Standard Model**

MODUS PONENDO PONENS see Modus Ponens

MODUS PONENS Modus ponens (or **modus ponendo ponens**, or **affirming the antecedent**, or **conditional elimination**) is the **rule of inference** that allows one to **infer** the **consequent** of a **conditional** from that conditional and the **antecedent** of that conditional. In symbols we have:

$$\frac{\begin{array}{l} P \to Q \\ P \end{array}}{Q}$$

See also: **Affirming the Consequent, Conditional Proof, Denying the Antecedent, Modus Tollens**

MODUS TOLLENDO TOLLENS see Modus Tollens

MODUS TOLLENS Modus tollens (or **modus ponendo tollens**, or **denying the consequence**) is the **rule of inference** that allows one to **infer** the **negation** of the **antecedent** of a **conditional** from that conditional and the negation of the **consequent** of that conditional. In symbols we have:

$$P \rightarrow Q$$
$$\underline{\sim Q}$$
$$\sim P$$

See also: **Affirming the Consequent, Conditional Proof, Denying the Antecedent, Modus Ponens**

MOLECULE see **Compound Formula**

MONADIC FIRST-ORDER LOGIC   Monadic first-order logic (or **monadic predicate logic**, or the **logic of attributes**) is the subsystem of **classical first-order logic** obtained when **monadic predicates**, but no **polyadic predicates**, are allowed into the **language**. Unlike **polyadic first-order logic**, logical theoremhood in monadic first-order logic is **decidable**.

See also: **Church's Theorem, Entscheidungsproblem**

MONADIC FUNCTION see **Unary Function**

MONADIC PREDICATE   A monadic predicate (or **unary predicate**) is a **predicate** that takes one **argument**, such as "x is red" or "x is tall." A predicate that takes more than one argument is a **polyadic predicate**.

See also: **Adicity, Monadic First-order Logic, Polyadic First-order Logic, Unary Function, Unary Relation**

MONADIC PREDICATE LOGIC see **Monadic First-order Logic**

MONADIC RELATION see **Unary Relation**

MONISM see **Logical Monism**

MONOMORPHISM   A monomorphism is a **homomorphism** between two **structures** that is also **injective**, or **one-to-one**.

See also: **Automorphism, Endomorphism, Epimorphism, Isomorphism**

MONOTONIC LOGIC   A **logic** is monotonic if and only if adding additional **statements** to the **premises** of a **valid argument** cannot make that argument **invalid**. In other words, a logic is monotonic if, for any **sets** of statements Δ and Σ, and any statement Φ, if:

$$\Delta \vDash \Phi$$

then:

$$\Delta \cup \Sigma \vDash \Phi$$

A logic where this can fail is a **non-monotonic logic**.

See also: **Monotonicity, Substructural Logic, Weakening**

MONOTONICITY   A **unary function** f mapping a **set** S to itself is monotonic relative to an **ordering** δ on that set if and only if, for any a and b in S such that $a \leq b$, we have $f(a) \leq f(b)$. More generally, if f is an n-ary function, then f is monotonic if and only if, whenever $a_1 \leq b_1$, $a_2 \leq b_2$, ... $a_n \leq b_n$, we have $f(a_1, a_2, \ldots a_n) \leq f(b_1, b_2, \ldots b_n)$.

Many formal results regarding **non-standard logics** depend on the fact that the **connectives** of such **logics** correspond to **truth functions** which are monotonic with respect to a particular ordering on the **truth values**.

See also: **Kleene Connectives, Monotonic Logic, Weakening**

MOOD see **Syllogistic Mood**

MORSE-KELLEY SET THEORY   Morse-Kelley set theory (or **Kelley-Morse set theory, or KM, or MK**) is an extension of **Von Neumann Bernays Gödel** set theory obtained by allowing arbitrary **formulas** to occur in the **class comprehension schema**.

See also: **Kripke-Platek Set Theory, Positive Set Theory, Zermelo Fraenkel Set Theory**

MULTI-MODAL LOGIC   A multi-modal logic is a **modal logic** with more than one primitive **modal operator** (standard modal logics are not multi-modal, since $\Box$ and $\Diamond$ are interdefinable, and only one needs to be taken as primitive). **Dynamic logic** is an example of a multi-modal logic, as are systems that combine **epistemic** and **alethic** **modal operators**.

See also: **Accessibility Relation, Fitch Paradox, Kripke Semantics, Kripke Structure**

MULTIPLICATIVE AXIOM see **Axiom of Choice**

MULTISET   A multiset (or **bag**) is a collection where **members** can occur more than once. In other words, when dealing with multisets (unlike the case with standard **sets**), the number of occurrences of an **element** matters. Thus, if we view {a, b, b, c} and {a, b, c} as multisets, then they are distinct, since the former contains, as elements, two occurrences of b, while the latter contains only one.

See also: **Non-Well-Founded Set, Sequence, Sequent Calculus**

MULTIVALENT LOGIC see **Many-Valued Logic**

MUTUALLY EXCLUSIVE see **Contrary**

N-ADIC FUNCTION see **N-ary function**

N-ADIC RELATION see **N-ary relation**

NAÏVE COMPREHENSION SCHEMA see **Comprehension Schema**

NAÏVE SET THEORY   Naïve set theory is the **set theory** obtained by adopting all instances of the **comprehension schema**:

$$(\exists x)(\forall y)(y \in x \leftrightarrow \Phi(y))$$

where Φ is any **formula** not containing x as a **free variable**. Within **classical logic**, naïve set theory is **inconsistent**, since one can derive the **Russell paradox** (and other **set-theoretic paradoxes**) within the **theory**. Consistent versions of naïve set theory within **paraconsistent logics** have been explored, however.

See also: **Burali-Forti Paradox, Vicious Circle Principle, Zermelo Fraenkel Set Theory**

NAND see **Sheffer Stroke**

N-ARY FUNCTION   An n-ary function (or **n-adic function**) is a

function which takes n **arguments** (where n is a **natural number**) as input. Thus, a 3-ary function takes three arguments as input.

See also: **Adicity, N-ary Relation**

N-ARY RELATION An n-ary relation (or **n-adic relation**) is a **relation** which takes n **arguments** (where n is a **natural number**). Thus, a 3-ary relation takes three arguments as input.

See also: **Adicity, N-ary Function**

NATURAL DEDUCTION Natural deduction is a type of **formal system** for **logic** modeled after patterns of actual reasoning. Typically, natural deduction systems have no **axioms**, and instead consist solely of **rules of inference**. In addition, the rules of inference in a natural deduction system often consist of pairs of rules for each **logical connective** – and **introduction rule** for inserting an instance of the connective and an **elimination rule** for removing an instance of the connective – plus other additional rules, such as **classical reductio ad absurdum**.

See also: **Sequent Calculus**

NATURAL LANGUAGE A natural language is any **language** that is used for general communication and that evolved naturally. Natural languages are to be distinguished from **formal languages**, which exist primarily as a tool for studying reasoning or other matters of **logical** interest, and were artificially constructed with these applications in mind. Thus, English and Chinese are natural languages, while **first-order arithmetic** and the λ-calculus are developed within formal languages.

See also: **Metalanguage, Translation**

NATURAL NUMBERS The natural numbers are the whole counting numbers (usually including zero), that is, $\{0, 1, 2, 3, \ldots\}$.

See also: **Arithmetic, Integers, Peano Arithmetic, Rational Numbers, Real Numbers**

NBG see **Von Neuman Bernays Gödel Set Theory**

NECESSARY CONDITION A is a necessary condition for B if and only if the **truth** of B is enough to guarantee the truth of A. Thus,

A is a necessary condition for B if and only if the **material conditional** B → A is true. If A is a necessary condition for B, then B is a **sufficient condition** for A.

See also: **Material Consequence, Material Equivalence, Material Implication**

NECESSITATION see Necessitation Rule

NECESSITATION RULE   Within **modal logic**, necessitation rule is the **rule of inference** that allows one to move from the claim that A is a **theorem**:

⊢ A

to the claim that "**necessarily** A" is a theorem:

⊢ □ A

Modal logics that satisfy both necessitation and the **distribution axiom** are **normal modal logics**.

See also: **K, Kripke Semantics, Kripke Structure**

NECESSITY   A **statement** is necessary if and only if it cannot be **false**. Necessary statements are contrasted with both **impossible** statements (which cannot be **true**) and **contingent** statements, which can be true, but which can also be false.

   Within **modal logic**, where **possibilities** are represented by **possible worlds**, a necessary statement is one where there is no **accessible** possible world in which it is false. This is represented in the **language** of modal logic as:

□ A

See also: **Actual World, Alethic Modal Logic, Modality**

NECESSITY OF IDENTITY   The necessity of identity is the following principle of **quantified modal logic**:

$(\forall x)(\forall y)(x = y \rightarrow (\Box\, x = y))$

See also: **Barcan Formula, Converse Barcan Formula, Identity, Necessity**

NEGATION   A negation is a **statement** of the form:

It is not the case that A.

or:

Not A.

Within **propositional logic**, negations are usually represented as:

~ A

or:

¬ A

The term "negation" is also used to **denote**, not the entire **statement**:

~ A

but rather the **logical connective** represented by "~."

Within **classical logic** negation has the following **truth table**:

P	~ P
T	F
F	T

See also: **Boolean Negation, Choice Negation, DeMorgan Negation, Double Negation, Exclusion Negation, Tilde**

NEGATION COMPLETENESS   A **theory** is negation complete if and only if, for any **formula** A in the **language** of the theory, either A is a **theorem** of the theory, or ~ A is a theorem. A theory that is not negation complete is **negation incomplete**.

See also: **Negation Consistency, ω-Completeness, Strong Completeness, Weak Completeness**

NEGATION CONSISTENCY   A theory is **negation consistent** (or **simply consistent**) if and only if it is not the case that there is some **formula** A such that both A and ~ A are **theorems** of the theory. A theory that is not negation consistent is **negation inconsistent**.

See also: **Negation Completeness, ω-Consistency, Post Consistency, Triviality**

NEGATION ELIMINATION see **Double Negation Elimination, Ex Falso Quodlibet**

NEGATION INCOMPLETENESS see **Negation Completeness**

NEGATION INCONSISTENCY see **Negation Consistency**

NEGATION INTRODUCTION see **Double Negation Introduction, Reductio ad Absurdum**

NEGATION NORMAL FORM A **formula** is in negation normal form if and only if all of its **negations** range only over **atomic formulas** and the only other **logical connectives** occurring in the formula are **conjunctions** and **disjunctions**. As a result, any formula in either **conjunctive normal form** or **disjunctive normal form** is in negation normal form, although not vice versa.

See also: **Prenex Normal Form, Skolem Normal Form**

NEGATIVE PROPOSITION The **quality** of a **categorical proposition** is negative – that is, the categorical proposition is a negative proposition – if and only if it denies that (some or all) **members** of the **class denoted** by the **subject term** are also members of the class denoted by the **predicate term**. Thus **E-propositions** and **O-propositions** are negative, while **A-propositions** and **I-propositions** are not negative. **Categorical propositions** that are not negative are **affirmative**.

See also: **Particular Proposition, Quality, Quantity, Square of Opposition, Universal Proposition**

NEO-FREGEANISM see **Mathematical Abstractionism**

NEO-LOGICISM see **Mathematical Abstractionism**

NEUMANN BERNAYS GÖDEL SET THEORY see **Von Neumann Bernays Gödel Set Theory**

NEUMANN GÖDEL BERNAYS SET THEORY see **Von Neumann-Bernays Gödel Set Theory**

NEW FOUNDATIONS New Foundations (or NF) is a **formal set theory** containing, as **axioms**:

> **Axiom of Extensionality:** $(\forall x)(\forall y)(x = y \leftrightarrow (\forall z)(z \in x \leftrightarrow z \in y))$

Stratified **Comprehension Schema**: For any **formula** Φ which does not contain y as a **free variable**, if Φ is **stratified**, then there is a **set** y where, for all x, x is a **member** of y if and only if Φx.

A formula is stratified if and only if **natural numbers** can be assigned to its **variables** in such a way that whenever:

x ∈ y

occurs in the formula, then the number assigned to y is exactly one greater than the number assigned to x.

See also: **Kripke-Platek Set Theory, Non-Well-Founded Set Theory, Positive Set Theory**

NF see **New Foundations**

NGB see **Von Neuman Bernays Gödel Set Theory**

NOMINALISM Nominalism is the view that **abstract objects, properties,** and **universals** do not exist. These apparent entities only have reality within **language**, in terms of the **predicates** used to collect together particular instances. Hence, on this view, abstract objects or properties exist "in name only."

See also: **Mathematical Abstractionism, Meinongianism, Platonism, Set-Theoretic Realism**

NON-ALETHIC MODAL LOGIC see **Alethic Modal Logic**

NON-CLASSICAL LOGIC see **Classical Logic, Deviant Logic, Non-Standard Logic**

NON-COMMUTATIVE LOGIC Non-commutative logics (or **ordered logics**) are **substructural logics** within which weakening:

$$\frac{\Delta \Rightarrow \Gamma}{\Delta, A \Rightarrow \Gamma}$$

$$\frac{\Delta \Rightarrow \Gamma}{\Delta \Rightarrow \Gamma, A}$$

and **permutation**:

$$\frac{\Delta, A, B \Rightarrow \Gamma}{\Delta, B, A \Rightarrow \Gamma}$$

$$\frac{\Delta \Rightarrow A, B, \Gamma}{\Delta \Rightarrow B, A, \Gamma}$$

fail.

See also: **Lambek Calculus, Sequent Calculus, Substructural Logic**

NON-CONTRADICTION see **Law of Non-Contradiction**

NON-DETERMINISTIC POLYNOMIAL TIME   A **function** is **computable** in non–deterministic polynomial time (or is of **complexity class NP**) if and only if there is a polynomial equation which takes the length of an **argument** as input and provides the number of computational steps necessary for a **non–deterministic Turing machine** to obtain the value of the function on that argument as output.

Although non–deterministic Turing machines can compute any function that **deterministic Turing machines** can compute (and vice versa), it is not known whether every function that can be computed in non–deterministic polynomial time can be computed in **deterministic polynomial time** – in other words, even though both types of Turing machine can compute the same functions, it might take much longer to compute some functions on a deterministic Turing machine than on a non–deterministic Turing machine. Settling this issue is perhaps the most important outstanding problem of **complexity theory**.

See also: **Automaton, Church–Turing Thesis, NP–Complete, Recursive Function Theory, Turing Computable Function**

NON-DETERMINISTIC TURING MACHINE   A non–deterministic Turing machine is a machine (usually conceived abstractly) which consists of (a) an **infinitely** long tape containing cells, each of which contains a symbol from a **finite** list (including a special symbol called the blank symbol), (b) a head that can read, write, and erase symbols in the cell at which it is located, and that can also move from a cell to either adjacent cell, (c) a state register which keeps track of the particular state the machine is in at any time, and (d) a table of instructions (sometimes called an **action table** or **transition function**) that, given a particular state and the symbol on the cell inhabited by the head, instructs the machine (d1) either to modify the symbol on the tape, or to move the head one cell to the left or right, and (d2) the new state that the machine is in (which need not be different from the previous state). The difference between a non-deterministic Turing machine and a **deterministic Turing machine** is that a non-deterministic Turing machine does not uniquely specify which action is to be taken based on the state of the machine and the symbol in the inhabited cell. Rather, the table of instructions can provide a number of actions which the machine can select from.

In determining which **functions** can be **computed** using non-deterministic Turing machines, we assume that the machine always makes the "best" choice when provided with more than one **possible** action to take. In other words, a function can be computed by a non-deterministic Turing machine if and only if, given a particular input, there is some **sequence** of choices such that the machine can compute the function on that input.

Non-deterministic Turing machines are **equivalent** – that is, can compute exactly the same functions or solve exactly the same problems – as a number of other formal models of computation, including deterministic Turing machines, **recursive functions**, and **register machines**.

See also: **Automaton, Effectively Computable, NP, NP-Complete, P**

NON-LOGICAL CONSTANT see **Logical Constant**

NON-LOGICAL VOCABULARY see **Logical Constant**

NON-MONOTONIC LOGIC see **Monotonic Logic**

NON-NORMAL MODAL LOGIC see **Normal Modal Logic**

NON-NORMAL WORLD see **Impossible World**

NO-NO PARADOX see **Open Pair**

NON-STANDARD ANALYSIS   Non-standard analysis is the study of **non-standard models** of the **axioms** of **analysis**, and, in particular, the study of such models that include **infinitesimals**. If the axioms in question are the first-order axioms for analysis, then the existence of such models is guaranteed by **compactness theorem** and the **Lowenheim-Skolem theorems**.

See also: **Downward Lowenheim-Skolem Theorem, Non-Standard Arithmetic, Non-Standard Model, Upward Lowenheim-Skolem Theorem**

NON-STANDARD ARITHMETIC   Non–standard arithmetic is the study of **non-standard models** of the **axioms** of **arithmetic**. If the axioms in question are the **first-order Peano axioms** for arithmetic, then the existence of such models is guaranteed by the **compactness theorem** and the **Lowenheim-Skolem theorems**.

See also: **Downward Lowenheim-Skolem Theorem, Non-Standard Analysis, Non-Standard Model, Upward Lowenheim-Skolem Theorem**

NON-STANDARD LOGIC   A non–standard logic (or **alternative logic**, or **non-classical logic**) is any **formal system** that fails to agree with **classical logic**. There are two ways in which such disagreement can occur. First, there might be a disagreement over principles – the non–standard logic might either reject some classical **logical truth**, or accept some classically unacceptable principle, or both. **Intuitionistic logic** is an example of this first sort of non–standard logic. Second, there might be a disagreement over the justification of these principles – that is, the non–standard logic might agree with classical logic regarding which principles should be accepted or rejected, but provide a different **semantics** from standard classical formalisms in order to justify these principles. **Supervaluational semantics** is an example of this second sort of non–standard logic.

See also: **Deviant Logic, Dialethic Logic, Many-Valued Logic, Paraconsistent Logic, Relevance Logic**

NON-STANDARD MODEL   A non–standard model of a **theory** T is a **model** of T which is not **isomorphic** to the **intended interpretation** of T. The **Lowenheim-Skolem theorems** guarantee that any **first-order theory** whose intended interpretation has an **infinite domain** has non-standard models.

See also: **Categorical, Downward Lowenheim-Skolem Theorem, Non-Standard Analysis, Non-Standard Arithmetic, Upward Lowenheim-Skolem Theorem**

NON-TRIVIALITY see **Triviality**

NON-WELL-FOUNDED SET   A non-well-founded set (or **hyper-set**) is a set whose **membership relation** is not **well-founded**. In other words, a non-well-founded set is a set which has either loops or **infinitely** descending chains in the membership relation on its **transitive closure**.

The simplest non-well-founded sets are the **universal set**, which has all objects as its members, and thus contains itself as a member, and Ω, the set that is its own **singleton** (i.e. $\Omega = \{\Omega\}$).

See also: **Anti-Foundation Axiom, New Foundations, Non-Well-Founded Set Theory, Positive Set Theory**

NON-WELL-FOUNDED SET THEORY   A non-well-founded set theory (or **Aczel set theory**) is any **set theory** that allows for the existence of **non-well-founded sets**. Non-well-founded set theories are most commonly obtained by replacing the **axiom of foundation** in **Zermelo Fraenkel set theory** (which rules out the existence of non-well-founded sets) with the **anti-foundation axiom**, or by adding some variant of the anti-foundation axiom.

See also: **New Foundations, Positive Set Theory, Universal Set, Well-Founded**

NOR see **Dagger**

NORMAL FORM see **Conjunctive Normal Form, Disjunctive Normal Form, Prenex Normal Form, Skolem Normal Form**

NORMAL MODAL LOGIC   A normal modal logic is any **modal logic** that contains the **distribution axiom K**:

$$\mathbf{K:} \quad \Box (A \to B) \to (\Box A \to \Box B)$$

and the **necessitation rule**: If:

$$\vdash A$$

then:

$$\vdash \Box A$$

See also: **B, D, K, S5, S4, T**

NP   In **complexity theory**, NP is the class of **recursive functions** whose values can be computed in **non-deterministic polynomial time**. In other words, a recursive function f is in NP if and only if there is a polynomial **function** g such that, given an input n, the number of steps a **non-deterministic Turing machine** will need in order to **compute** f(n) is no more than g(n).

See also: **Automaton, Effectively Computable, NP-Complete, P, Recursive Function Theory**

NP-COMPLETE   In **complexity theory**, NP-complete (or **NPC**) is a **subset** of the **set** of **functions** whose values can be computed in **non-deterministic polynomial time**. A function f is a **member** of NP-complete if and only if it is in **NP** and every function in NP is reducible to f. NP-complete functions play an important role in complexity theory, because if any NP-complete function is in **P** (the set of functions computable in **deterministic polynomial time**), then every NP function (including all of the NP-complete functions) is in P.

See also: **Automaton, Effectively Computable, Recursive Function Theory**

NPC see **NP-Complete**

N-TUPLE see **Ordered N-Tuple**

NULL SET see **Empty Set**

NULL SET AXIOM see **Axiom of Empty Set**

NUMERAL   A numeral is a **singular term** that **refers** to a **natural number**.

See also: **Arithmetic, Arithmetization, Gödel Numbering, Hilbert's Program**

NUMERICAL QUANTIFIER   A numerical quantifier is an expression of one of the following three forms:

"There are at least n x's such that ..."

"There are at most n x's such that ..."

"There are exactly n x's such that ..."

where n is any (possibly **infinite**) **cardinal number**. These **quantifiers** are typically represented as:

$(\exists_{\geq n}x)\dots$

$(\exists_{\leq n}x)\dots$

$(\exists_n x)\dots$

If n is **finite**, then the numerical quantifiers in question can be defined within **first-order logic recursively**. For example:

$$(\exists_0 x)(Fx) \quad =_{df} \quad \sim (\exists x)(Fx)$$

$$(\exists_{n+1}x)(Fx) \quad =_{df} \quad (\exists y)(Fy \wedge (\exists_n x)(x \neq y \wedge Fx))$$

Numerical quantifiers for infinite n are beyond the expressive power of first-order logic and are usually constructed using the resources of **generalized quantifiers**.

See also: **Arithmetic, Bounded Quantifier, Infinitary Logic, ω-Rule, Plural Quantification**

O

ω ω is the first **infinite ordinal number**, that is, the ordinal number of the **natural numbers** on their standard **ordering**.

See also: **Cardinal Number, Transfinite, Transfinite Ordinal Number, Well-ordering**

OBJECT LANGUAGE see **Metalanguage**

OBJECTUAL QUANTIFIER An objectual quantifier is a **quantifier** that is interpreted as ranging over **objects**. Consider a **universally quantified sentence** $(\forall x)\Phi(x)$. If we interpret the **quantifier** objectually, then the sentence will be **true** in a **model** if and only if every object in the **domain** of the model **satisfies** the **open formula** $\Phi(x)$. **Substitutional quantifiers** offer an alternative to the objectual interpretation of the quantifier, although the two are **equivalent** if every object in the domain has a **name** in the **language** in question.

See also: **Existential Quantifier, First-Order Logic, Generalized Quantifier, Numerical Quantifier, Universal Quantifier**

OBVERSE   The obverse of a **categorical proposition** is obtained by replacing the **predicate term** of the **proposition** with its **complement,** and changing the **quality** of the proposition from **negative** to **affirmative** (or vice versa). For example, the obverse of the **A-proposition:**

> All men are mortal.

is:

> No men are non–mortal.

In **categorical logic,** the obverse of a categorical proposition must have the same **truth value** as the original proposition.

See also: **Contrapositive, Converse, Obversion**

OBVERSION   Obversion is the process of taking the **obverse** of a **categorical proposition**. It also refers to the **immediate inference,** within **categorical logic,** where one infers, from a **proposition,** the obverse of that proposition.

See also: **Contraposition, Contrary, Conversion, Subalternation, Subcontrary**

ω-COMPLETENESS   A **theory** of **arithmetic** is ω–complete if and only if, for any **predicate** Φ in the **language,** if for each **numeral** n, we can **prove** Φ(n), then we can prove (∀x)Φ(x). A theory of arithmetic that is not ω–complete is **ω-incomplete.**

See also: **Gödel's First Incompleteness Theorem, Gödel's Second Incompleteness Theorem, Limitation Result, Negation Completeness, ω-Rule**

ω-CONSISTENCY   A **theory** of **arithmetic** is ω–consistent if and only, for any **predicate** Φ in the **language,** if, for each **numeral** n, we can **prove** Φ(n) then we cannot prove ~ (∀x)Φ(x). A theory of arithmetic that is not ω–consistent is **ω-inconsistent.**

See also: **Gödel's First Incompleteness Theorem, Gödel's Second Incompleteness Theorem, ω-Completeness, ω-Rule, Post Consistency**

ω-INCOMPLETENESS see ω-Completeness

ω-INCONSISTENCY see ω-Consistency

ONE-ONE see **One-to-One**

ONE-TO-ONE   A **function** f is one-to-one (or **one-one**, or **injective**) if and only if, for any two distinct **members** of the domain x and y, $f(x) \neq f(y)$. In other words, a one-to-one function does not map two distinct members of the **domain** to the same member of the **range**.

See also: **Bijection, Injection, Onto, Permutation, Surjection**

ONE-TO-ONE ONTO see **Bijective**

ONTIC VAGUENESS   Ontic vagueness refers to the view that there are **vague** objects in the world, and, as a result, there is vagueness concerning **identity** claims between objects, or vagueness with regard to whether an object exists or not.

See also: **Borderline Case, Higher-Order Vagueness, Semantic Vagueness, Sorites Paradox, Sorites Series**

ONTO   A **function** f is onto (or **surjective**) if and only if, for any **member** x of the **range** of the function, there is a member y of the **domain** of the function such that $f(y) = x$. In other words, an onto function "hits" every member of its range.

See also: **Bijection, Injection, One-to-One, Permutation, Surjection**

OPACITY see **Referential Opacity**

OPEN FORMULA   An open formula is a **formula** that contains one or more **free variables**, that is, **variables** that are not **bound** by a **quantifier**. A formula that is not an open formula is a **closed formula**.

See also: **Bound Variable, First-order Variable, Higher-order Variable, Open Term**

OPEN PAIR   The open pair (or the **no-no paradox**) is the following pair of **statements** which display a circular pattern of **reference**:

S_1: S_2 is false.
S_2: S_1 is false.

Given **bivalence** and the **law of non-contradiction**, one can **prove** that exactly one of S_1 and S_2 is **true**, and one is **false**. The puzzle arises when we consider which of the two statements is **true**. Since the two statements are semantically **indistinguishable**, there seems to be no reason to prefer the claim that it is S_1, and not S_2, that is true (or vice versa). Additionally, if two statements which are semantically indistinguishable ought to have the same **semantic value**, then we are faced with a genuine **paradox**.

See also: **Curry Paradox, Liar Paradox, Semantically Closed Language, Truth-Teller, Yablo Paradox**

OPEN TERM   An open term is a **term** that contains one or more **free variables**, that is, **variables** that are not **bound** by **quantifiers**. A term that is not an open term is a **closed term**.

See also: **Bound Variable, First-order Variable, Higher-order Variable, Open Formula**

OPERATION see **Logical Constant**

OPERATOR see **Logical Constant**

O-PROPOSITION   An O-proposition is a **categorical proposition** asserting that there is at least one object which is a **member** of the **class designated** by the **subject term** which is not a member of the class designated by the **predicate term**. In other words, an O-proposition is a **proposition** whose **logical form** is:

>   Some P is not Q.

The **quality** of an O-proposition is **negative**, and its **quantity** is **particular**. An O-proposition **distributes** its predicate term, but not its subject term.

See also: **A-Proposition, E-Proposition, I-Proposition, Square of Opposition**

OR see **Disjunction**

ORDER see **Ramified Type Theory**

ORDER TYPE   Two **partially ordered sets** $<A, \leq >$ and $<B, \propto >$ have the same order type if and only if they are order-**isomorphic**, that is, there is a **one-to-one onto function** f from A to B such that, for any x and y in A, $x \leq y$ if and only if $f(x) \propto f(y)$. If $<A, \leq >$ is a

well-ordered set, then the order type of <A, ≤ > is an **ordinal number**.

See also: **Burali-Forti Paradox, Cofinality, Transfinite Ordinal Number**

ORDERED LOGIC see **Non-Commutative Logic**

ORDERED N-TUPLE An ordered n-tuple (or **n-tuple**) is a **set-theoretic** construction that allows us to treat n objects as a single "thing" without losing sight of which object is which. For example, given three distinct objects x, y, and z, their **ordered triple** (i.e. ordered 3-tuple), written <x, y, z>, is an object whose first **element** is x, whose second element is y, and whose third element is z.

Given a particular set-theoretic **definition** of **ordered pair**, we can define ordered n-tuples **inductively** as:

$$<a_1, a_2, a_3 \ldots, a_{n-1}, a_n> =_{df} <a_1, <a_2, a_3, \ldots, a_{n-1}, a_n>>$$

or as:

$$<a_1, a_2, a_3 \ldots, a_{n-1}, a_n> =_{df} <<a_1, a_2, a_3, \ldots, a_{n-1}>, a_n>$$

The notion of ordered n-tuple can be generalized to the case of **infinitely** many objects using **transfinite induction**.

See also: **Inductive Definition, Sequence, Unordered Pair**

ORDERED PAIR An ordered pair is a **set-theoretic** construction that allows us to treat two objects as a single "thing" without losing sight of which object is which. For example, given distinct objects x and y, the ordered pair of x and y, written <x, y>, is an object whose first **element** is x and whose second element is y. The set-theoretic **definition** of ordered pair most commonly used today is the **Kuratowski ordered pair**, where:

$$<x, y> = \{\{x\}, \{x, y\}\}$$

See also: **Axiom of Pairing, Ordered N-Tuple, Unordered Pair**

ORDERED TRIPLE see **Ordered N-Tuple**

ORDINAL see **Ordinal Number**

ORDINAL ARITHMETIC Ordinal arithmetic is the **theory** governing the extension of the standard **functions** of **arithmetic**, such as addition and multiplication, to **infinite ordinal numbers**.

See also: **Cardinal Arithmetic, König's Lemma**

ORDINAL NUMBER   An ordinal number is the **number** assigned to the **order type** of a **well-ordered set**. For **finite sets**, the ordinal number will be the same as the **cardinal number**, and is just a **natural number**, for example, for three objects a, b, and c ordered by < where a < b < c, the ordinal number is 3.

The ordinal number of the **set** of natural numbers on their standard ordering (i.e. $0 < 1 < 2 < \ldots < n < n+1 < \ldots$) is ω. ω is the first **infinite** ordinal number. If we consider the ordering on the natural numbers that is **identical** to the standard ordering except that we move 0 from the "beginning" to the "end," then we obtain the next ordinal number, $\omega + 1$, the **ordinal successor** of ω.

Continuing in this way, we obtain all of the **countably infinite** ordinal numbers. If we consider **uncountably infinite sets**, we can obtain **transfinite ordinal numbers** (assuming the **axiom of choice**, which implies that any set can be well-ordered).

See also: **Burali-Forti Paradox, Cofinality, Limit Ordinal, Ordinal Arithmetic, Ordinal Successor**

ORDINAL PREDECESSOR see **Ordinal Successor**

ORDINAL SUCCESSOR   Within **set theory**, the ordinal successor of an **ordinal number** α is the ordinal number occurring immediately after α on the standard ordering. Typically, the ordinal successor of α is **defined** as:

$$S(\alpha) \quad = \quad \alpha \cup \{\alpha\}$$

If n is the ordinal successor of m, then m is the **ordinal predecessor** of n.

See also: **Cardinal Successor, Cofinality, Limit Ordinal, Transfinite Induction, Transfinite Recursion**

OR ELIMINATION see **Disjunctive Syllogism**

OR INTRODUCTION see **Addition**

ω-RULE   The ω-rule is an **infinitary rule of inference** for **arithmetic** that allows one to conclude:

$(\forall x)\Phi(x)$

if one has, as **premises**, all instances of:

$\Phi(n)$

where n is a **natural number**. In other words, the ω–rule allows one to conclude that Φ holds of all natural numbers if and only if one can **prove**, of each natural number, that Φ holds of it.

See also: **Infinitary Logic, ω–Completeness, ω–Consistency**

OSTENSIVE DEFINITION   An ostensive definition is a **definition** that furnishes an expression with meaning by pointing out, or otherwise indicating, either the **referent** of that expression (if the expression is a **singular term**) or typical, exemplary, or paradigmatic instances of objects that the expression applies to (if, e.g., the expression is a **predicate**).

See also: **Explicit Definition, Impredicative Definition, Intensional Definition, Persuasive Definition, Stipulative Definition**

OVERLAP   In **mereology**, two objects a and b overlap if and only if there is some object c such that c is a **part** of both a and b. In symbols, we have:

$$Oxy \quad = \quad (\exists z)(Pzx \wedge Pzy)$$

See also: **Composition, Intersection, Mereological Fusion, Proper Parthood, Underlap, Unrestricted Fusion**

P   In **complexity theory**, P is the class of **recursive functions** whose values can be **computed** in **deterministic polynomial time**. In other words, a recursive function f is in P if and only if there is a polynomial **function** g such that, given an input n, the number of steps a **deterministic Turing machine** will need in order to **compute** f(n) is no more than g(n).

See also: **Automaton, Effectively Computable, NP, NP-Complete, Recursive Function Theory**

PAIR see **Ordered Pair, Unordered Pair**

PAIRING AXIOM see **Axiom of Pairing**

PAIRING FUNCTION   A pairing function is any **binary function** that maps each distinct pair of objects in the **domain** onto a unique object. In other words, a pairing function f is a **total function** such that:

$$(\forall x)(\forall y)(\forall z)(\forall w)(f(x, y) = f(z, w) \leftrightarrow (x = z \wedge y = w))$$

A pairing function can exist only if the domain in question is **infinite** – thus, an **axiom** asserting the existence of a pairing function is equivalent to an axiom asserting the existence of **infinitely** many objects.

See also: **Axiom of Infinity, Infinity Axiom, Ordered Pair, Unordered Pair**

PAIRWISE DISJOINT   A collection of **sets** is pairwise disjoint if and only if, for any two sets A and B in the collection, there is no x such that x is a **member** of A and x is a **member** of B. In other words, a collection of sets is pairwise disjoint if and only if any two sets in the collection are **disjoint**.

See also: **Exclusive, Exhaustive, Intersection, Overlap**

PARACONSISTENT LOGIC   A paraconsistent logic is any **non-standard logic** where **ex falso quodlibet**:

$$\frac{A \quad \sim A}{B}$$

is not a **valid rule of inference**. In other words, within para-consistent logics, **contradictions** do not result in **triviality**.

Any non-trivial **dialethic logic** is also a paraconsistent logic, although not vice versa.

See also: **Dialetheism, First-Degree Entailment, Relevance Logic, Strong Paraconsistency, Weak Paraconsistency**

PARADOX   A paradox is an **argument** that proceeds from apparently **true premises**, through apparently unobjectionable reasoning, to a patently **false** or even **contradictory conclusion**.

See also: **Antinomy, Epistemic Paradox, Insolubilia, Paradox of Denotation, Semantic Paradox, Set-Theoretic Paradox**

PARADOX OF DENOTATION A paradox of denotation is a **paradox** that uses **definite descriptions** in an essential way. The most widely discussed example of a paradox of denotation is the **Berry paradox**, which concerns the puzzle that arises when one attempts to determine what **natural number** is **denoted** by the expression:

> The smallest natural number that cannot be uniquely specified in fewer than 100 characters.

Other paradoxes of denotation include the **König paradox** and the **Richard paradox**.

See also: **Epistemic Paradox, Semantic Paradox, Set-Theoretic Paradox**

PARADOX OF KNOWABILITY see **Fitch Paradox**

PARADOX OF THE HEAP see **Sorites Paradox**

PARADOX OF THE KNOWER see **Knower's Paradox**

PARADOX OF THE LIAR see **Liar Paradox**

PARADOX OF VAGUENESS see **Sorites Paradox**

PARADOXES OF MATERIAL IMPLICATION The paradoxes of material implication (or **paradoxes of relevance**) are not **paradoxes** in the strict sense. Rather, the paradoxes of material implication involve the puzzling nature of a number of **logical truths** in **classical propositional logic** that involve the **material conditional**. First, the claim that any **truth** is a **material consequence** of any **formula** whatsoever:

> $A \rightarrow (B \rightarrow A)$

Second, the claim that any **falsehood** has any **statement** whatsoever as a **material consequence**:

> $\sim A \rightarrow (A \rightarrow B)$

Dissatisfaction with these aspects of classical logic has been one of the primary motivations behind the development of a number of **non-standard logics**, including **paraconsistent logics, relevant logics,** and **conditional logics.**

See also: **Peirce's Law, Strong Paraconsistency, Weak Paraconsistency**

PARADOXES OF MOTION see **Zeno Paradoxes**

PARADOXES OF RELEVANCE see **Paradoxes of Material Implication**

PARAMETER A parameter is an expression whose **referent** is assumed to be fixed relative to a particular situation, but whose value can vary across situations. Thus, parameters differ from **singular terms** or **constants,** whose **denotation** is constant across situations, and from **variables,** which range over all entities of the appropriate sort within a particular situation.

See also: **Axiom Schema, Constructible Sets, Schema**

PARAMETER THEOREM see **S-M-N Theorem**

PARAMETRIZATION THEOREM see **S-M-N Theorem**

PART see **Parthood**

PARTHOOD Parthood is the central notion of **mereology.** An exact **definition** of parthood is difficult, and thus mereologists typically satisfy themselves with defining the notion **implicitly** in terms of one or another **axiomatization** of mereology. Nevertheless, we can say informally that an object x is a part of object y if and only if x is a component of y, or x is contained in y, or y presupposes x, or x is one of the objects that y is **composed** of.

In formal mereology the **binary parthood relation** P is generally assumed to impose a **partial ordering** on objects. In other words, the parthood relation is:

Reflexive:	$(\forall x)(Pxx)$
Transitive:	$(\forall x)(\forall y)(\forall z)((Pxy \wedge Pyz) \rightarrow Pxz)$
Antisymmetric:	$(\forall x)(\forall y)((Pxy \wedge Pyx) \rightarrow x = y)$

Additional principles are often assumed.

See also: **Mereological Fusion, Overlap, Proper Parthood, Underlap, Unrestricted Fusion**

PARTIAL FUNCTION see **Total Function**

PARTIAL LOGIC   A partial logic is a **non-standard logic** where either the mapping from **statements** to **truth values** is (or can be) a **partial function** (thus allowing for statements that receive no truth value, in which case the **logic** in question is a **gap** logic), or where the mapping from **singular terms** to objects in the **domain** is (or can be) a partial function (thus allowing for singular terms that do not **denote**, in which case the logic in question is a **free logic**).

See also: **Existence Predicate, Many-Valued Logic, Relational Semantics**

PARTIAL ORDER see **Partial Ordering**

PARTIAL ORDERING   A partial ordering (or **partial order**, or **partially ordered set**, or **poset**) is any **set** A and **binary relation** R on A such that R is:

> **Reflexive:** $(\forall x)(Rxx)$
>
> **Transitive:** $(\forall x)(\forall y)(\forall z)((Rxy \wedge Ryz) \rightarrow Rxz)$
>
> **Antisymmetric:** $(\forall x)(\forall y)((Rxy \wedge Ryx) \rightarrow x = y)$

See also: **Boolean Algebra, Lattice, Linear Ordering, Mereology, Parthood, Pre-Ordering, Mereology, Strict Ordering, Well-Ordering**

PARTIALLY ORDERED SET see **Partial Ordering**

PARTICULAR PROPOSITION   The **quantity** of a **categorical proposition** is particular if it makes a claim about some, but not all, of the **members** of the **class** denoted by the **subject term** of the proposition. Thus **I-propositions** and **O-propositions** are particular, while **A-propositions** and **E-propositions** are not particular. Categorical propositions that are not particular are **universal**.

See also: **Affirmative Proposition, Negative Proposition, Quality, Square of Opposition**

PARTITION   A partition of a non-empty **set** X is a collection of non-empty sets Y such that the sets in Y are **exclusive** and **exhaustive** with respect to X. In other words, Y is a collection of sets such that:

(1) There is no object z and sets S, P in Y such that z is a **member** of both S and P.

(2) For any object z, z is a member of X if and only if there is a set S in Y such that z is a member of S.

More intuitively, Y consists of a "division" of X into **subsets** which do not overlap and which cover all of X. Any **equivalence relation** E on a set X imposes a partition on X – namely, the **equivalence classes** of X relative to E.

See also: **Disjoint, Pairwise Disjoint**

PEANO ARITHMETIC   Peano arithmetic (or **Peano-Dedekind Arithmetic**, or the **Peano Postulates**) is the most widely studied **axiomatization** of **arithmetic**:

(1) $(\forall x)S(x) \neq 0$

(2) $(\forall x)(\forall y)(S(x) = S(y) \rightarrow x = y)$

(3) $(\forall x)(x + 0 = x)$

(4) $(\forall x)(\forall y)(x + S(y) = S(x + y))$

(5) $(\forall x)(x \cdot 0 = 0)$

(6) $(\forall x)(\forall y)(x \cdot S(y) = (x \cdot y) + x)$

(7) For any **predicate** Φ:

$$(\Phi(0) \wedge (\forall x)(\Phi(x) \rightarrow \Phi(S(x)))) \rightarrow (\forall x)\Phi(x)$$

where $S(x)$ is the **arithmetic successor function**. The final principle is not an axiom, but is an **axiom schema**, coding up **infinitely** many instances of **mathematical induction** (one for each distinct predicate Φ).

See also: **Arithmetization, Diagonalization Lemma, Gödel's First Incompleteness Theorem, Gödel's Second Incompleteness Theorem, Robinson Arithmetic**

PEANO-DEDEKIND ARITHMETIC see **Peano Arithmetic**

PEANO POSTULATES see **Peano Arithmetic**

PEIRCE DAGGER see **Dagger**

PEIRCE'S LAW Within **propositional logic**, Peirce's law is the principle:

$$((A \rightarrow B) \rightarrow A) \rightarrow A$$

See also: **Intermediate Logic, Material Implication, Paradoxes of Material Implication**

PERMUTATION₁ A permutation is a **bijection** from a **set** to itself. In other words, a permutation maps each **member** x of a set A onto another member y of A; maps no two members x and y of the set A onto the same member of A, and, for any member y of A, there is a member x of A such that x is mapped onto y.

Given an **ordering** on the set in question, we can view a permutation as providing a re-ordering of the set. Thus, if we order the members of the set A = {x, y, z} as <x, y, z>, then the permutation f:

$$f(x) = x$$
$$f(y) = z$$
$$f(z) = y$$

provides us with the new ordering <x, z, y>.

See also: **Automorphism, Endomorphism, Epimorphism, Homomorphism, Isomorphism**

PERMUTATION₂ Permutation (or **exchange**) is the **structural rule** that allows one to exchange two **formulas** that are on the same side of the arrow. Thus, by applying permutation we can move from:

$$\Delta, A, B, \Gamma \Rightarrow \Sigma$$

to:

$$\Delta, B, A, \Gamma \Rightarrow \Sigma$$

or we can move from:

$$\Delta \Rightarrow \Gamma, A, B, \Sigma$$

to:

$$\Delta \Rightarrow \Gamma, B, A, \Sigma$$

See also: **Commutativity, Non-Commutative Logic, Sequent Calculus, Substructural Logic, Weakening**

PERMUTATION INVARIANT A **function** or **operation** is permutation invariant if and only if the result of applying it to a **domain** is the same as applying it to any **permutation** of the **domain**. For example, if R is a **binary relation** on a domain D, then R is permutation invariant if and only if, for any permutation f on D, R holds of objects x and y if and only if R holds of f(x) and f(y).

Often, the distinction between **logical constants** (such as **disjunction** and **universal quantification**) and **non-logical vocabulary** is defined as follows: the logical constants are exactly the operations and functions that are permutation invariant.

See also: **First-order Logic, Generalized Quantifier, Higher-order Logic, Logical Connective, Objectual Quantifier, Substitutional Quantifier**

PERSUASIVE DEFINITION A persuasive definition is a **definition** that purports to provide the common understanding of an expression while actually providing the meaning that the author would like the reader to associate with the expression.

See also: **Explicit Definition, Impredicative Definition, Intensional Definition, Ostensive Definition, Stipulative Definition**

PETITIO PRINCIPII see **Begging the Question**

Π-FORMULA Within the **arithmetical hierarchy** (or **Kleene hierarchy**) a Π-formula (or Π_1 formula) is a **formula** Φ such that Φ is **logically equivalent** to some formula of the form:

$$(\forall x_1)(\forall x_2) \ldots (\forall x_m)\Psi$$

where Ψ is a formula containing only **bounded quantifiers**.

See also: **Finitary Arithmetic, Π-Sentence, Σ-Formula, Σ-Sentence**

Π₁-FORMULA see **Π-Formula**

PHILONIAN CONDITIONAL see **Material Conditional**

PHILOSOPHICAL LOGIC Philosophical logic involves the use of **formal systems** as a tool for solving, or contributing to the solution of, philosophical problems (which might, or might not, involve **arguments** or reasoning). Thus, it differs from **philosophy of logic**, which is the philosophical study of formal systems as models of the **consequence relation**.

See also: **Logic, Mathematical Logic**

PHILOSOPHY OF LOGIC Philosophy of logic is the philosophical study of **formal systems** as models of the **consequence relation**. Thus, it differs from **philosophical logic**, which is the use of formal systems in attempts to solve philosophical problems.

See also: **Logic, Mathematical Logic**

PLATONISM Platonism is the metaphysical thesis that **abstract objects** exist. In particular, in the philosophy of mathematics, Platonism amounts to a belief in the existence of abstract objects as the subject matter of mathematics – that is, that **natural numbers**, **sets**, spaces, etc. exist, and are the objects **referred** to by working mathematicians.

See also: **Mathematical Abstractionism, Meinongianism, Nominalism, Set-Theoretic Realism**

PLATO'S BEARD Plato's beard refers to the problem of how we can deny the existence of some object or objects, since in order to do so, one must apparently describe or directly **refer** to those things in the denial, as a result accepting, at least implicitly, their existence.

Bertrand Russell's method of **definite descriptions** is typically taken to solve the problems posed by Plato's beard.

See also: **Free Logic, Indefinite Description**

PLURAL QUANTIFICATION Plural quantification is **quantification** over pluralities of objects. Thus, the **statement**:

> There is a car in the lot.

involves singular quantification over objects, while:

> There are some cars in the lot.

involves plural quantification.

Defenders of plural quantification point out that our understanding of such constructions does not seem to commit us to any
entities over and above the objects involved – in other words, the
second statement above does not seem to involve **sets**, or **concepts**,
or other supposedly problematic notions any more than does the first
statement. As a result, plural quantification has been suggested as a
promising means for understanding **second-order quantifiers** and
perhaps **higher-order quantifiers** generally.

See also: **Branching Quantifier, Comprehension Schema,
Geach-Kaplan Sentence**

PLURALISM see **Logical Monism**

POLISH NOTATION   Polish notation is a notation for **formulas** in
propositional logic where each **logical connective** is written to
the left of its **argument** or arguments – that is, in Polish notation all
logical connectives are written in **prefix notation**. Thus, instead of
writing:

$$(A \wedge B) \vee (C \wedge D)$$

we would write:

$$\vee \wedge A\,B \wedge C\,D$$

Originally, Polish notation used upper-case letters for connectives
and lower-case letters for **statements** instead of the modern
notation, so the above would have appeared as:

$$D\,C\,a\,b\,C\,c\,d$$

One of the main reasons why Polish notation is of technical interest
is that it eliminates the need for parentheses, since formulas in Polish
notation are unambiguous without such **punctuation**.

See also: **Infix Notation, Suffix Notation**

POLYADIC FIRST-ORDER LOGIC   Polyadic first-order logic (or
polyadic predicate logic, or the **logic of relations**, or **full
predicate logic**) is the system of **classical first-order logic**
obtained when **polyadic predicates** (as opposed to only **monadic
predicates**) are allowed into the **language**. Unlike **monadic first-
order logic, theoremhood** in polyadic first-order logic is not
decidable.

See also: **Church's Theorem, Entscheidungsproblem**

POLYADIC PREDICATE see **Monadic Predicate**

POLYADIC PREDICATE LOGIC see **Polyadic First-order Logic**

POLYSYLLOGISM   A polysyllogism (or **sorites**) is an **argument** consisting of a **sequence** of **syllogisms**, usually **categorical syllogisms**.

See also: **Categorical Logic, Term Logic**

POSET see **Partial Ordering**

POSITIVE PROPOSITION see **Affirmative Proposition**

POSITIVE SET THEORY   Positive set theory is a **formal set theory** obtained by assuming:

> **Axiom of Extensionality:** $(\forall x)(\forall y)(x = y \leftrightarrow (\forall z)(z \in x \leftrightarrow z \in y))$
>
> **Axiom of Empty Set:** $(\exists x)(\forall y)(y \notin x)$
>
> **Axiom of Infinity:** $(\exists x)(\Phi \in x \wedge (\forall y)(y \in x \rightarrow y \cup \{y\} \in x))$
>
> Positive **Naïve Comprehension Schema**:
>
> $(\exists x)(\forall y)(y \in x \leftrightarrow \Phi(y))$

(where Φ can contain only the membership and identity symbols, conjunction, disjunction, and the existential and universal quantifiers).

In other words, positive set theory is the result of restricting the **comprehension schema** to the positive formulas – those not containing **negation** or the **conditional**.

Positive set theory differs from more standard set theories in a number of ways, the most striking of which is that it implies the existence of the **universal set** (the set containing all objects, including itself, as **members**). As a result, positive set theory is a **non-well-founded set theory**.

See also: **New Foundations, Non-Well-Founded Set, Well-Founded**

POSSIBILIA see **Mere Possibilia**

POSSIBILISM see **Modal Realism**

POSSIBILITY   A **statement** is possible if it can be **true**. Possible statements should be contrasted with **contingent** statements, which can be true, but which can also be **false**. All contingent statements are possible, but not vice versa.

Within **modal logic**, where possibilities are represented by **possible worlds**, a possible statement is one where there is some **accessible** possible world in which it is true. This is represented in the **language** of modal logic as:

$$\Diamond A$$

See also: **Actual World, Alethic Modal Logic, Impossibility, Mere Possibilia, Necessity**

POSSIBLE WORLD   A possible world is, intuitively speaking, a way the world could have been other than the way that it is. Possible worlds are used to explain the **truth conditions** of **modal** claims. Thus, "**necessarily** Φ" is **true** if and only if Φ is true at every possible world, and "**possibly** Φ" is true if and only if Φ is true at some possible world.

Although the need for introducing possible worlds in order to explain the truth conditions of modal expressions is widely agreed upon, there is vast disagreement regarding the exact nature of possible worlds. **Modal realists** believe that possible worlds are actual places, of the same sort as the actual world, whereas **modal actualists** believe that possible worlds are (usually abstract) bits of the **actual world**, such as maximal states of affairs.

See also: **Accessibility Relation, Impossible World, Mere Possibilia, Modal Agnosticism, Modal Fictionalism**

POSSIBLE WORLDS SEMANTICS see **Kripke Semantics**

POST COMPLETENESS see **Strong Completeness**

POST CONSISTENCY   A **theory** is Post consistent (or **absolutely consistent**) if and only if there is at least one **statement** in the language of the theory that is not a **theorem**. A theory that is not Post consistent is **Post inconsistent** (or **absolutely inconsistent**).

See also: **Gödel's First Incompleteness Theorem, Gödel's Second Incompleteness Theorem, Limitation Result, Metatheorem, ω-Consistency**

POSTFIX NOTATION see **Suffix Notation**

POST HOC, ERGO PROPTER HOC   Post hoc ergo propter hoc (Latin for "after this, therefore because of this") is an **informal fallacy** which occurs when the reasoner concludes that event A caused event B merely because event A preceded event B.

POST INCOMPLETENESS see **Strong Completeness**

POST INCONSISTENCY see **Post Consistency**

POTENTIAL INFINITY see **Complete Infinity**

POWER see **Cardinality**

POWERSET   Within **set theory**, the powerset of a **set** A is the set whose **members** are exactly the **subsets** of A. For example, if the original set is {a, b, c}, then the powerset of this set is:

$$\{\varnothing, \{a\}, \{b\}, \{c\}, \{a, b\}, \{a, c\}, \{b, c\}, \{a, b, c\}\}$$

See also: **Axiom of Powerset, Cantor's Theorem, Continuum Hypothesis, Generalized Continuum Hypothesis, Rank**

POWERSET AXIOM see **Axiom of Powerset**

Pr(A/B) see **Conditional Probability**

PRAGMATICS   Pragmatics studies the properties of expressions and utterances that can vary from use to use, or from context to context. This distinguishes it from **logic** and **semantics**, which typically study those aspects of **language** which are constant from use to use, or context to context. Thus, pragmatics (as opposed to **semantics**) takes into account the situation in which an assertion occurs, the intentions of the person making the utterance, and the background assumptions at play in the discourse within which the utterance is embedded.

See also: **Compositionality, Contextualism**

PREDECESSOR see **Arithmetic Successor, Cardinal Successor, Ordinal Successor**

PREDICATE   A predicate is an expression that denotes a **concept**, or, alternatively, an expression that denotes a **unary propositional function**.

See also: **Existence Predicate, Monadic Predicate, Open Formula, Polyadic Predicate, Predicate Functor**

PREDICATE FUNCTOR   A predicate functor is an expression which, when applied to a **predicate**, yields another predicate. Loosely put, predicate functors are the formal analogue of adverbs.

See also: **λ-Calculus, Monadic Predicate, Polyadic Predicate**

PREDICATE FUNCTOR LOGIC   Predicate functor logic is a **logic** which eliminates the need for **quantified variables**, instead relying on the addition of **predicate functors** to the **language** – that is, expressions which, when applied to a predicate, yield another predicate. Predicate functor logic is, in its standard formulation, equivalent to **first-order logic**.

See also: **Monadic Predicate, Polyadic Predicate**

PREDICATE LOGIC see **First-order Logic**

PREDICATE TERM   Within **categorical logic**, the predicate term of a **categorical proposition** is the **term** that occurs second in the proposition. Thus, in the **A-proposition**:

All men are mortal.

the predicate "is mortal" is the predicate term.

See also: **Major Term, Middle Term, Minor Term, Subject Term**

PREDICATIVE DEFINITION see **Impredicative Definition**

PREFIX NOTATION   A **function** symbol, **relation** symbol, or **logical constant** is an instance of prefix notation if it occurs to the left of its **arguments**. Thus, **successor function** is typically represented in prefix notation, since we often denote the successor of x as S(x), and **negation** is typically represented in prefix notation, since we denote the negation of A as ~ A.

See also: **Infix Notation, Polish Notation, Suffix Notation**

PRELINEARITY AXIOM Within **propositional logic**, the prelinearity axiom is the **formula**:

$$(P \rightarrow Q) \vee (Q \rightarrow P)$$

Extending **intuitionistic logic** through the addition of the prelinearity axiom results in the **intermediate logic** known as **Gödel-Dummett logic**.

See also: **Kreisel-Putnam Logic, Logic of Weak Excluded Middle, Scott Logic**

PREMISE In an **argument**, a premise (or **premisse**) is a **statement** that is intended to provide **evidence** or **support** for the **conclusion**. In a formal **proof** the premises are those statements that are assumed at the beginning of the proof (if any), from which all later statements follow according to **rules of inference** or **rules of replacement**.

See also: **Deductive Argument, Double Turnstile, Inductive Argument, Logical Form, Single Turnstile**

PREMISSE see **Premise**

PRENEX NORMAL FORM A **formula** in the **language** of **first-order logic** is in prenex normal form if and only if the formula consists of a **sequence** of **quantifiers** followed by a quantifier-free formula Φ where the scope of each quantifier is all of Φ and no quantifier in the initial sequence is a **vacuous quantifier**. The quantifier-free formula following the initial sequence of quantifiers is the **matrix** of the prenex normal form formula. Thus:

$$(\forall x)(\exists y)(\forall z)((Fx \wedge Gxy) \vee Hzx)$$

is in prenex normal form. Every formula in **classical first-order logic** is **logically equivalent** to one in prenex normal form.

See also: **Conjunctive Normal Form, Disjunctive Normal Form, Negation Normal Form, Skolem Normal Form**

PRE-ORDER see **Pre-Ordering**

PRE-ORDERING A pre-ordering (or **pre-order**, or **quasi-order**, or quasi-ordering) is any **set** A and **binary relation** R on A such that R is:

Reflexive: $(\forall x)(Rxx)$

Transitive: $(\forall x)(\forall y)(\forall z)((Rxy \wedge Ryz) \rightarrow Rxz)$

See also: **Linear Ordering, Partial Ordering, Strict Ordering, Well-Ordering**

PRIMITIVE RECURSION   Primitive recursion is one of the simple **function**-building operations of **recursive function theory**. Given a **binary recursive function** f and a **ternary** recursive function g the primitive recursion of f and g is the binary function h such that:

$$h(x, 0) \;\;=\;\; f(x)$$
$$h(x, y+1) \;\;=\;\; g(x, y, h(x, y))$$

See also: **Composition, Identity Function, Minimization, Successor Function, Zero Function**

PRIMITIVE RECURSIVE FUNCTION   A primitive recursive function is any **function** that can be constructed from the basic functions of **recursive function theory** (the **zero function**, the **successor function**, and the **identity functions**) plus the function-building operations **composition** and **primitive recursion**.

See also: **Course of Values Recursion, Effectively Computable Function, Recursive Function**

PRIMITIVE RECURSIVE RELATION   A primitive recursive relation is any **relation** on the **natural numbers** whose **characteristic function** is a **primitive recursive function**.

See also: **Recursive Function, Recursive Function Theory, Recursive Relation**

PRIMITIVE RECURSIVE SET   A primitive recursive set is any **set** S of **natural numbers** whose **characteristic function** is a primitive recursive function.

See also: **Definable Set, Effectively Enumerable Set, Enumerable Set, Enumeration, Recursively Set, Recursively Enumerable Set**

PRINCIPLE OF BIVALENCE see **Bivalence**

PRINCIPLE OF EXCLUDED MIDDLE see **Excluded Middle**

PRINCIPLE OF CONSTRUCTIVE CHOICES see **Markov's Principle**

PRINCIPLE OF NON-CONTRADICTION see **Law of Non-Contradiction**

PROBABILITY CALCULUS   The probability calculus is a system of rules providing a method for assigning **probabilities** to **compound statements** based on the probabilities of simpler statements. In order to assign probabilities to compound statements using the probability calculus, one must not only know the probabilities of the simple statements involved, but also the probabilities of **conditional probability** statements of the form:

$$Pr(B/A)$$

(intuitively, the probability that B is **true** given that A is true). Within the probability calculus, the rules for the propositional connectives are as follows:

$$Pr(\sim A) \quad = \quad 1 - Pr(A)$$

$$Pr(A \wedge B) \quad = \quad Pr(A) \bullet Pr(B/A)$$

$$Pr(A \vee B) \quad = \quad Pr(A) + Pr(B) - Pr(A \wedge B)$$

See also: **Bayes' Theorem, Degree-Theoretic Semantics, Probability Logic, Probability Theory, Ramsey Test**

PROBABILITY LOGIC Probability logics are **formal systems** intended to capture **inferences** involving **statements** whose **probability** is strictly between 0 and 1. Thus, statements in such logics are assigned probabilities instead of **truth values**, and the **consequence relation** of such a logic will preserve the probability of the **premises** in the **conclusion**. Typically, probability logics reduce to standard **classical logic** on the assumption that all statements have probabilities of either 0 or 1.

See also: **Bayes' Theorem, Conditional Probability, Degree-Theoretic Semantics, Probability Calculus, Probability Theory, Ramsey Test**

PROBABILITY THEORY Probability theory is the branch of mathematics that studies random events or events for which we can only determine their likelihood, and not determine whether they have or have not occurred with certainty. Two tools that are useful for the philosophical study of probability are **probability logics** and the **probability calculus**.

See also: **Bayes' Theorem, Conditional Probability, Ramsey Test**

PRODUCT see **Cartesian Product**

PROJECTION FUNCTION see **Identity Function**

PROOF A proof (or **demonstration**) is a **finite sequence** of **statements** where each statement in the list is either an **axiom** or the result of applying a **rule of inference** to one or more preceding statements. The final statement is the **conclusion** of the proof.

See also: **Deductive Argument, Derivation, Formal Proof, Natural Deduction, Rule of Replacement**

PROOF BY CASES see **Classical Dilemma**

PROOF BY INDUCTION see **Induction on Well-Formed Functions, Mathematical Induction, Transfinite Induction**

PROOF-THEORETIC CONSEQUENCE see **Deductive Consequence**

PROOF-THEORETIC EQUIVALENCE see **Deductively Equivalent**

PROOF-THEORETIC IMPLICATION see **Deductive Implication**

PROOF-THEORETIC VALIDITY see **Deductive Validity**

PROOF-THEORETICALLY EQUIVALENT see **Deductively Equivalent**

PROOF THEORY Proof theory is the branch of mathematical logic that studies proofs within a formal system. Important results in proof theory include the **cut elimination theorem**, Gödel's **first**

incompleteness theorem and Gödel's second incompleteness theorems.

See also: **Deduction Theorem, Independence Result, Limitation Result, Metalogic, Model Theory**

PROPER CLASS   A proper class is a collection that is too ill-behaved to be a **set**. Different **set theories** posit different collections to be the proper classes, but the **Russell paradox** (and related **set-theoretic paradoxes**) show that some collections must not be sets.

See also: **Absolute Infinite, Global Choice, Global Well-Ordering, Set, Von Neumann Bernays Gödel Set Theory**

PROPER PARTHOOD   In **mereology**, an object x is a proper part of an object y if and only if x is a **part** of y and y is not a part of x. In symbols, we have:

$$PPxy \quad = \quad Pxy \wedge \sim Pyx$$

If we assume, as is typical, that the parthood **relation** is a **partial ordering**, then this is equivalent to defining proper parthood as parthood plus non-**identity**:

$$PPxy \quad = \quad Pxy \wedge x \neq y$$

See also: **Composition, Mereological Extensionality, Mereological Fusion, Overlap, Underlap, Unrestricted Fusion**

PROPER SUBSET   A **set** A is a proper subset of a set B if and only if every **member** of A is a member of B, and there is some member of B that is not a member of A. **Equivalently**, A is a proper subset of B if and only if A is a **subset** of B, and A is not **identical** to B.

See also: **Powerset, Set Theory**

PROPERTY see **Concept**

PROPOSITION₁   A proposition is any **statement** in **propositional logic**, that is, either a **propositional letter** or a **compound formula** built up from propositional letters and **logical connectives**.

See also: **Compound Statement, Formation Rules, Formula, Subformula, Syntax, Well-Formed Formula**

PROPOSITION₂   A proposition is the object that is the meaning, or content, of a **statement** or assertion. While there is vast disagreement amongst philosophers and logicians as to whether or not propositions exist, and over the nature of propositions if they do exist, believers in propositions typically take them to be the objects of **propositonal attitudes** such as belief and desire – that is, on this view, when we believe something, or desire for something to be true, it is the proposition that we believe, or desire to become true.

See also: **Atomic Sentence, Categorical Proposition, Propositional Function, Propositional Letter, Propositional Logic**

PROPOSITIONAL ATTITUDE   A propositional attitude is a relation holding between a person and a **proposition** in virtue of the person having certain attitudes towards that proposition. Thus, examples of propositional attitudes include belief, desire, and knowledge.

See also: **Referential Opacity**

PROPOSITIONAL CONNECTIVE see **Logical Connective**

PROPOSITIONAL FUNCTION   A propositional function is the **function** denoted by an expression containing one or more **free variables**. The **domain** of the function is the set of appropriate **arguments** that can be substituted for the **free variable** (or **sequences** of such arguments, if there is more than one free variable), and the **range** is the set of **truth values**. Thus, if R represents the predicate "is red," then the propositional function denoted by "Rx" is the function that maps the red objects to the true, and maps any non-red objects to the false.

The term "propositional function" is also sometimes used to refer to the expression containing free variables itself, instead of to the corresponding function from arguments to truth values.

See also: **Characteristic Function, Primitive Recursive Function, Proposition, Recursive Function, Truth Function**

PROPOSITIONAL LETTER   A propositional letter (or **atom**, or **atomic letter**, or **sentence letter**, or **sentential variable**) is any (usually upper-case) letter used within **propositional logic** to represent a primitive **statement**. **Compound statements** are constructed within propositional logic by combining propositional letters with **logical connectives**.

See also: **Atomic Formula, Atomic Sentence, Formation Rules, Logical Constant, Proposition, Well-Formed Formula**

PROPOSITIONAL LOGIC   Propositional logic (or **sentential logic**) is the **logic** containing **propositional letters**, representing simple statements, and **logical connectives**, which are used to form **compound statements** by combining simpler ones. Typically, propositional logic is formulated using **conjunction** ($\wedge$), **disjunction** ($\vee$), **material implication** ($\rightarrow$), and **negation** ($\sim$), although other connectives have been studied. Thus, if S is the propositional letter representing the English sentence:

It is snowing.

and R is the propositional letter representing:

It is raining.

then:

R $\vee$ S

represents the compound statement:

Either it is raining or it is snowing.

See also: **First-order Logic, Logical Consequence, Proposition, Statement**

PROSENTENTIAL   An expression is prosentential if it stands in for the name of, or a **description** of, a **statement** in the same way that a pronoun stands in for the name of, or a description of, a noun.

See also: **Demonstrative, Indexical**

PROSENTENTIAL THEORY OF TRUTH   The prosentential theory of truth is the view that, given any **statement** A, "A is **true**" is a **prosentential** expression, picking out A indirectly in the same manner that the pronoun "he" can indirectly denote a person. As a result, prosentential theorists deny that there is a substantial **property** called "truth" that attaches to statements, and thus the view is a species of **deflationism**.

See also: **Disquotationalism, Redundancy Theory of Truth**

PROVABILITY LOGIC   Provability logic (or **GL**) is a **modal logic** that formalizes **provability** within **first-order arithmetic** (or within any **formal system** strong enough to interpret arithmetic, and for which the **Gödel incompleteness theorems** hold). Within provability logic □P is interpreted as "P is provable." Provability logic is the **normal modal logic** whose additional **axiom** is:

L: $\Box(\Box A \rightarrow A) \rightarrow \Box A$

Provability logic is **valid** on any **frame** in which the **accessibility relation** is **transitive** and **converse-well-founded**. A particularly surprising fact about provability logic is that the axiom **T**:

$\Box A \rightarrow A$

is not a **theorem**.

See also: **Doxastic Modal Logic, Epistemic Modal Logic, Provability Predicate**

PROVABILITY PREDICATE   Within **first-order arithmetic**, the provability predicate (often written "**Bew**") is the **recursive predicate** that holds of a **natural number** if and only if that natural number is the **Gödel number** of a **statement** that is **provable** within the arithmetic system in question.

See also: **Arithmetization, Diagonalization, Gödel's Second Incompleteness Theorem, Gödel Sentence, Löb's Theorem**

Π-SENTENCE   Within the **arithmetical hierarchy** (or **Kleene hierarchy**) a Π-sentence (or Π_1 **sentence**) is any **statement** Φ such that Φ is **logically equivalent** to some statement of the form:

$(\forall x_1)(\forall x_2) \ldots (\forall x_m)\Psi$

where Ψ is a formula containing only **bounded quantifiers**. In other words, a Π-sentence is a **Π-formula** with no **free variables**.

See also: **Finitary Arithmetic, Σ-Formula, Σ-Sentence**

Π_1-SENTENCE see **Π-SENTENCE**

PSEUDO MODUS PONENS see **Assertion**

PUNCTUATION   Punctuation refers to any linguistic device used to eliminate **ambiguity** from expressions in a **language**. Within **formal systems**, punctuation usually takes the form of parentheses or other bracketing devices (for example, {. }, [,], <, >), and is used to guarantee unique readability – that is, that every **well-formed formula** of the system has a unique, unambiguous **interpretation**.

See also: **Polish Notation, Quotation**

PURE FIRST-ORDER LOGIC Pure first-order logic (or **pure predicate logic**) is the system of **first-order logic** that contains no **function symbols, relations,** or **constants** other than the **identity relation**.

See also: **Inclusive First-order Logic, Monadic First-order Logic, Polyadic First-order Logic, Quantified Modal Logic**

PURE PREDICATE LOGIC see **Pure First-order Logic**

PURE SET THEORY Any **set theory** that disallows the existence of objects that are not **sets** is a pure set theory. In other words, a pure set theory only **quantifies** over sets, and not over **urelements**.

See also: **Zermelo Fraenkel Set Theory**

PUTNAM'S MODEL-THEORETIC ARGUMENT Putnam's model-theoretic argument attempts to show that the **Lowenheim-Skolem theorems** imply that there are too many **models** of our **language** – that is, too many ways in which our expressions could link up to the world – for there to be determinate facts about **truth** and meaning. As a result Putnam argues that we must embrace a version of antirealism regarding the connection between our language and the world.
See also: **Compactness, Downward Lowenheim Skolem Theorem, Non-Standard Model, Upward Lowenheim Skolem Theorem**

Q see **Robinson Arithmetic**

QED see **Quod Erat Demonstrandum**

QUALITY Within **categorical logic**, the quality of a **categorical proposition** is determined by whether or not the **proposition**

affirms or denies that (some or all) **members** of the **class denoted** by the **subject term** are also members of the class denoted by the **predicate term**. The quality of **A-propositions** and **I-propositions** is **affirmative**, since they involve the claim that some or all of the members of the class denoted by the subject term are also members of the class denoted by the predicate term. The quality of **E-propositions** and **O-propositions** is **negative**, since they involve the claim that some or all of the members of the class denoted by the subject term are not members of the class denoted by the predicate term. More simply put, the quality of a categorical proposition is negative if the proposition involves a **negation**, and is affirmative **otherwise**.

See also: **Particular Proposition, Quantity, Square of Opposition, Universal Proposition**

QUANTIFIED MODAL LOGIC Quantified modal logic is the **formal system** obtained either by **extending propositional modal logics** with the addition of **quantifiers**, or by extending **first-order logic** with the addition of **modal operators**. Quantified modal logic is vastly more complicated than either of these subsystems, from both a technical perspective and a philosophical perspective. In particular, the status of the following purported "laws" are of particular interest within **quantified modal logic**:

   The Necessity of Identity: $(\forall x)(\forall y)(x = y \to \Box(x = y))$

   The Barcan Formula: $\Box(\forall x)\Phi \to (\forall x)\Box\Phi$

   The Converse Barcan Formula: $(\forall x)\Box\Phi \to \Box(\forall x)\Phi$

See also: **Counterpart Theory, Mere Possibilia, Transworld Identity**

QUANTIFIER A quantifier is a **determiner** used to express a definite or indefinite number or amount. Within **formal systems** the most common quantifiers are the **existential quantifier** ($\exists$ – used to express **existential generalizations** of the form "there exists at least one object x such that ...) and the **universal quantifier** ($\forall$ – used to express **universal generalizations** of the form "for any object x, ..."). Universal and existential quantifiers can be used to **quantify** over objects, in which case they are **first-order quantifiers** (the **variables** ranged over by **first-order quantifiers** are usually taken from the end of the alphabet and written in lower case). Quantifiers can also be used to quantify over **concepts, relations, properties,** or other **higher-order** entities, in which case they are called **second-** or **higher-order quantifiers** (the variable bound by such a higher-order quantifier is usually written in upper case, in order to distinguish it from first-order quantifiers and the variables they bind). Other sorts of quantifier have been studied, including **generalized quantifiers** and **numerical quantifiers**.

See also: **Bounded Quantifier, Branching Quantifier, Objectual Quantifier, Plural Quantification, Substitutional Quantifier, Vacuous Quantifier**

QUANTIFIER ELIMINATION see **Elimination of Quantifiers**

QUANTIFIER SHIFT FALLACY   The quantifier shift fallacy is the **formal fallacy** that occurs when the reasoner mistakenly moves from a claim of the form:

   $(\forall x)(\exists y)\Phi xy$

to a claim of the form:

   $(\exists y)(\forall x)\Phi xy$

The fallacy becomes evident if we let "Φ" represent the **relation** of child to father. Then the first **statement** becomes the **truth** that every person has a father, while the second statement becomes the **false** claim that someone is everyone's father.

See also: **Existential Quantifier, First-order Logic, Scope, Universal Quantifier**

QUANTITY   The quantity of a **categorical proposition** is determined by whether or not the **proposition** makes a claim about all or merely some of the **members** of the **class denoted** by the **subject term** of the **proposition**. The quantity of **A-propositions** and **E-propositions** is **universal**, since they involve the **quantifiers** "all" and "no" respectively. The quantity of **I-propositions** and **O-propositions** is **particular**, since they involve the quantifier "some."

See also: **Affirmative Proposition, Negative Proposition, Quality, Square of Opposition**

QUANTUM LOGIC   Quantum logic is a **nonstandard logic** whose development was motivated by puzzles regarding measurement and observation within quantum physics. The most notable aspect of quantum logic is that **distributivity** fails, and thus:

A ∧ (B ∨ C)

does not entail:

(A ∧ B) ∨ (A ∧ C)

See also: **Absorbsion, Deviant Logic**

QUASI-ORDER see **Pre-Ordering**

QUASI-ORDERING see **Pre-Ordering**

QUINE-PUTNAM INDISPENSABILITY ARGUMENT see **Indispensability Argument**

QUINE'S DICTUM   Quine's dictum is the thesis according to which we can determine which objects we ought to believe in merely by determining which **theory** is our best theory, and then determining what sorts of objects fall in the range of the **existential quantifiers** in that theory. Quine sums up the dictum as:

"To be is to be the value of a **variable**."

See also: **Bound Variable, Existential Import, Existential Variable, Objectual Quantifier, Ramsey Sentence, Substitutional Quantifier**

QUOD ERAT DEMONSTRANDUM   Quod erat demonstrandum (or **QED**), which means "that which was to be **proved**" in Latin, is a phrase that is sometimes written at the end of a proof to indicate that the proof was successfully carried out.

See also: **Corollary, Demonstration, Formal Proof, Lemma**

QUOTATION   Quotation is a device, usually represented using matched pairs:

"

and

"

used in order to speak about expressions themselves, instead of what those expressions **denote**. Thus:

> Red is a color.

> "Red" contains three letters.

are **true**, and:

> "Red" is a color.

> Red contains three letters.

are **false**.

See also: **Punctuation, Use**

RAA see **Reductio ad Absurdum**

RAMIFIED THEORY OF TYPES see **Ramified Type Theory**

RAMIFIED TYPE THEORY   A ramified type theory (or **ramified theory of types**) is a **type theory** that divides entities into a simple **hierarchy** of objects, **classes** of objects, classes of classes of objects, etc. like a simple type theory, but further divides these types into **orders**. For example, on the **simple theory of types** all collections of individuals of type 1 are on a par, being of type 2. On the ramified theory of types we further subdivide these collections in terms of the resources needed to specify them. Thus, a type 2 entity (that is, a collection of **individuals**) will be of order 1 if it can be defined merely in terms of individuals and **logical** resources, while a type 2 entity whose definition requires reference to other type 2 entities is a type 2 entity of order 2.

The technical difficulties associated with the ramified theory of types led to the introduction of the **axiom of reducibility**, which essentially reduces the ramified theory of types to the simple theory of types.

See also: **Type Theory, Vicious Circle Principle**

RAMSEY SENTENCE   A Ramsey sentence (or **Carnap-Ramsey**

Sentence) is the **statement** obtained by replacing all **non-logical terms** in the original statement with **variables**, and then binding the resulting variables with **existential quantifiers**. Thus, beginning with:

Fab

we first obtain:

Xyz

and then:

($\exists$X)($\exists$y)($\exists$z)Xyz

Ramsey sentences are thought to be useful in terms of isolating the exact ontological commitments of a **theory**.

See also: **Quine's Dictum**

RAMSEY TEST   The Ramsey test is a method for connecting **conditional probabilities** to the acceptability, or assertability, of **conditionals**. The Ramsey test asserts that the acceptability of a conditional

P → Q

(in situations where we lack definitive knowledge regarding the truth conditions of P and Q) is the degree of belief we assign to the **conditional probability**:

Pr(Q/P)

that is, the **probability** that we assign to Q given the hypothesis that P is true.

See also: **Bayes' Theorem, Conditional Probability, Probability Calculus, Probability Logic, Probability Theory**

RANGE   The range of a **function** (or **right field**, or **co-domain**, or **converse domain**, or **counterdomain**) is the **set** of objects that may serve as values (outputs) of the function. Note that the **image** of a function can be a **proper subset** of the range of that function – that is, not every member of the range of a function needs to be "hit" by that function.

See also: **Domain, Field, Fixed Point, Signature**

RANK The rank (or **stage**) of a **set** is defined by **transfinite induction** on sets as follows:

The rank of the **empty set** is 0.

The rank of a set S is the least **ordinal number** greater than the rank of any **member** of S.

Intuitively, the rank of a set is a measure of how far up in the **cumulative hierarchy** a set first appears.

See also: **Ad Infinitum, Cantor's Theorem, Iterative Conception of Set**

RATIONAL NUMBERS A rational number is a **real number** that can be expressed as a fraction x/y, where both x and y are **integers**. A real number that is not a rational number is an **irrational number**. Examples of irrational numbers include $\sqrt{2}$ and π.

See also: **Dense, Natural Number, Real Number**

REAL NUMBERS The real numbers are the result of closing the **rational numbers** under the operation of taking **least upper bounds** (or **greatest lower bounds**). Alternatively, the real numbers are any numbers appearing on the number line. Thus $1, -1$, $\pi, e, 2$, etc. are all real numbers.

See also: **Analysis, Integers, Natural Numbers, Non-Standard Analysis**

RECURSION see **Course of Values Recursion, Primitive Recursion, Recursive Definition, Recursive Function Theory, Transfinite Recursion**

RECURSION THEOREM$_1$ The recursion theorem states that, given **any** set A, any **member** b of A, and any **function** g from A to A, there is a function f from the **natural numbers** to A such that:

$$f(0) \quad = \quad b$$

$$f(n+1) \quad = \quad g(f(n)$$

In other words, the recursion theorem legitimates the method of defining a function via **recursion**. A variant of the recursion theorem is particularly useful when g is a **recursive function**, since the resulting function f will also be recursive.

See also: **Course of Values Recursion, Primitive Recursion, Recursive Function Theory, Transfinite Recursion**

RECURSION THEOREM$_2$ The recursion theorem states that, if f_x is the **n-ary recursive function** whose **Gödel code** is x, and g is any n+1-ary **partial recursive function**, then there exists an **integer** e such that:

$$f_e(x_1, x_2, \ldots x_n)$$

and:

$$g(e, x_1, x_2, \ldots x_n)$$

compute the same function.

See also: **Arithmetization, Course of Values Recursion, Primitive Recursion, Recursive Function Theory**

RECURSION THEORY see **Recursive Function Theory**

RECURSIVE DEFINITION$_1$ A recursive definition (or **inductive definition**) of a **set** is a **definition** that proceeds in three steps. First, some initial **members** of the set are identified. Second, a condition is provided which states that certain objects are members of the set if they have certain specified **relations** to objects that are members of the set. Third, no object may be a member of the set unless its inclusion is mandated by the previous steps.

For example, the set of Bob's ancestors (including himself) A can be defined recursively as follows:

(1) Bob is in A.

(2) If x is in A, and y is a parent of x, then y is in A.

(3) A is the smallest set satisfying (1) and (2).

See also: **Inductive Set, Recursion Theorem**

RECURSIVE DEFINITION$_2$ A recursive definition (or **inductive definition**) of a function on the natural numbers is a function whose value for a particular argument is determined in terms of the values the function took for earlier arguments. For example, the Fibonacci sequence can be defined as the range of the following recursive function:

$$f(0) \quad = \quad 0$$

$$f(1) \quad = \quad 1$$

$$f(n+2) \quad = \quad f(n+1) + f(n)$$

See also: **Explicit Definition, Impredicative Definition, Recursion Theorem**

RECURSIVE FUNCTION A recursive function is any **function** that can be constructed from the basic functions of **recursive function theory** (the **zero function**, the **successor function**, and the **identity functions**) plus the function-building operations: **composition, primitive recursion**, and **minimization**.

See also: **Ackermann Function, Characteristic Function, Primitive Recursive Function, Recursive Relation, Recursive Set**

RECURSIVE FUNCTION THEORY Recursive function theory (or **computability theory**) is the study of the **recursive functions**, and of particularly important sub-classes of these functions, such as the **primitive recursive functions**. One of the central results in recursive function theory is the **proof** that all functions **computable** by a **Turing machine** are **recursive functions**, and vice versa. Also important is the **Church-Turing thesis**, which asserts that the functions that can be computed by **finite** reasoners (i.e. all **effective functions**) are exactly the recursive functions.

See also: **Automaton, Complexity Theory, Deterministic Turing Machine, Non-Deterministic Turing Machine**

RECURSIVE RELATION A recursive relation (or **decidable relation**) is any **relation** on the **natural numbers** whose **characteristic function** is a **recursive function**.

See also: **Primitive Recursive Relation, Recursive Function Theory, Recursive Set**

RECURSIVE SET A recursive set (or **decidable set**) is any **set of natural numbers** whose **characteristic function** is a **recursive function**.

See also: **Primitive Recursive Set, Recursive Function Theory, Recursive Relation**

RECURSIVE THEORY see **Recursively Axiomatizable Theory**

RECURSIVELY AXIOMATIZABLE THEORY   A **theory** is a recursively axiomatizable theory (or **recursive theory**) if and only if there is an **axiomatization** of that theory such that the **set** of **axioms** is a **recursive set**.

See also: **Finitely Axiomatizable Set, Recursive Function Theory, Semi-Decidable Set**

RECURSIVELY ENUMERABLE SET   A **set** of **natural numbers** A is recursively enumerable (or **semi-decidable set**, or **Turing recognizable set**) if there is a **recursive unary function** whose **image** is A.

See also: **Definable Set, Enumerable Set, Primitive Recursive Set, Recursive Set**

RED HERRING   Red herring (or **ignoratio elenchi**) is an **informal fallacy** which occurs when the reasoner presents an **argument** for a **conclusion** that is related to, but distinct from, the conclusion that the reasoner is presenting himself as arguing for. Notice that in an occurrence of the red herring fallacy the argument presented might be **valid** or **inductively strong** – the problem is that the reasoner has (perhaps successfully) argued for conclusion that is irrelevant to the point at issue.

See also: **Enthymeme, Informal Fallacy**

REDUCIBILITY see **Axiom of Reducibility**

REDUCTIO see **Classical Reductio ad Absurdum, Reductio ad Absurdum**

REDUCTIO ABSURDUM see **Reductio ad Absurdum**

REDUCTIO AD ABSURDUM   Reductio ad absurdum (or **RAA**, or **reductio**, or **reductio absurdum**, or **indirect proof**, or **negation introduction**) is the **rule of inference** that allows one to **infer** the **negation** of a **formula** from a **derivation** whose assumption is the formula in question (without the negation), and which terminates in a **contradiction**. In symbols we have:

$$\frac{\overline{P}}{\begin{array}{c} \vdots \\ \vdots \\ \underline{Q \wedge \sim Q} \end{array}}{\sim P}$$

where the horizontal line above P indicates that this assumption has been **discharged** – that is, that the **proof** no longer depends on it.

Reductio ad absurdum should be distinguished from the stronger **rule of inference classical reductio ad absurdum**.

See also: **Double Negation Elimination, Double Negation Introduction, Excluded Middle, Introduction Rule, Natural Deduction**

REDUNDANCY THEORY OF TRUTH The redundancy theory of truth is the view that, given any **statement** A, "A is **true**" has the same **meaning** as A. Thus, redundancy theorists defend the following **schema** (sometimes called the **equivalency thesis**):

For any statement A:

"'A' is true" has the same meaning as "A"

As a result, redundancy theorists deny that there is a substantial **property** called "truth" that attaches to statements, and thus the view is a species of **deflationism**.

See also: **Convention T, Disquotationalism, Minimalism, Prosentential Theory of Truth**

REFERENCE Reference is the **relation** that holds between a **singular term** and the object (if any) that it picks out.

See also: **Co-Referential, Denotation, Free Logic, Referential Opacity, Semantic Value, Slingshot Argument**

REFERENTIAL OPACITY An expression is referentially opaque if and only if one cannot substitute **co-referential** terms within the **scope** of the expression while preserving the **truth value** of the resulting **statements**. For example, "believes that" is referentially opaque. Even assuming that "Jim" and "president of the club" are co-referential, it does not follow that:

Bob believes that Jim is powerful.

and:

Bob believes that the president of the club is powerful.

must have the same truth value, since Bob might be unaware of the fact that Jim is **identical** to the president of the club.

See also: **Denotation, Propositional Attitude, Reference, Semantic Value**

REFLECTION PRINCIPLE Within **set theory**, a reflection principle states that any **property** holding of the entire universe of **sets** also holds when restricted to some particular set. Typically, reflection principles take the form:

$$\Phi \rightarrow (\exists x)\Phi^x$$

where:

$$\Phi^x$$

is the result of restricting all of the **quantifiers** in Φ to members of x.

Reflection principles are quite strong, implying the existence of **large cardinal numbers**, such as **inaccessible cardinals**. In addition, if one assumes the **axiom of choice**, then reflection principles imply **global well-ordering**.

See also: **Cumulative Hierarchy, Global Choice, Iterative Conception of Set, Limitation-of-Size Conception of Set**

REFLEXIVITY A **binary relation** R is reflexive if and only if, for any object x, we have:

Rxx

See also: **Coreflexivity, Irreflexivity T**

REFUTATION A refutation of a **statement** Φ is a **proof** that takes Φ as a **premise** and has a **contradiction** as its **conclusion**. Thus, a refutation of Φ is a proof that the **truth** of Φ leads to a contradiction (or, intuitively, is a proof that Φ cannot be true).

See also: **Classical Reductio ad Absurdum, Counterexample, Countermodel, Reductio ad Absurdum**

REGISTER COMPUTABLE A **function** is register computable (or abacus computable) if and only if it can be **computed** by a **register machine**. The register computable functions are exactly the **recursive functions** (and thus are exactly the functions computable by a **Turing machine**).

See also: **Automaton, Deterministic Turing Machine, Non-Deterministic Turing Machine, Recursive Function Theory**

REGISTER MACHINE   A register machine (or **abacus machine**) is a machine (usually conceived abstractly) which consists of (a) an unbounded or **infinite** collection of registers that can hold any number of counters, (b) an unbounded or infinite collection of counters, (c) a table of instructions where each instruction specifies a particular register, specifies the arithmetic function to be performed on that register (e.g. "add a counter," "double the number of counters"), and specifies the next instruction to be performed. Register machines can compute exactly the same functions as **Turing machines**.

See also: **Automaton, Deterministic Turing Machine, Non-Deterministic Turing Machine, Register Computable Function, Recursive Function Theory**

REGULAR CARDINAL   A regular cardinal is **cardinal number** γ where the **cofinality** of γ is equal to γ itself (i.e. $\mathrm{co}(\gamma) = \gamma$). A cardinal number that is not regular is a **singular cardinal**.

See also: **Cardinal Arithmetic, Cardinal Successor, Large Cardinal, Limit Ordinal, Strongly Inaccessible Cardinal, Weakly Inaccessible Cardinal**

REGULAR ORDINAL   A regular ordinal is a **limit ordinal** number γ where the **cofinality** of γ is equal to γ itself (i.e. $\mathrm{co}(\gamma) = \gamma$). An ordinal number that is not regular is a **singular ordinal**.

See also: **Limit Ordinal, Order Type, Ordinal Arithmetic, Ordinal Successor**

REGULARITY see **Axiom of Foundation**

REGULARITY AXIOM see **Axiom of Foundation**

RELATIONAL SEMANTICS₁ see **Kripke Semantics**

RELATIONAL SEMANTICS₂   A relational semantics is a **semantics** that represents the **semantic** status of a **statement** in terms of a **relation** holding, or not, between it and one of the **truth values**. Unlike standard semantics, which are typically formulated in terms of a **function** mapping each statement onto a unique truth value, relational semantics provides a natural framework within which one can treat **truth value gaps** or **truth value glut logics**, since a statement might be related to neither classical truth value, or both truth values, respectively.

See also: **Analethic Logic, Dialethic Logic, First-Degree Entailment, Many-Valued Logic, Paraconsistent Logic, Relevance Logic**

RELATIVE COMPLEMENT   The relative complement of two **sets** A and B (or the **complement** of B relative to A, or the **difference** of A and B), usually written as "A \ B" or "A − B," is the set that contains, as **members**, exactly the members of A that are not members of B. In other words, the complement of B relative to A is:

$$\{x : x \in A \text{ and } x \notin B\}$$

See also: **Symmetric Difference**

RELATIVE CONSISTENCY PROOF   A relative consistency proof is a **proof** that some **formal system** S is **consistent** which is carried out within another formal system S*. As a result of **Gödel's second incompleteness theorem**, in most cases S* needs to be significantly stronger than S in order to carry out a relative consistency proof of S in S*. As a result, relative consistency proofs do not provide us with unqualified assurance that the system in question is consistent. Instead, a relative consistency proof of S in S* tells us that if S* is consistent, then so is S.

See also: **Forcing, Independence Result, Inner Model, Limitation Result**

RELEVANCE LOGIC   A relevance logic (or **relevant logic**) is a **nonstandard logic** where the **truth** of a **conditional**:

$$P \to Q$$

requires that the **antecedent** P must be relevant to the **conclusion** Q. Relevance logics are primarily motivated by the **paradoxes of material implication**, and their **semantics** are usually a variation of **Kripke semantics**. Most relevance logics are **paraconsistent logics**.

See also: **Dialethic Logic, First-Degree Entailment, Impossible Worlds, Relational Semantics, Strong Paraconsistency, Weak Paraconsistency**

RELEVANT LOGIC see **Relevance Logic**

REPLACEMENT see **Axiom(s) of Replacement**

REPLACEMENT AXIOM see **Axiom(s) of Replacement**

REPLACEMENT RULE see **Rule of Replacement**

REPRESENTATION   A n+1-ary **predicate** P represents an n-ary **function** f if and only if we have:

$Px_1, x_2, \ldots x_n, y$ is **true** if and only if $f(x_1, x_2, \ldots x_n) = y$

Similarly, a **unary predicate P** represents a **set** S if and only if:

Px is true if and only if x is a **member** of S

See also: **Definable, Primitive Recursive Function, Primitive Recursive Set, Recursive Function, Recursive Set**

RESTRICTION see **Axiom of Foundation**

RESTRICTION AXIOM see **Axiom of Foundation**

RETRODUCTION see **Abduction**

REVERSE MATHEMATICS   Reverse mathematics is the project of determining how much mathematics can be reduced to **finitary mathematics**, in light of **Gödel's incompleteness theorems** and the failure of **Hilbert's Program** to reduce all of mathematics to **finitary** constructions. This is accomplished through a detailed investigation designed to find the weakest **formal systems** of **arithmetic** and **analysis** within which various classic mathematical results can be **proven**.

REVISION THEORY OF TRUTH   The revision theory of truth is an account of the **Liar paradox** (and other **semantic paradoxes**) which avoids the **contradiction** by treating **Tarski's T-schema** for the **truth predicate** as a circular **definition** of **truth**. According to the revision theory, such circular definitions should be treated as rules for revising one's initial hypothesis regarding the truth or **falsity** of **statements**. As a result, true statements are those that stabilize on the value true after sufficiently many revisions, while false statements are statements that stabilize on the false. **Paradoxical** statements, which never stabilize but forever oscillate between the two values, are prevented from implying contradictions by a sophisticated account of the correct **logic** for reasoning about such definitions.

See also: **Convention T, Correspondence Theory of Truth, Semantic Paradox, Semantically Closed Language, Tarski's Indefinability Theorem**

RICHARD PARADOX   The Richard paradox (or **Richard's paradox**) is **the paradox of denotation** that arises as follows. Since our **language** is **countably infinite**, we can **enumerate** all expressions which **denote** a unique **real number**. Given such an enumeration, we can construct a real number r as follows. For the ith digit in the decimal expansion of r, pick 5 if the ith place in the decimal expansion of the ith entry in our list is not 5, and pick 6 otherwise. This **diagonalization** construction picks out a unique real number which is not on our list (since, for the real number denoted by the nth expression on the list, our number disagrees with it at the nth decimal place). **Contradiction**.

See also: **Berry Paradox, König Paradox**

RICHARD'S PARADOX see **Richard Paradox**

RIGHT FIELD see **Range**

RIGID DESIGNATOR   A rigid designator is any **referring** expression that refers to the same objects in every **possible world** in which it refers at all. Thus, **definite descriptions** such as:

> The tallest man on earth.

are typically not rigid designators. **Singular terms**, however, are thought by many to rigidly designate.

See also: **Counterpart Theory, Necessity of Identity, Reference, Transworld Identity**

ROBINSON ARITHMETIC Robinson arithmetic (or **Q**) is a **finitely axiomatized** sub-system of **Peano arithmetic**. One standard axiomatization of Robinson arithmetic consists of the following seven **axioms**:

(1) $(\forall x)S(x) \neq 0$

(2) $(\forall x)(\forall y)(S(x) = S(y) \rightarrow x = y)$

(3) $(\forall y)(y = 0 \vee (\exists x)(Sx = y)$

(4) $(\forall x)(x + 0 = x)$

(5) $(\forall x)(\forall y)(x + S(y) = S(x + y))$

(6) $(\forall x)(x \cdot 0 = 0)$

(7) $(\forall x)(\forall y)(x \cdot S(y) = (x \cdot y) + x)$

(where $S(x)$ is the **arithmetic successor function**). Speaking somewhat loosely, Robinson arithmetic is Peano arithmetic without **mathematical induction**.

See also: **Gödel's First Incompleteness Theorem, Gödel's Second Incompleteness Theorem**

ROSS PARADOX The Ross paradox (or **Ross's Paradox**) is a puzzle that arises in **deontic modal logic**. If we assume that the deontic obligation operator O obeys the rules for a **normal modal logic**, and as a result we have the **distributivity axiom K**:

$$O(P \rightarrow Q) \rightarrow (O(P) \rightarrow O(Q))$$

then we obtain:

$$O(P) \rightarrow O(P \vee Q)$$

(since $P \rightarrow (P \vee Q)$ is a **classical logical truth**). Letting P be "Jon pays the rent" and Q be "Jon burns down the building," however, it follows that Jon's obligation to pay the rent entails an obligation that he can fulfill by burning down the building.

See also: **Paradox**

ROSS'S PARADOX see **Ross Paradox**

RULE OF INFERENCE A rule of inference (or **inference rule**) is an explicit rule within a **formal system** for generating a new line in a **derivation** from previously obtained lines.

See also: **Elimination Rule, Harmony, Introduction Rule, Natural Deduction, Rule of Replacement**

RULE OF REPLACEMENT   A rule of replacement (or **replacement rule**) is an explicit rule within a **formal system** for replacing a line in a **derivation** with a new line **logically equivalent** to the original line.

See also: **Elimination Rule, Harmony, Introduction Rule, Natural Deduction, Rule of Inference**

RUSSELL PARADOX   The Russell paradox (or **Russell's paradox**) concerns the intuitive idea that **sets** can be **members** of themselves. If we accept the **comprehension schema** for sets:

$$(\exists x)(\forall y)(y \in x \leftrightarrow \Phi(y))$$

then we are guaranteed that, for any **predicate** Φ, there will be a set that contains exactly the objects that **satisfy** Φ. One condition we can plug into the comprehension schema is being a set that is not a member of itself. The resulting instance of the comprehension schema is:

$$(\exists x)(\forall y)(y \in x \leftrightarrow y \notin y)$$

The set whose existence is asserted by this principle is the **Russell set**, which we shall represent as R. Thus:

$$(\forall y)(y \in R \leftrightarrow y \notin y)$$

Now, the Russell set is itself an object, and we can thus ask whether it is a member of itself. The principle above, however, has the following as a **logical consequence**:

$$R \in R \leftrightarrow R \notin R$$

In other words, the Russell set is a member of itself if and only if it is not. This is a **contradiction**, and we can thus see that the comprehension schema is **inconsistent**.

See also: **Absolute Infinite, Grelling Paradox, Indefinite Extensibility, Naïve Set Theory, Vicious Circle Principle**

RUSSELL SET   The Russell set (or **Russell's set**) is the (supposed) **set** which contains, as **members**, any set that does not contain itself as a member. In symbols, letting R be the Russell set, we have:

$(\forall x)(x \in R \leftrightarrow x \notin x)$

The existence of the Russell set follows from the **comprehension schema,** and also follows from **Basic Law V.** One need merely ask whether the Russell set is a member of itself to see that the existence of the Russell set leads to a **contradiction** (this is the **Russell paradox**).

See also: **Grelling Paradox, Heterological, Indefinite Extensibility, Iterative Conception of Set, Limitation-of-Size Conception of Set, Set-Theoretic Paradox**

RUSSELLIAN PROPOSITION see **Singular Proposition**

RUSSELL'S PARADOX see **Russell Paradox**

RUSSELL'S SET see **Russell Set**

SALVE VERITATE   Salve veritate is Latin for "saving the **truth**." Two expressions are interchangeable salve veritate if and only if they can be substituted for one another in other expressions without affecting the **truth values** of those expressions.

See also: **Indeterminacy of Translation, Propositional Attitude, Referential Opacity, Slingshot Argument**

SATISFACTION   Satisfaction is the **relation** that holds between an **n-ary predicate** and any **n-tuple** of objects such that the predicate is "**true**" of those objects. The notion of "truth" at issue here is spelled out in different ways in different **formal semantics**.

See also: **Truth-in-a-Model, Variable**

SATISFIABILITY   A **theory** is satisfiable if there is some **interpretation** that makes all **statements** in the theory **true**. A theory that is not satisfiable is **unsatisfiable**.

See also: **Interpretation, Model, Model Theory, Truth-in-a-Model**

SCHEMA   A schema is a **formula** expressed in some **formal language** except for the occurrence of one or more **metalinguistic variables**. These metalinguistic variables can be replaced by any expression of the appropriate logical type from the formal language in question in order to form an instance of the schema (sometimes additional constraints on acceptable substitutions are imposed). As a result, the schema typically represents **infinitely** many different formulas within the formal language.

See also: **Axiom(s) of Replacement, Axiom of Separation(s), Axiom Schema, Comprehension Schema, Mathematical Induction, T-schema**

SCHEMA T see **T-schema**

SCOPE   The scope of a **logical connective** occurring within a **formula** is the smallest **well-formed formula** that contains the logical constant in question. Intuitively, the scope of a logical constant is the portion of the formula over which that operator has some effect.

The scope of a **quantifier** is the **variable** occurrences within the formula that are **bound** by that quantifier.

See also: **Formation Rules, Quantifier Shift Fallacy, Vacuous Quantifier**

SCOTT LOGIC   Scott logic is the **intermediate logic** obtained by adding all instances of:

$$((\sim \sim A \rightarrow A) \rightarrow (A \vee \sim A)) \rightarrow (\sim \sim A \vee \sim A)$$

to **intuitionistic propositional logic**. Scott logic (along with **Kreisel-Putnam logic**) is one of the few intermediate logics known to **satisfy** the **disjunction property**.

See also: **Gödel-Dummett Logic, Logic of Weak Excluded Middle**

SEA BATTLE see **Aristotle's Sea Battle**

SECOND-ORDER LOGIC   Second-order logic is the **formal system** that results from **extending first-order logic** by adding additional **quantifiers** that range over **concepts** or properties of objects. Second-order logic differs from **higher-order logic** more generally in that some higher-order logics also allow quantification over concepts of concepts, concepts of concepts of concepts, etc.

Consider the **statement**:

Alice is nice.

We can formalize this as:

Na

Within first-order logic, we can **infer** from this that something is nice:

$(\exists x)Nx$

Within second-order logic, however, we can also infer that there is something – that is, some concept – that Alice has:

$(\exists X)Xa$

See also: **Aristotelian Second-order Logic, Comprehension Schema, Geach-Kaplan Sentence, Many-Sorted Logic, Plural Quantification**

SELF-CONTRADICTORY see **Contradiction**

SELF-REFERENCE   An expression displays self-reference if it contains a **singular term** or other **referring** expression that refers to the statement itself. The most famous instance of self-reference is the **Liar sentence**:

This sentence is false.

See also: **Fixed Point, Gödel Sentence, Liar Paradox, Yablo Paradox**

SEMANTIC CONCEPTION OF TRUTH see **Convention T**

SEMANTIC CONSEQUENCE see **Logical Consequence**

SEMANTIC EQUIVALENCE see **Logically Equivalent**

SEMANTIC IMPLICATION see **Logical Implication**

SEMANTIC PARADOX   A semantic paradox (or **logical paradox**) is a **paradox** that arises from basic intuitions regarding **truth,**

satisfaction, **reference**, or related **semantic** notions. Examples of semantic paradox include the **Liar paradox**, the **Yablo paradox**, and the **paradoxes of denotation**.

See also: **Curry Paradox, Insolubilia, Open Pair, Semantically Closed Language, Tarski's Indefinability Theorem, Truth-Teller**

SEMANTIC TABLEAU   A semantic tableau (or **truth-tree**) is a method for testing **arguments** for **validity** by constructing a branching, **tree**-like structure. In essence, a tableau unpacks the **truth-conditions** of the **premises** and the **negation** of the **conclusion** of an argument, reducing them to their simplest constituent **parts** according to a fixed set of rules. If the argument is valid, then every branch of the tableau will contain a **contradiction**, while if some branch of the tree is not closed off in this way, then this shows that the argument is **invalid**.

See also: **Logical Consequence, Logical Validity, Semantics**

SEMANTIC VAGUENESS   **Vagueness** is semantic if and only if it is a result of some sort of inadequacy in the **language** we use to describe the world and not due to any indeterminacy in the world itself. For example, on might think that the **predicate** "is tall" is vague, not because there is any imprecision or "fuzziness" in the exact heights of objects, but because the rules for correctly applying the predicate "is tall" do not specify how one is to apply it in **borderline cases**.

See also: **Forced March Sorites, Higher-order Vagueness, In Rebus Vagueness, Ontic Vagueness, Sorites Paradox, Sorites Series**

SEMANTIC VALIDITY see **Logical Validity**

SEMANTIC VALUE   The semantic value of an expression is the entity (if any) which the **formal semantics** assigns to that expression. Thus, **singular terms** have objects as their semantic value, and **statements** have **truth values** as their semantic values. In some systems **predicates** have **sets** as their semantic values and **logical connectives** have **functions** from **sequences** of truth values to truth values – that is, **truth functions** - as their semantic values.

See also: **Denotation, Designated Value, Reference, Slingshot Argument**

SEMANTICALLY CLOSED LANGUAGE   A semantically closed language is any **language** where:

(1) Every expression of the language has a name in the language.

(2) The language contains a **predicate** T (a **truth predicate**) which holds of (the name of) a **statement** if and only if that statement is **true**.

(3) All instances of the **T-schema**:
$$T(<\Phi>) \leftrightarrow \Phi$$
expressible in the language are true.

Alfred Tarski proved that any semantically closed language enables one to construct a version of the **Liar paradox**, and is thus **inconsistent**.

See also: **Bivalence, Law of Non-Contradiction, Semantic Paradox, Tarski's Indefinability Theorem**

SEMANTICALLY EQUIVALENT see **Logically Equivalent**

SEMANTICS   Semantics studies the properties of expressions, utterances, and **statements** that do not vary from use to use, or from context to context – this distinguishes it from **pragmatics**, which takes such variation into account. Thus, semantics is concerned with the (context-independent) meaning of expressions and statements, and their **referents**, as well as with the **logical** connections between expressions.

See also: **Formal Semantics, Model Theory, Pragmatics**

SEMI-DECIDABLE SET see **Recursively Enumerable Set**

SEMI-DECIDABLE THEORY   A **theory** is semi-decidable if and only if the **set** of **Gödel codes** of **theorems** of that theory is a **recursively enumerable set**.

See also: **Arithmetization, Effectively Enumerable Set, Finitely Axiomatizable Theory, Recursively Axiomatizable Theory**

SENSE   Sense is one of the two aspects of the content of an expression identified by Gottlob Frege. Frege considered cases such as:

Hesperus is identical to Phosphorus

(where both terms refer to Venus) and wondered how such **statements** could be informative or significant, since the two **singular terms** being equated **refer** to the same object. He concluded that the content of an expression could be divided into two aspects: its sense (i.e. its meaning, or mode of presentation) and its referent (i.e. the object picked out). The puzzle is then solved, since the informativeness of the **identity** claim above results from learning that two expressions with different senses nevertheless refer to the same object.

See also: **Definition, Intension, Intensional Logic**

SENTENCE LETTER see **Propositional Letter**

SENTENTIAL LOGIC see **Propositional Logic**

SENTENTIAL VARIABLE see **Propositional Letter**

SEPARATION see **Axiom(s) of Separation**

SEPARATION AXIOM see **Axioms(s) of Separation**

SEQUENCE   A sequence (or **string**) is a **set** of objects along with a **linear ordering** on them. Thus, unlike sets (without an ordering) and **multisets**, in a sequence the order in which the **elements** occur matters, and as a result, unlike sets (but like multisets), multiple occurrences of the same element matter.

See also: **Ordered N-tuple, Ordered Pair, Sequent, Sequent Calculus**

SEQUENT   A sequent is an **ordered triple** consisting of three parts: a **sequence** (or sometimes a **set**, or **multi-set**, etc.) of **formulas**, followed by an arrow, followed by a second sequence (or set, or multiset, etc.) of formulas. Thus:

A, B $\Rightarrow$ A $\wedge$ B, C

is a sequent. A sequent is meant to represent the claim that if all the **members** of the first sequence (or set, or multiset, etc.) are **true,** then at least one member of the second sequence (or set, or multiset, etc.) will be true. Thus, the above sequent represents the claim that if both A and B are true, then at least one of A ∧ B and C will be true.

See also: **Contraction, Cut, Permutation, Sequent Calculus, Structural Rule, Weakening**

SEQUENT CALCULUS Sequent calculus is a **formal system** consisting of **rules of inference** for combining one or more **sequents** into a new sequent. For example, the **cut** rule in the sequent calculus tells us that if we have two sequents of the form:

$$\Gamma \Rightarrow \Delta, A$$

and:

$$A, \Pi \Rightarrow \Sigma$$

then we can infer the new sequent:

$$\Gamma, \Pi \Rightarrow \Delta, \Sigma$$

(effectively, "cutting" A out of the inference). Cut is what is known, within the sequent calculus, as a **structural rule**. Other important structural rules include **weakening**, **contraction**, and **permutation**.

See also: **Abelian Logic, Affine Logic, Cut Elimination, Substructual Logic**

SERIALITY A **relation** R is serial (or **entire**) if and only if, for any x, there is a y, such that:

$$Rxy.$$

See also: **Axiom of Choice, D, Function**

SET A set is a collection of objects. In other words, the set-forming operation allows us to combine a number of objects into a single object: the set containing them. The objects combined in this way to form the set are the **members** of the set.

Curly brackets {} are often used to **denote** sets. Thus, the set of **natural numbers** strictly between 2 and 6 can be represented as:

$$\{3, 4, 5\}$$

and the set of all natural number greater than 4 can be represented as:

$$\{x \mid x > 4\}$$

(This can be read as "The set of all x such that x is greater than 4.")

See also: **Cartesian Product, Multiset, Non-Well-Founded Set, Subset, Urelement**

SET-THEORETIC HIERARCHY see **Cumulative Hierarchy**

SET-THEORETIC PARADOX   A set-theoretic paradox is a **paradox** that arises from basic intuitions regarding the nature of **sets**. Examples of set-theoretic paradoxes include the **Russell paradox**, the **Cantor paradox**, and the **Burali-Forti paradox**.

See also: **Absolute Infinite, Indefinite Extensibility, Iterative Conception of Set, Limitation-of-Size Conception of Set, Naïve Set Theory, Vicious Circle Principle**

SET-THEORETIC REALISM   Set-theoretic realism is a version of **platonism** about mathematical objects which asserts that **sets** actually exist and are epistemically accessible to us.

See also: **Mathematical Abstractionism, Meinongianism, Nominalism, Platonism**

SET-THEORETIC SUCCESSOR see **Cardinal Successor, Ordinal Successor**

SET THEORY   Set theory is the mathematical study of **sets**. Set theory proceeds by formulating an axiomatization of **sets**, usually containing "$\in$" as its only **non-logical** expression, such as **Zermelo Fraenkel set theory** or **Von Neumann Bernays Gödel set theory**, and then studying the formal properties of this system. Typically, in order to be considered a set theory, the **theory** will need to entail the **axiom of extensionality**:

$$(\forall x)(\forall y)(x = y \leftrightarrow (\forall z)(z \in x \leftrightarrow z \in y))$$

Most of the other common **axioms** of set theory have been rejected in at least one set theory, however.

See also: **Kripke-Platek Set Theory, Morse-Kelley Set Theory, Naïve Set Theory, Non-Well-Founded Set Theory, Positive Set Theory**

S5   The **modal logic** S5 is the **normal modal logic** whose additional **axioms** are:

T: $\Box A \to A$

5:   $\Diamond A \to \Box \Diamond A$

The modal logic S5 is **valid** on any **frame** in which the **accessibility relation** is **symmetric, transitive,** and **reflexive.**

See also: **Kripke Semantics, Kripke Structure, Modality, S4**

Σ-FORMULA Within the **arithmetical hierarchy** (or **Kleene hierarchy**) a Σ-formula (or Σ_1 **formula**) is a **formula** Φ such that Φ is **logically equivalent** to some formula of the form:

$(\exists x_1)(\exists x_2) \ldots (\exists x_m) \Psi$

where Ψ is a formula containing only **bounded quantifiers**.

See also: **Finitary Arithmetic, Π-Formula, Π-Sentence, Π-Sentence**

S4 The **modal logic** S4 is the **normal modal logic** whose additional **axioms** are:

T: $\Box A \to A$

4:   $\Box A \to \Box \Box A$

The modal logic S4 is **valid** on any **frame** in which the **accessibility relation** is **transitive** and **reflexive.**

See also: **Kripke Semantics, Kripke Structure, Modality, S4**

SHARPENING Within **supervaluational semantics**, a sharpening (or **admissible sharpening**), relative to a **predicate** Φ, is any **model** that assigns an **extension** E and **anti-extension** A to Φ such that, for any object x in the **domain** of the model, x is either in the extension E or in the anti–extension A. In other words, a sharpening, relative to a predicate Φ, is a model that treats Φ classically. In applications of supervaluational semantics to **vague predicates**, a sharpening represents a way of making the application conditions of Φ precise.

See also: **Borderline Case, Sorites Paradox, Sorites Series, Supertrue**

SHEFFER DAGGER see **Dagger**

SHEFFER STROKE   The Sheffer stroke (or **alternate denial**) is the **binary logical connective** represented by "|" (or sometimes "↑") whose **truth table** is:

P	Q	P | P
T	T	F
T	F	T
F	T	T
F	F	T

Intuitively, "P | Q" can be read as "either not P or not Q" or "not both P and Q" and is known as the **NAND** operation in computer science and in **Boolean algebra**.

The Sheffer stroke is an **expressively complete** connective – that is, every truth table in **propositional logic** can be represented by an expression containing only **propositional letters, punctuation,** and the **Sheffer stroke**. For example, the **disjunction** of P and Q (i.e. "P ∨ Q") can be represented as:

(P | P) | (Q | Q)

and the **negation** of P (i.e. "~ P") can be represented as:

(P | P)

See also: **Boolean Operator, Dagger**

SIGNATURE   The signature of a **formal system** is a formal way of representing the **non-logical vocabulary** of the **language** of that **formal system**. Typically, a signature consists of three **elements**: a **set** of **function** symbols, a set of **relation** symbols, and a function mapping any function symbol or relation symbol contained in these sets onto a **natural number** – the **adicity**, or number of **arguments**, of the function or relation.

See also: **Binary Function, Binary Relation, N-ary Function, N-ary Relation, Unary Function, Unary Relation**

SIMPLE FORMULA see **Atomic Formula**

SIMPLE ORDERING see **Linear Ordering**

SIMPLE SENTENCE see **Atomic Sentence**

SIMPLE THEORY OF TYPES see **Simple Type Theory**

SIMPLE TYPE THEORY A simple type theory (or the **simple theory of types**) is a **type theory** that divides objects into a simple **hierarchy** of objects, classes of objects, classes of classes of objects, etc. Simple type theories are contrasted with **ramified type theories**, which further stratifies these simple types into **orders**.

See also: **Axiom of Reducibility, Type Theory, Vicious Circle Principle**

SIMPLIFICATION see **Conjunction Elimination**

SIMPLY CONSISTENT see **Negation Consistent**

SIMPLY FINITE see **Simply Infinite**

SIMPLY INFINITE A **set** S is simply infinite if and only if there is no **natural number** n such that there is a **one-to-one onto function** from {0, 1, 2, … n-1, n} to S. A set is **simply finite** if there is such an n.

A set being simply infinite should be contrasted with its being **Dedekind infinite**, since the two notions are only **equivalent** if one assumes the **axiom of choice**.

See also: **Absolute Infinite, Complete Infinity, Countably Infinite**

SINGLE TURNSTILE The single turnstile symbol ⊢ is used to represent the **deductive consequence relation**. If Δ is a **set** of **statements**, and Φ a single statement, then:

Δ ⊢ Φ

holds if Φ is a deductive consequence of Δ.

See also: **Consequence Relation, Deductive Validity, Double Turnstile, Logical Consequence**

SINGLETON Within **set theory**, the singleton of an object A is the **set** that contains exactly A as a **member**. The singleton of an object A is usually written as {A}.

See also: **Axiom of Infinity, Axiom of Pairing, Axiom of Zermelo Infinity, Ordered Pair, Unordered Pair**

SINGULAR CARDINAL see **Regular Cardinal**

SINGULAR ORDINAL see **Regular Ordinal**

SINGULAR PROPOSITION   A singular proposition (or **Russellian proposition**) is a **proposition** that involves a particular object in virtue of that object being a constituent of the proposition. Thus, that Bob is bald is a singular proposition involving Bob himself in this direct manner. The proposition that the tallest man alive is tall is not singular, since it does not involve the tallest man in this direct way.

See also: **Constant, Individual, Singular Term, Statement**

SINGULAR TERM   A singular term is a linguistic expression that **denotes** an object. Singular terms come in two varieties: **constants**, each of which denotes a particular object, and **first-order variables**, which, when used together with **quantifiers**, can range over many objects.

See also: **Bound Variable, Existential Variable, Higher-order Variable, Individual, Open Term, Universal Variable**

SITUATION   A situation is a **part** of a world. Situations are, within **situation semantics**, the analogue of **models** within more traditional approaches to **semantics**.

See also: **Mereology, Proper Parthood, Semantics, Situation Semantics, Structure**

SITUATION SEMANTICS   Situation semantics is a **formal semantics** which interprets **statements** as **true** or **false** relative to **situations**. Situations are **structures** that are **parts** of the world, and, as a result, a situation, unlike a traditional **possible world**, will not always assign **truth** or **falsity** to every statement – in particular, it will fail to assign a **truth value** to statements that concern aspects of the world that are not contained in the situation.

Situation semantics allows for the situation itself to be a constituent of the situation, so that we can interpret statements that concern the situation of evaluation itself. As a result, recent formulations of situational semantics have made use of **non-well-founded set theory**.

See also: **Model Theory, Non-Well-Founded Set, Self-Reference, Semantics**

SITUATIONAL SEMANTICS see **Situation Semantics**

SKOLEMIZATION Skolemization is the process by which a **formula** in the **language** of **first-order logic** is transformed into one which is in **Skolem normal form**. Skolemization is achieved by eliminating each **existential quantifier**, and replacing each **existential variable** with a **function** term $f(x_1, x_2, \ldots x_n)$ where f is a new function symbol and $x_1, x_2, \ldots x_n$ are the **universal variables** within whose **scope** the eliminated existential variable occurred.

See also: **Prenex Normal Form, Skolem Normal Form**

SKOLEM-LOWENHEIM THEOREM see **Downward Lowenheim-Skolem Theorem, Upward Lowenheim-Skolem Theorem**

SKOLEM NORMAL FORM A **statement** in the **language** of **first-order logic** is in Skolem normal form if and only if it is in **prenex normal form** and contains no **existential quantifiers**. Every statement in the language of **first-order logic** can be transformed into a statement in Skolem normal form which is **satisfiable** if and only if the first is (although the two formulas might not be **logically equivalent**). This process is called **skolemization**.

See also: **Conjunctive Normal Form, Disjunctive Normal Form, Negation Normal Form**

SKOLEM PARADOX The Skolem paradox (or **Skolem's paradox**) is a direct result of the **downward Lowenheim-Skolem theorem**, which states that any **theory**, such as **set theory**, that has an **infinite model**, has a **countably infinite** model. Standard set theories (such as **Zermelo Fraenkel set theory**), however, have, as a **theorem**, a statement asserting the existence of **uncountable sets**. The **paradox** thus arises when we ask how there can be a countably infinite model of a theory that asserts the existence of uncountably infinite sets, and thus asserts the existence of uncountably many objects.

See also: **Cantor's Theorem, Intended Interpretation, Non-Standard Model, Upward Lowenheim-Skolem Theorem**

SKOLEM'S PARADOX see **Skolem Paradox**

SLINGSHOT ARGUMENT A slingshot argument is any one of a

number of **arguments** whose **conclusion** is that all **true statements denote** the same object, if they denote at all.

See also: **Co-Referential, Gödel's Slingshot Argument, Reference, Semantic Value**

SLIPPERY SLOPE   Slippery slope is an **informal fallacy** which occurs when the reasoner attempts to support a **conclusion** by appealing to a **chain** of **inferences**, or some other sort of "chain reaction," which is not in fact likely to hold. Note that much of the persuasiveness of a slippery slope argument stems from the fact that each link in the chain might be likely, even though the likelihood of the entire chain coming about may be low.

See also: **Informal Fallacy, Polysyllogism, Sorites Paradox, Sorites Series**

S-M-N THEOREM   The S-M-N theorem (or **iteration theorem**, or **parameter theorem**, or **parametrization theorem**, or S_{mn} **theorem**, or **translation lemma**) states that, given any **m+n-ary total recursive function** f, each of the total recursive n-ary functions formed by fixing the first m **arguments** as **parameters** are also recursive, and can be **effectively** constructed from the original m+n-ary function and the parameter.

See also: **Effectively Computable Function, Partial Function, Primitive Recursive Function, Recursive Function Theory**

S_{mn} **THEOREM** see **S-M-N theorem**

Σ_1 **FORMULA** see Σ-**Formula**

Σ_1 **SENTENCE** see Σ-**Sentence**

SOPHISM   A sophism is a **fallacious argument** used to convince someone of a **false conclusion** based on reasoning that is confusing or is somehow likely to lead the reader astray. The notion traces to the sophists, a group of rhetoric teachers in ancient Greece who taught their students methods of persuasion, usually for careers in public life.

See also: **Antinomy, Formal Fallacy, Informal Fallacy, Insolubilia, Paradox, Sophisma**

SOPHISMA   Within medieval logic, a sophisma (plural: **sophismata**) was any one of a number of ambiguous, puzzling, or **paradoxical statements** that were thought to need philosophical treatment and some sort of solution. A number of the sophismata involved **self-reference** and are closely related to the **Liar paradox**.

See also: **Epistemic Paradox, Insolubilia, Semantic Paradox, Sophism, Truth Predicate**

SOPHISMATA see **Sophisma**

SORITES see **Polysyllogism**

SORITES PARADOX   The Sorites paradox (or **paradox of vagueness**, or **paradox of the heap**) concerns **predicates**, such as "heap," "bald," or "red," where there is some imprecision involved in the distinction between definite instances of that predicate and definite instances of the negation of the predicate. For example, the predicate "bald" is **tolerant**: small changes to an object, such as the addition or subtraction of a single hair, do not turn a clear instance of a bald man into a clear instance of a non-bald man. The following three claims are inconsistent, however:

(1) A man with 0 hairs on his head is bald.

(2) For any **natural number** n, if a man with n hairs on his head is bald, then a man with n+1 hairs on his head is bald.

(3) A man with 100,000 hairs on his head is not bald.

(1) and (3) are obviously true, so the problem must lie either with (2), or with the reasoning that leads to the **contradiction**. (2), however, just expresses the idea that "bald" is tolerant.

See also: **Borderline Case, Forced March Sorites, Higher-Order Vagueness, In Rebus Vagueness, Ontic Vagueness, Semantic Vagueness, Sorites Series**

SORITES SERIES   Given a particular **vague predicate** Φ, a Sorites series is a **sequence** of objects $a_1, a_2, a_3 \ldots a_n$ such that, for each i, the difference between a_i and a_{i+1} is small enough not to affect the justice with which Φ applies, yet where a_1 is a clear instance of Φ, and a_n is a clear instance of $\sim \Phi$. In other words, a Sorites series is a sequence of objects that gives rise to the **Sorites paradox**.

See also: **Borderline Case, Forced March Sorites, Higher-order Vagueness, In Rebus Vagueness, Semantic Vagueness**

SOUND see **Sound Deductive Argument, Soundness**

SOUND DEDUCTIVE ARGUMENT   A sound deductive argument is a **valid deductive argument** where all the **premises** are **true**. A valid deductive argument that is not a sound deductive argument is an **unsound deductive argument**.

See also: **Deductive Consequence, Logical Consequence, Validity**

SOUNDNESS   A **formal system** is **sound** relative to a **formal semantics** if, and only if, given a **set** of **statements** Δ and a statement Φ, if there is a **derivation** of Φ from Δ:

$$\Delta \vdash \Phi$$

then Φ is a **logical consequence** of Δ:

$$\Delta \vDash \Phi$$

See also: **Double Turnstile, Metatheorem, Single Turnstile, Strong Completeness, Weak Completeness**

SQUARE OF OPPOSITION   The square of opposition is a geometrical representation of the various **logical relations** that hold between the four types of **categorical proposition** found in **categorical logic**:

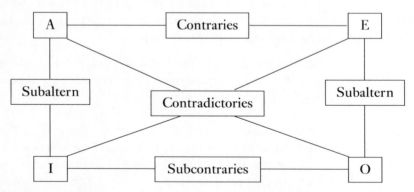

The square of opposition represents the fact that corresponding **A-propositions** and **E-propositions** are **contraries**, corresponding **I-propositions** and **O-propositions** are **subcontraries**, corresponding A-propositions and O-propositions are **contradictories**, and corresponding E-propositions and I-propositions are also contradictories.

The square of opposition also codifies the idea that an I-proposition is the **subaltern** of an A-proposition (and the A-proposition is thus the **superaltern** of an I-proposition), and that an O-proposition is the subaltern of the corresponding E-proposition.

See also: **Categorical Logic, Existential Import, Immediate Inference, Term Logic, Venn Diagram**

Σ-SENTENCE Within the **arithmetical hierarchy** (or **Kleene hierarchy**) a Σ-sentence (or Σ_1 **sentence**) is any **statement** Φ such that Φ is **logically equivalent** to some statement of the form:

$$(\exists x_1)(\exists x_2) \dots (\exists x_m) \, \Psi$$

where Ψ is a formula containing only **bounded quantifiers**. In other words, a Σ-sentence is a **Σ-formula** with no **free variables**.

See also: **Finitary Arithmetic, Π-Formula, Π-Sentence**

STAGE see **Rank**

STAGE THEORY see **Cumulative Hierarchy, Iterative Conception of Set**

STATEMENT A statement is a **sentence** that receives a **truth value** (or, within some **gap logics**, is a sentence that could receive a truth value, even if it happens not to). More informally, a statement is a declarative sentence, as opposed, for example, to questions and commands.

See also: **Categorical Proposition, Compound Statement, Imperative, Interrogative, Well-Formed Formula**

STIPULATIVE DEFINITION A stipulative definition is a **definition** that provides a new meaning for a pre-existing expression with a pre-existing meaning. Stipulative definitions are typically used temporarily, for the sake of some **argument** or to give examples, since there can be no question of the definition being correct or incorrect. Instead, a stipulative definition, in effect, provides us with a new expression, and a novel meaning for that expression, where the new expression exactly resembles, in its spelling and grammatical role, an old, familiar expression.

See also: **Explicit Definition, Impredicative Definition, Intensional Definition, Ostensive Definition, Persuasive Definition**

STRATIFIED   A **formula** of **set theory** is stratified if and only if **natural numbers** can be assigned to its **variables** in such a way that whenever:

$$x \in y$$

occurs in the formula, then the natural number assigned to y is exactly one greater than the natural number assigned to x.

See also: **New Foundations**

STRAW MAN   Straw man is an **informal fallacy** which occurs when the reasoner, in attempting to demonstrate the inadequacy of another person's **argument**, attacks instead a misinterpreted or misleading version of the original argument.

See also: **Ad Hominem**

STRICT CONDITIONAL   A strict conditional is a **statement** of the form:

If A then B

which is true if and only if, at every **possible world**, either A is **false** or B is **true**. Letting "⊃" temporarily stand for the **material condition**, a strict conditional can be **defined** as:

$$A \rightarrow B \quad =_{df} \quad \Box(A \supset B)$$

where "□" is the necessity operator.
    The term "strict conditional" is also used to **denote**, not the entire statement:

$$A \rightarrow B$$

but rather the **logical operator** represented by "→."

See also: **Counterfactual Conditional, Counternecessary Conditional, Indicative Conditional, Subjunctive Conditional**

STRICT IMPLICATION   Strict implication is the **relation** that holds between statements A and B if and only if:

$$A \rightarrow B$$

is true, where the conditional in question is the **strict conditional**. In other words, strict implication is the relation that holds between two statements if and only if, at every **possible world**, either the first statement is **false** or the second statement is **true**. The **formula**:

$$A \rightarrow B$$

is also said to be a strict implication, if the relation of strict implication holds between A and B (in that order).

See also: **Deductive Implication, Logical Implication, Material Implication**

STRICT ORDER see **Strict Ordering**

STRICT ORDERING   A strict ordering (or **strict total ordering**, or **strict order**, or **strict total order**) is a binary relation R on a set of objects S which is:

> **Asymmetric:** $\quad (\forall x)(\forall y)(Rxy \rightarrow \sim Ryx)$
>
> **Transitive:** $\quad (\forall x)(\forall y)(\forall z)((Rxy \wedge Ryz) \rightarrow Rxz)$
>
> **Trichotomous:** $\quad (\forall x)(\forall y)(Rxy \vee Ryx \vee x = y)$

Given a strict ordering, one can **define** a **linear ordering** R* as:

R^*xy if and only if Rxy or $x = y$

See also: **Linear Ordering, Partial Ordering, Pre-Ordering, Well-Ordering**

STRICT TOTAL ORDER see **Strict Ordering**

STRICT TOTAL ORDERING see **Strict Ordering**

STRING see **Sequence**

STROKE see **Sheffer Stroke**

STRONG COMPLETENESS₁   A **formal system** is strongly complete relative to a **formal semantics** if and only if, given a set of **statements** Δ and a statement Φ, if Φ is a **semantic consequence**

of Δ:

$$\Delta \vDash \Delta$$

then Φ is a deductive consequence of Δ:

$$\Delta \vdash \Phi$$

The strong completeness of a **formal system** implies the **weak completeness** of that same formal system, although not vice versa.

See also: **Deductive Consequence, Logical Consequence, Metatheorem, Negation Completeness, ω-Completeness, Soundness**

STRONG COMPLETENESS₂ A **formal system** is **strongly complete** (or **Post complete**) if and only if, whenever Φ is a **statement** in the **language** of that formal system that is not a **theorem** of the formal system, the addition of all **substitution instances** of Φ to the formal system renders the formal system **inconsistent**. A formal system that is not strongly complete is **Post incomplete**.

See also: **Metatheorem, Negation Completeness, ω-Completeness, Soundness, Weak Completeness**

STRONG COUNTEREXAMPLE   Within **intuitionistic logic** and **intuitionistic mathematics**, a strong counterexample is a **proof** of the **negation** of an instance of some variant of the **law of excluded middle**. The simple formulation of excluded middle, that is:

$$P \vee \sim P$$

has no strong counterexamples in this sense (assuming intuitionistic logic is **consistent**), since:

$$\sim \sim (P \vee \sim P)$$

is a **theorem** of intuitionistic logic. Nevertheless, intuitionists have been able to prove theorems with a form very similar to the negation of excluded middle, such as theorems of the form:

$$\sim (\forall x)(Px \vee \sim Px)$$

within intuitionistic **real analysis**.

See also: **Bivalence, Free Choice Sequence, Weak Counterexample, Weak Excluded Middle**

STRONG INDUCTIVE ARGUMENT   A strong inductive argument is an **inductive argument** where it is improbable (but **possible**) for the **premises** to be **true** and the **conclusion** to be **false**. An inductive argument that is not a strong inductive argument is a **weak inductive argument**.

See also: **Abduction, Cogent Inductive Argument, Fallacy, Informal Fallacy**

STRONG KLEENE CONNECTIVES   The strong Kleene connectives are **logical connectives** for **three-valued logic** which have the following **truth tables** (where N is the third value):

P	~ P
T	F
N	N
F	T

P	Q	P ∧ Q
T	T	T
T	N	N
T	F	F
N	T	N
N	N	N
N	F	F
F	T	F
F	N	F
F	F	F

P	Q	P ∨ Q
T	T	T
T	N	T
T	F	T
N	T	T
N	N	N
N	F	N
F	T	T
F	N	N
F	F	F

Typically, the **conditional** "A → B" is, in this context, defined as "~ A ∨ B."

See also: **Analethic Logic, Choice Negation, K₃, Logic of Paradox, Supervaluational Semantics**

STRONG KLEENE LOGIC see **K₃**

STRONG MATHEMATICAL INDUCTION   Strong mathematical induction (or **complete induction**) is a version of **mathematical induction** where one proves that some **property** holds of all **natural numbers** by (a) proving that the property holds of some **basis set** (typically 0, 1, or all the natural numbers less than n for some n), and then (b) proving that, if the property holds of all natural numbers less than n, for an arbitrary n, then the property holds of n itself.

See also: **Induction on Well-Formed Formulas, Transfinite Induction, Weak Mathematical Induction**

STRONG NEGATION   The term "strong negation" has, at various times, been used to refer to either **exclusion negation** or **choice negation**.

See also: **Boolean Negation, Bottom, DeMorgan Negation, Falsum, Negation, Tilde**

STRONG PARACONSISTENCY   Strong paraconsistency is the view that there are **possible worlds** – that is, real ways the world could be (including perhaps the **actual world**) – where **contradictions** are **true**, or where some **statements** are both **true** and **false**. Strong paraconsistency should be contrasted with **weak paraconsistency** – the view that true contradictions, and worlds that contain them, are merely a formal tool used to study reasoning. Most **relevant logics** are formulated from a weak paraconsistency viewpoint, while **dialethic logics** such as the **logic of paradox** reflect a strong paraconsistent viewpoint.

See also: **Dialetheism, Impossible Worlds, Paraconsistent Logic, Ternary Semantics, Truth Value Glut**

STRONG SUPPLEMENTATION PRINCIPLE   The strong supplementation principle states that, given two objects such that the second is not a **part** of the first, there must be a third object that is a part of the second object but does not **overlap** the first object. In symbols, with "P" representing the **binary** parthood **relation**, we have:

$$(\forall x)(\forall y)(\sim Pyx \rightarrow (\exists z)(Pzy \wedge \sim (\exists w)(Pwx \wedge Pwz)))$$

The strong supplementation principle implies the **weak supplementation principle**, but not vice versa.

See also: **Extensional Mereology, General Extensional Mereology, Mereological Extensionality, Mereological Fusion**

STRONGLY CONNECTED   A **relation** R is strongly connected (or **total**) if and only if, for all x and y, either:

>   Rxy

or:

>   Ryx

See also: **Connected, Trichotomy**

STRONGLY INACCESSIBLE CARDINAL   A **cardinal number** κ is strongly inaccessible if and only if:

(1) κ is an uncountably infinite cardinal number.

(2) κ is a regular cardinal.

(3) for all $\gamma < \kappa$, $2^{\gamma} < \kappa$.

Standard **Zermelo Fraenkel set theory** implies that all strongly inaccessible cardinals are **weakly inaccessible cardinals**, and the **generalized continuum hypothesis implies** that all weakly inaccessible cardinals are strongly inaccessible cardinals.

See also: **Large Cardinal, Large Cardinal Axiom, Reflection Principle**

STRUCTURAL RULE   A structural rule is a **rule of inference** that does not refer specifically to any **logical connective** or operator. Structural rules are typically studied within **sequent calculus**, although the notion has broader applicability. Examples of structural rules include **contraction, cut, weakening**, and **permutation**.

See also: **Abelian Logic, Affine Logic, Cut Elimination, Non-Commutative Logic, Sequent, Substructual Logic**

STRUCTURE see **Model**

SUBALTERN   Given a pair of **categorical propositions** standing in the **relation** of **subalternation** – that is, a **universal proposition** and the corresponding **particular proposition** of the same **quality** – then the particular proposition is the subaltern of the pair and the universal proposition is the **superaltern**.

See also: **Square of Opposition, Superaltern**

SUBALTERNATION   In **categorical logic**, subalternation is the **relation** that holds between a **universal proposition** and the corresponding **particular proposition** of the same **quality**. Thus, subalternation holds between the **A-proposition**:

All A are B.

and the **I-proposition**:

Some A are B.

and subalternation also holds between the **E-proposition**:

No A are B.

and the **O-proposition**:

Some A are not B.

In each of these cases, the universal proposition is the **superaltern** of the pair, while the particular proposition is the **subaltern**.

Within categorical logic, if subalternation holds between two categorical propositions, then the second proposition is entailed by the first, although this **inference** depends on the assumption of **existential import** – the idea that if all P's are Q's, then there is at least one thing that is a P and also a Q.

See also: **Contraposition, Conversion, Immediate Inference, Obversion, Square of Opposition**

SUBCONTRARIES see **Subcontrary**

SUBCONTRARY   A pair of **statements** are subcontrary (or **subcontraries**) when it is **impossible** for them simultaneously to be **false**, but it is **possible** for them simultaneously to be **true**.

Within **categorical logic** subcontrary is a term of art, expressing the relationship that holds between an **I-proposition** and the corresponding **O-proposition**. This is just a special case of the more general usage, however.

See also: **Contradictory, Contrary, Square of Opposition**

SUBFORMULA   A subformula of a **formula** Φ is a **formula** Ψ such that Ψ is a **part** of Φ. Typically, if Ψ is a subformula of Φ, then Φ will have been obtained by combining Ψ with other formulas using the **formation rules** of the **language** in question.

See also: **Compound Formula, Compound Statement, Open Formula, Syntax, Well-Formed Formula**

SUBJECT TERM   The subject term of a **categorical proposition** is the **categorical term** that occurs first in the **proposition**. Thus, in the **A-proposition**:

> All men are mortal.

the **predicate** "is a man" is the subject term.

See also: **Major Term, Middle Term, Minor Term, Predicate Term**

SUBJUNCTIVE CONDITIONAL   A subjunctive conditional is a **conditional** that expresses what would have been the case had the **antecedent** been **true**. Subjunctive conditionals thus should be distinguished from **material conditionals** which express what is the case if, in fact, the antecedent is true. For example, the subjunctive conditional:

> If Archimedes had not been a mathematician, then he would have been a pool shark.

is **false**, since if Archimedes had not been a mathematician, pool shark would not have been his second choice of career. The similar material conditional:

> If Archimedes is not a mathematician, then he is a pool shark.

is true, however.

Typically subjunctive conditionals are equated with **counterfactual conditionals**, although occasionally the term counterfactual conditional is reserved for subjunctive conditionals with false antecedents (i.e. those that actually are counterfactual).

See also: **Conditional Logic, Counterfactual Logic, Counternecessary Conditional, Indicative Conditional, Strict Conditional**

SUBLANGUAGE   A **language** L is a sublanguage of a language L* if and only if the **set** of **well-formed formulas** in L is a **subset** of the set of well-formed formulas of L*. If L is a sublanguage of L*, then L* is a **superlanguage** of L.

See also: **Metalanguage, Object Language, Sublogic, Subtheory**

SUBLOGIC   A **logic** L is a sublogic of a logic L* if and only if:

    (1) The **set** of **well-formed formulas** in the **language** of L is a **subset** of the set of well-formed formulas in the language of L* (i.e. the language of L is a **sublanguage** of the language of L*).

    (2) For every **formula** Φ and set of formulas Δ, if Δ implies Φ according to L, then Δ implies Φ according to L*.

If L is a sublogic of L*, the L* is a **superlogic** of L.

See also: **Formal System, Intermediate Logic, Subtheory**

SUBSET   A set A is a subset of another set B if and only if every member of A is also a member of B. If A is a subset of B, then B is a **superset** of A.

See also: **Axiom of Separation, Proper Subset**

SUBSTITUTION₁   Substitution is the process of replacing one or more occurrences of a **metalinguistic variable** in a **schema** with an object language expression of the appropriate type. The resulting **object language formula** is a **substitution instance** of the schema.

See also: **Axiom(s) of Replacement, Axiom(s) of Separation, Comprehension Schema, Derived Rule, Mathematical Induction, T-schema**

SUBSTITUTION₂ see **Axiom of Replacement**

SUBSTITUTION INSTANCE see **Substitution**

SUBSTITUTIONAL QUANTIFIER   A substitutional quantifier is a **quantifier** that is **interpreted** as ranging over **statements**. Consider a **universally quantified sentence** $(\forall x)\Phi(x)$. If we interpret the quantifier substitutionally, then the sentence will be **true** in a **model** if and only if the model **satisfies** every **closed formula** $\Phi(t)$, where t is a **term** in the **language**. Substitutional quantifiers offer an alternative to the **objectual** interpretation of the **quantifier**, although the two understandings of quantification are **equivalent** if every object in the domain has a name in the **language** in question.

See also: **Existential Quantifier, First-Order Logic, Generalized Quantifier, Numerical Quantifier, Objectual Quantifier, Universal Quantifier**

SUBSTRUCTURAL LOGIC Substructural logics are **nonstandard logics** where one or more of the **structural rules** (such as **cut, contraction, weakening**, and **permutation**) are absent. Typically, substructural logics are formulated within **sequent calculus**. Many **relevant logics** are substructural logics, and substructural logics are also of interest in **computability theory**.

See also: **Abelian Logic, Affine Logic, Cut Elimination, Non-Commutative Logic, Sequent**

SUBTHEORY A **theory** T is a subtheory of a theory T* if and only if T is a **subset** of T*. If T is a subtheory of T*, then T* is a **supertheory** of T.

See also: **Metalanguage, Object Language, Sublanguage, Sublogic**

SUCCESSOR see **Arithmetic Successor, Cardinal Successor, Ordinal Successor**

SUCCESSOR CARDINAL see **Cardinal Successor**

SUCCESSOR FUNCTION The successor function is one of the **simple function-building operations** of **recursive function theory**. The successor function is the **function** which, when applied to the **natural number** n as argument, provides n+1 as output – that is, it maps each natural number to its **arithmetic successor**.

See also: **Composition, Identity Function, Minimization, Primitive Recursion, Zero Function**

SUCCESSOR ORDINAL see **Ordinal Successor**

SUFFICIENT CONDITION see **Necessary Condition**

SUFFIX NOTATION A **function** symbol, **relation** symbol, or **logical constant** is an instance of suffix notation (or **postfix notation**) if it occurs to the right of its **arguments**. For example, within set theory one version of the notation for **cardinal successor** occurs in suffix notation, since we can **denote** the cardinal successor of κ as κ^{+}.

See also: **Infix Notation, Polish Notation, Prefix Notation**

SUM see **Union**

SUMSET see **Union**

SUMSET AXIOM see **Axiom of Union**

SUPERALTERN see **Subaltern**

SUPERINTUITIONISTIC LOGIC see **Intermediate Logic**

SUPERLANGUAGE see **Sublanguage**

SUPERLOGIC see **Sublogic**

SUPERSET see **Subset**

SUPERTASK A supertask is a situation in which **infinitely** many distinct actions are carried out in a **finite** amount of time.

See also: **Complete Infinity, Potential Infinity, Zeno Paradoxes**

SUPERTHEORY see **Subtheory**

SUPERTRUE Within supervaluational semantics, a **statement** is supertrue in a **supervaluational model** M if and only if it is **true** on all **admissible sharpenings** of that model.

See also: **Anti-Extension, Extension, Sorites Paradox, Sorites Series**

SUPERVALUATIONAL SEMANTICS Supervaluational semantics is a **formal semantics** used to formalize **languages** containing

vague predicates. Within a supervaluational **model**, each predicate is assigned an **extension** E and an **anti-extension** A where E and A are **exclusive** but not necessarily **exhaustive** – that is, E and A cannot overlap, and there might be objects which are members of neither E nor A. Intuitively, the extension E of a predicate Φ is the set of objects that Φ is definitely **true** of, and the anti-extension A is the set of objects that Φ is definitely not true of.

Truth and **falsity** are typically evaluated within a supervaluational model using the **truth tables** for the **strong Kleene connectives** where instances of a predicate falling in neither the extension or the anti-extension are treated as having the **truth value gap**. Supervaluational semantics differs from more traditional **three-valued logics**, however, in that it adds a notion of **supertruth** to the semantics: Given two supervaluational models M and M*, M* is an **admissible sharpening** of M if and only if, for any predicate Φ, if E and A are the extension and anti-extension of Φ in M, and E* and A* are the extension and anti-extension of Φ in M*, then:

(1) E is a **subset** of E* and A is a subset of A*.

(2) E* and A* are exclusive and exhaustive – that is, every object is in exactly one of E* and A*.

Intuitively, sharpenings are just **classical models** that "agree," in the relevant sense, with the supervaluational models that they are sharpenings of. A statement is supertrue on a model if and only if it is true on every sharpening of that model. If we formulate **logical consequence** in terms of preservation of supertruth, then supervaluational semantics validates **classical logic**.

See also: **Borderline Case, Degree-Theoretic Semantics, Epistemicism, Sorites Paradox, Sorites Series**

SUPPOSITION   Within medieval **logic**, supposition is a concept that was used to explain troubling aspects of our **language** – aspects that often resulted in **paradoxes** or other puzzles. Supposition is a **relation** between an expression and the object or concept that the expression is being used to talk about, where the supposition of the expression need not be its literal **reference**. For example, in the **imperative**:

Drink another glass.

the supposition of the word "glass" is not the actual glass (which cannot be drunk), but the liquid that is the contents of the glass.

See also: **Antimony, Sophism, Sophisma**

SUPPRESSED EVIDENCE Suppressed evidence is an **informal fallacy** which occurs when the reasoner, in attempting to support a **conclusion**, ignores or is unaware of a piece of **evidence** that would support the **negation** of the **conclusion** at least as well as the argument presented supports the conclusion itself.

See also: **Bias, Enthymeme, Red Herring**

SUPREMUM see **Least Upper Bound**

SURJECTION A surjection is a **surjective,** or **onto, function.**

See also: **Bijection, Injection**

SURJECTIVE see **Onto**

SYLLOGISM A syllogism is any **argument** with two **premises.**

See also: **Categorical Syllogism, Disjunctive Syllogism, Hypothetical Syllogism, Polysyllogism**

SYLLOGISTIC FIGURE The syllogistic figure (or **figure**) of a **categorical syllogism** is the arrangement of the **syllogistic terms** in the categorical syllogism. Letting A be the **major term,** B be the **minor term,** and C be the **middle term,** a categorical syllogism is in the first figure if its **logical form** is:

        [Quantifier]   C are A
        [Quantifier]   B are C
        [Quantifier]   B are A

the second figure if its logical form is:

        [Quantifier]   A are C
        [Quantifier]   B are C
        [Quantifier]   B are A

the third figure if its logical form is:

        [Quantifier]   C are A
        [Quantifier]   C are B
        [Quantifier]   B are A

and the fourth figure if its logical form is:

[Quantifier]   A are C
[Quantifier]   C are B
[Quantifier]   B are A

The logical form of a categorical syllogism can be specified uniquely in terms of the syllogistic figure and **syllogistic mood** of the categorical syllogism.

See also: **Barbara, Major Premise, Minor Premise, Predicate Term, Subject Term**

SYLLOGISTIC MOOD The syllogistic mood (or **mood**) of a **categorical syllogism** is the arrangement of **A-propositions, E-propositions, I-propositions,** and **O-propositions** as the **premises** and **conclusion** of the **argument**. Thus, the syllogistic mood of the categorical syllogism **Barbara**:

All B's are C's
All A's are B's
All A's are C's

is AAA, since both its **major premise** and **minor premise** are A-propositions and its conclusion is also an A-proposition. Similarly, a categorical syllogism that consisted of an O-proposition as its major premise, an O-proposition as its minor premise, and an I-proposition as its conclusion would have OOI as its syllogistic mood. The **logical form** of a categorical syllogism can be specified uniquely in terms of the **syllogistic figure** and syllogistic mood of the categorical syllogism.

See also: **Barbara, Major Term, Middle Term, Minor Term**

SYLLOGISTIC TERMS see **Major Term, Middle Term, Minor Term, Predicate Term, Subject Term**

SYMMETRIC DIFFERENCE The symmetric difference of two **sets** A and B (written "A Δ B") is the set that contains, as **members**, exactly the objects that are members of one or the other, but not both, of A and B. In other words, the symmetric difference of A and B is:

$$\{x : x \in A \text{ and } x \notin B, \text{ or } x \in B \text{ and } x \notin A \}$$

See also: **Complement, Relative Complement**

SYMMETRY A **relation** R is symmetric if and only if, for any objects x and y, if:

> Rxy

then:

> Ryx

See also: **Antisymmetry, Asymmetry, B**

SYNCATEGOREMATIC TERMS Syncategorematic terms are expressions which, on their own, signify nothing, but contribute to more complex **expressions** in which they occur by indicating how other expressions are to be combined in order to obtain a **meaningful** whole. Within **logic**, the most important syncategorematic terms are the **logical constants**. **Modal operators** are also syncategorematic terms. Expressions which are not syncategorematic (i.e. those that have independent meaning, such as **predicates** and **singular terms**) are **categorematic** terms.

See also: **Logical Connectives**

SYNTACTIC CONSEQUENCE see **Deductive Consequence**

SYNTACTIC EQUIVALENCE see **Deductively Equivalent**

SYNTACTIC IMPLICATION see **Deductive Implication**

SYNTACTIC SYSTEM see **Formal System**

SYNTACTIC VALIDITY see **Deductive Validity**

SYNTACTICALLY EQUIVALENT see **Deductively Equivalent**

SYNTAX   The syntax of a **formal system** is the **set** of rules governing what is to count as a meaningful expression within the **language** of that **formal system**. In other words, the syntax of a language is the set of **formation rules** governing what is to count as a **well-formed formula** in the language.

See also: **Logical Connective, Logical Constant, Punctuation**

SYNTHETIC see **Analytic**

$\boxed{\text{T}}$

T The **modal logic** T is the **normal modal logic** whose sole additional **axiom** is:

T: $\Box P \rightarrow P$

In **possible worlds semantics**, the modal logic T is **valid** on any **frame** in which the **accessibility relation** is **reflexive**.

T also refers to the axiom that is characteristic of the modal logic T. The axiom **T** is satisfied on any frame in which the accessibility relation is **reflexive**.

See also: **Kripke Semantics, Kripke Structure, Modality**

TABLEAU see **Semantic Tableau**

TARSKIAN HIERARCHY The Tarskian hierarchy is a view of **language**, developed to avoid the **Liar paradox** and related **semantic paradoxes** and puzzles, based on an **infinite hierarchy** of languages. Within the hierarchy, each language L has a unique language L* "above" it – its **metalanguage**. No language contains a **truth predicate** applying to all of the **statements** within that language. Instead, for each language L in the hierarchy, the metalanguage L* for that language contains a truth predicate that applies to all statements in L, and satisfies the **T-schema** for all statements in L.

See also: **Classical Logic, Convention T, Semantic Paradox, Semantically Closed Language, Tarski's Indefinability Theorem**

TARSKIAN MODEL see **Model**

TARSKI BICONDITIONAL see **T-schema**

TARSKI SCHEMA see **T-schema**

TARSKI'S CONVENTION T see **Convention T**

TARSKI'S INDEFINABILITY THEOREM Tarski's indefinability theorem (or **Tarski's theorem**) states that **arithmetical truth** cannot be **defined** in arithmetic – that is, there is no **predicate**

definable in arithmetic that holds of exactly the **Gödel numbers** of the **truths** of arithmetic.

The indefinability theorem is closely related to **Gödel's incompleteness theorems,** and is also at the heart of much research on the **Liar paradox.**

See also: **Convention T, Semantic Paradox, Semantically Closed Language, Truth Predicate, T-schema**

TARSKI'S THEOREM see **Tarski's Indefinability Theorem**

TAUTOLOGY   A tautology is a **statement** of **propositional logic** that receives all T's on its **truth table.** In other words, a tautology is a formula of propositional logic that must be **true,** no matter what the **truth values** its constituent **propositional letters** are **assigned.**

See also: **Logical Truth, Theorem, Truth-in-a-Model, Valid**

TEMPORAL LOGIC see **Temporal Modal Logic**

TEMPORAL MODAL LOGIC Temporal modal logic (or **chonological logic,** or **temporal logic,** or **tense logic**) is that branch of **modal logic** that studies the **unary modal operators** "it will always be the case that Φ," "it will be the case that Φ," "it has always been the case that Φ," "it was the case that Φ." The notions are typically formalized as "G Φ," "F Φ," "H Φ," and "P Φ," respectively.

See also: **Alethic Modal Logic, Dynamic Logic, Normal Modal Logic**

TENSE LOGIC see **Temporal Modal Logic**

T-EQUIVALENCE see **T-schema**

TERM see **Categorical Term, Singular Term**

TERM LOGIC   Term logic is a loose designation for **categorical logic** and the various techniques that grew out of categorical logic, but which pre-dated Gottlob Frege's introduction of the modern notions of **quantification** and **variables.**

See also: **Categorical Proposition, Categorical Syllogism, Polysyllogism, Square of Opposition, Venn Diagram**

TERNARY FUNCTION A ternary function (or **triadic function**) is a **function** that takes three **arguments**, such as "the point equidistant from points x, y, and z."

See also: **Adicity, Ternary Relation**

TERNARY RELATION A ternary relation (or **triadic relation**) is a **relation** that takes three **arguments**, such as "x is between y and z."

See also: **Adicity, Ternary Function**

TERNARY SEMANTICS A ternary semantics is a **possible worlds semantics** that makes use of a **ternary relation** on **possible worlds** instead of, or in addition to, the more standard **binary accessibility relation**. Ternary semantics have been most widely applied in the development of **relevant logics**.

See also: **Impossible World, Paraconsistent Logic, Paradoxes of Material Implication, Strong Paraconsistency, Weak Paraconsistency**

TERTIUM NON DATUR see **Excluded Middle**

THEOREM₁ A theorem (or **logical theorem**) is a statement that can be **proven** within a **formal system** with no assumptions or premises. In other words, a theorem is a **deductive consequence** of the **empty set** within a **formal system**.

See also: **Derivation, Formal Proof, Logical Truth, Tautology**

THEOREM₂ A theorem, relative to a **theory**, is a **statement** that can be **proven** using, as assumptions, only axioms of that particular theory. In other words, a theorem of a theory is a **deductive consequence** of that theory. Since theories are, by **definition**, closed under **deductive implication**, this is **equivalent** to saying that a statement is a theorem of a particular theory if and only if it is a **member** of that theory.

See also: **Derivation, Formal Proof, Proof Theory, Single Turnstile, Theory**

THEORY A theory is a **set** of **statements** in a **formal language** which is closed under **deductive implication**. In other words, if T is a theory, and Φ is a **deductive consequence** of T, then Φ must be a **member** of T.

See also: **Formal Proof, Proof Theory, Single Turnstile, Theorem, Transitive Closure**

THINNING see **Weakening**

THREE-VALUED LOGIC A three-valued logic is a **many-valued logic** whose **formal semantics** is based on three **truth values** instead of the traditional two truth values, **true** and **false**. Popular options for the third value include "neither true nor false" – the **truth value gap** – and "both true and false" – the **truth value glut**.

See also: **Analethic Logic, K₃, Logic of Paradox**

TILDE "Tilde" is the name of the **negation** symbol "~."

See also: **Boolean Negation, Choice Negation, DeMorgan Negation, Double Negation, Exclusion Negation**

TOKEN A token of a multiply instantiated entity, like a **statement**, is an individual occurrence of that entity. Tokens are distinguished from the general entity of which they are instances – the **type**. Thus, the following list contains two tokens but only one type:

Snow is white.

Snow is white.

TOLERANT A predicate Φ is tolerant if and only if small changes in the relevant underlying properties of an object x do not affect the justice with which Φ applies to x. Thus, the predicate "bald" is tolerant, since one hair more or less does not transform a clear instance of baldness into a clear instance of non-baldness. **Vagueness** is often tied to the tolerance of vague predicates.

See also: **Borderline Case, Forced March Sorites, Higher-Order Vagueness, Sorites Paradox, Sorites Series**

TONK Tonk is the **binary logical connective** which has the following as its **introduction rule** and **elimination rule**:

$$\frac{A}{A * B} \text{*Intro} \qquad \frac{A * B}{B} \text{*Elim}$$

This connective is meant to be a **counterexample** to **inferentialism**. The supposed connective tonk is **defined** in terms of the **rules of inference** that govern it, yet it arguably has no meaning, since the addition of tonk to any **formal system** that has a **transitive consequence relation** renders that logic **trivial**.

See also: **Harmony, Proof Theory**

TOP   The maximal **element** in a **lattice** or **Boolean algebra** is the top, and is usually symbolized as "1" or "T."

See also: **Bottom, Falsum, Partial Ordering, Verum**

TOPOI see **Topos**

TOPOS   A topos (Greek for commonplace; plural: **topoi**) is an important species of **category**. The formal **definition** of "topos" is beyond the scope of this dictionary. Roughly speaking, however, a topos is a category whose **structure** is sufficiently rich in a particular way. The category of **sets** is a topos, as are many other central mathematical **structures**. Topoi (sometimes "toposes") can also be thought of as **topological spaces**, which further bridges the gap between topology and geometry on the one hand, and **logic** and **set theory** on the other.

See also: **Categorical Logic, Category Theory, Topos Theory**

TOPOS THEORY   Topos theory is the branch of **category theory** that studies a particular type of **category** called a **topos**.

See also: **Categorical Logic**

TOTAL see **Strongly Connected**

TOTAL FUNCTION   A total function is a **function** whose value is defined for all **arguments**. In other words, a total function provides an output for all of its **possible** inputs. A function that is not defined for all arguments – that is, a function that is not total – is a **partial function**.

See also: **Minimization, Recursive Function Theory**

TOTAL ORDER see **Linear Ordering**

TOTAL ORDERING see **Linear Ordering**

TRANSFINITE CARDINAL NUMBER   A transfinite cardinal number is a **cardinal number** of an **infinite set**.

See also: ℵ, ℶ, **c**, **Dedekind Infinite**, **Transfinite Ordinal Number**

TRANSFINITE HIERARCHY see **Cumulative Hierarchy**

TRANSFINITE INDUCTION   Transfinite induction is a form of **proof by induction** where one **proves** that a certain **property** holds of all **elements** of some **well-ordered** collection, such as the **class** of **ordinal numbers**, the class of **cardinal numbers**, or the class of **sets**. Here we will sketch the steps for applying transfinite induction to the ordinal numbers – the case for cardinal numbers or sets is similar. The **basis step** amounts to proving that the property in question P holds of the initial elements of the **well-ordered** collection, in this case the **empty set**. The **inductive step** then consists in proving that both:

> If P holds of an ordinal number α, then P holds of the **ordinal successor** of α.

> If P holds of all ordinal numbers less than some **limit ordinal** γ, then P holds of γ.

If both claims can be demonstrated, then this is **sufficient** to show that the property holds of all ordinal numbers.

See also: **Cardinal Successor, Limit Cardinal, Mathematical Induction**

TRANSFINITE NUMBER see **Transfinite Cardinal Number, Transfinite Ordinal Number**

TRANSFINITE ORDINAL NUMBER   A transfinite ordinal number is an **ordinal number** of a **well-ordering** on an **infinite set**.

See also: **Dedekind Infinite**, ω, **Transfinite Cardinal Number**

TRANSFINITE RECURSION   Transfinite recursion is a **set-theoretic** method of constructing a **sequence** of objects X_γ for each **ordinal number** γ. Given a **function** g from **sets** to sets, transfinite recursion guarantees that there is a function f from ordinal numbers to sets such that:

$$f(0) \quad = \quad g(0)$$

$$f(\alpha+1) \quad = \quad g(f(\alpha))$$

$$f(\gamma) \quad = \quad g(\{f(x) : x < \gamma\}) \quad \text{[when } \gamma \text{ a limit ordinal]}$$

X_γ is then $f(\alpha)$.

See also: **Limit Ordinal, Ordinal Successor, Recursive Definition**

TRANSITION FUNCTION see **Action Table**

TRANSITIVE CLOSURE₁ The transitive closure of a **relation** R on a **set** A is the smallest **transitive relation** R* on A such that R* contains R. In other words, the transitive closure of R on A is the smallest relation R* such that:

(1) For any x and y in A, if Rxy, then R*x, y.

(2) For any x, y, and z in A, if R*xy and R*yz, then R*xz.

See also: **Ancestral, Hereditary**

TRANSITIVE CLOSURE₂ The transitive closure of a **set** A under a **relation** R is the smallest set A* such that:

(1) A is a **subset** of A*.

(2) For any x and y, if x is a **member** of A* and Rxy, then y is a member of A*.

One particularly important instance of this notion of transitive closure is the transitive closure of a set under the **membership relation**, which is sometimes called simply the transitive closure of the set (without any mention of the relation in question). The transitive closure of a set A, in this sense, is the smallest set A* such that:

(1) A is a subset of A*.

(2) For any x and y, if x is a member of A*, and y is a member of x, then y is a member of A*.

In other words, the transitive closure of a set A is the smallest set that contains the members of A, and the members of the members of A, and the members of the members of the members of A, and so on.

See also: **Well-Formed Formula**

TRANSITIVE SET   A transitive set is a **set** that contains each of the **members** of its members. In other words, if A is transitive, and B is a member of A, then any member of B is also a member of A.

See also: **Inductive Set, ω, Ordinal Arithmetic, Ordinal Number**

TRANSITIVITY   A **relation** R is transitive if and only if, for any objects x, y, and z, if:

Rxy

and:

Ryz

then:

Rxz

See also: **Cut, 4, Hypothetical Syllogism, S4**

TRANSLATION   A translation is a function from the expressions of one **language** to the expressions of another language. Translations are typically intended to preserve either the meanings or the **truth conditions** of the translated expressions.

See also: **Indeterminacy of Translation, Natural Language**

TRANSLATION LEMMA see **S-M-N Theorem**

TRANSPOSITION   Within **propositional logic**, transposition is the **rule of replacement** that allows one to replace a **formula** of the form:

$(P \rightarrow Q)$

with:

$(\sim Q \rightarrow \sim P)$

or vice versa.

See also: **Conditional Proof, Contraposition, Modus Ponens, Modus Tollens**

TRANS-WORLD IDENTITY   Trans-World identity (or **cross-world identity**) is a framework that allows us to interpret **modal** claims about objects. To see the puzzle at hand, consider the **statement**:

> Roy is a mathematician.

This statement, while **false** (assuming it is about the author), is certainly not **impossible**. Thus, according to **possible worlds semantics**, there must be a **possible world** in which it is **true**. Taken at face value, this would mean that, in that possible world, Roy exists and is a mathematician. But this is absurd, since Roy exists solely in the **actual world** and cannot also exist in a possible one.

Trans-world identity solves this problem by arguing that Roy (and any other object) can exist in more than one possible world and can have different, incompatible **sets** of **properties** in different worlds.

See also: **Counterpart Theory, Mere Possibilia**

TRICHOTOMY   A **relation** R is trichotomous (or **comparable**) if and only if, for any objects x and y, either:

> Rxy

or:

> Ryx

or:

> $x = y$

See also: **Connected, Strongly Connected, Trichotomy Law**

TRICHOTOMY AXIOM see **Trichotomy Law**

TRICHOTOMY LAW The trichotomy law (or **axiom of trichotomy**, or **trichotomy axiom**) states that, given any two **cardinal numbers** a and b (including **transfinite** cardinal numbers), exactly one of the following three conditions holds:

> $a > b$
>
> $b > a$
>
> $a = b$

The trichotomy law is equivalent, within set theory, to the **axiom of choice**.

See also: **Cardinal Arithmetic, Well-Ordered, Well-Ordering Principle, Zorn's Lemma**

TRIVIALITY   A theory is trivial if it has all **statements** as **theorems**. In the presence of the **rule of inference ex falso quodlibet** triviality is equivalent to **inconsistency**. A theory that is not trivial is a **non-trivial theory**.

See also: **Dialetheism, Dialethic Logic, Negation, Negation Consistency, Paraconsistent Logic**

TRUTH   Truth is the **relation** that holds between a **statement** and the world when what that statement says about the world is actually the case. Typically, if a sentence fails to be true, then it is **false**, although many **non-standard logics** allow for statements to fall into **semantic** categories other than the traditional true and false.

See also: **Bivalence, Designated Value, Law of Non-Contradiction, Truth Value Gap, Truth Value Glut**

TRUTH CONDITIONS   The truth conditions of a **statement** are what must obtain for that statement to be true. Truth conditions are different from meanings, since two statements with distinct meanings could have the same truth conditions (e.g. "1 + 1 = 2" and "0 = 0").

See also: **BHK-Interpretation, Formal Semantics, Model Theory, Truthmaker, Truth Table**

TRUTH FUNCTION   A truth function is any **function** from **sequences** of **truth values** to individual truth values. **Logical connectives** often correspond to a particular truth functions, and this fact is exemplified in their **truth tables**. For example, **conjunction** (∧), in **classical logic**, corresponds to the truth function f where:

$$f(<T, T>) \quad = \quad T$$
$$f(<T, F>) \quad = \quad F$$
$$f(<F, T>) \quad = \quad F$$
$$f(<F, F>) \quad = \quad F$$

Typically, however, not every possible truth function is codified by a unique connective.

See also: **Boolean Algebra, Dagger, Expressive Completeness, Propositional Function, Sheffer Stroke**

TRUTH FUNCTIONAL   A logical **connective** is truth functional if and only if the **truth value** of a **compound formula** containing that connective as its **main connective** is a **function** of the truth values of the constituent **subformulas** joined by that connective. Alternatively, a connective is truth functional if and only if knowing the truth values of the constituent formulas is enough to know the truth value of the compound formula obtained by joining those constituent formulas with the connective in question. All of the connectives of **classical logic** are truth functional, as are the connectives of most **many-valued logics**, although truth functionality fails in some other types of **non-standard logics**.

See also: **Classical Logic, Degree-theoretic Semantics**

TRUTH-IN-A-MODEL   A **statement** in the **language** of **first-order logic** is true-in-a-model if and only if that statement is assigned the value **true** by that **model**. A sentence that is true-in-a-model need not be literally true, or vice versa. Instead, truth-in-a-model is a means of modeling how truth works in **natural languages**.

See also: **Interpretation, Logical Consequence, Logical Truth, Logical Validity, Model Theory**

TRUTH-IN-AN-INTERPRETATION see **Truth-in-a-Model**

TRUTHMAKER   A truthmaker for a **statement** is an entity in virtue of which that statement is **true**. Some philosophers have argued that any true statement requires a truthmaker – that is, that for any expression P, P is true if and only if there is an x such that x is a truthmaker for P.

In addition to truthmakers, some philosophers have argued that **false** statements require **falsemakers**: entities in virtue of which the statements are false.

See also: **Correspondence Theory of Truth, Deflationism, Truth Predicate**

TRUTH PREDICATE   A truth predicate is a **predicate** that holds of a **statement** (or, in some cases, appropriate analogues of such statements such as **Gödel numbers**) if and only if the statement is **true**. A number of **limitation results**, including **Tarski's indefinability theorem**, impose limits on when a language can contain its own truth predicate.

See also: **Convention T, Factivity, Semantic Paradox, Semantically Closed Language, T-Schema**

TRUTH TABLE   A truth table is a chart codifying the **truth function** which corresponds to a particular **logical connective**. For example, the truth table for **conjunction** is:

P	Q	P ∧ Q
T	T	T
T	F	F
F	T	F
F	F	F

This table represents the fact that conjunction corresponds to the truth function that outputs **true** if both inputs are true (the top row of the table), and outputs **false** if either of the inputs is false (the other three rows).

See also: **Propositional Logic, Truth Conditions, Truth Functionality**

TRUTH-TELLER   The truth-teller is the **self-referential statement**:

This statement is **true**.

Although not **paradoxical** in the traditional sense, the truth-teller is nevertheless puzzling, since from a logical perspective it could either be true or **false** – on either option the relevant **T-schemas** come out true – and there seems to be no other relevant information regarding which of the two values it actually takes.

See also: **Bivalence, Liar Paradox, Open Pair, Semantically Closed Language**

TRUTH-TREE see **Semantic Tableau**

TRUTH VALUE   A truth value is a **semantic value** assigned to a statement. In **classical logic** the only truth values are **true** and **false**, although **many-valued logics** add additional truth values, such as neither-true-nor-false (the **truth value gap**) and both-true-and-false (the **truth value glut**).

See also: **Designated Value**

TRUTH VALUE GAP   A **semantics** for a **formal language** has a truth value gap if and only if some **statements** do not receive a **truth value** according to that semantics. From a formal perspective, truth value gaps are often represented, for the sake of convenience, as a third value, the **gap** value neither–true–nor–false.

See also: **Analethic Logic, First-Degree Entailment, K₃, Strong Kleene Connectives, Supervaluational Semantics, Weak Kleene Connectives**

TRUTH VALUE GLUT   A **semantics** for a **formal language** has a truth value glut if and only if some **statements** receive more than one **truth value** according to that semantics; usually such statements will receive both the value **true** and the value **false**. From a formal perspective, truth value gluts are often represented, for the sake of convenience, as a third value, the **glut** value neither–true–nor–false.

See also: **Dialethic Logic, First-Degree Entailment, Law of Non-Contradiction, Logic of Paradox, Strong Kleene Connectives, Weak Kleene Connectives**

T-SCHEMA   The T-schema (or **schema T**, or **Tarski biconditional**, or **Tarski schema**, or **T-equivalence**) is the following **schema**:

> Where T is the **truth predicate**, A is any **statement**, and n is any name of A:
>
> $$T(n) \leftrightarrow A$$

The T-schema plays a central role in a number of lines of thought regarding **truth**. For example, Tarski's **Convention T** asserts that an adequacy condition on any definition of a truth predicate is that it allows us to prove any instance of the T-schema. **Minimalists** about truth argue that the T-schema is true by **definition**, and that there is nothing more to say about truth.

Particular instances of the T-schema are **Tarski biconditionals**.

See also: **Axiom Schema, Deflationism, Semantically Closed Language, Tarski's Indefinability Theorem**

TUPLE see **N-Tuple**

TU QUOQUE   Tu quoque (Latin for "you as well") is an **informal fallacy** which occurs when the reasoner, in attempting to demonstrate the inadequacy of another person's **argument**, accuses the person presenting the argument of not acting in accordance with their own **conclusion**, implying (incorrectly) that this is a reason for rejecting the argument.

See also: **Ad Hominem**

TURING COMPUTABLE FUNCTION A **function** is Turing computable if and only if it can be computed by a **deterministic Turing machine**. The Turing computable functions are exactly the **recursive functions**, and the **Church-Turing thesis** hypothesizes that these are exactly the functions that are **effectively computable** – that is, computable in the intuitive sense of computable.

See also: **Automaton, Deterministic Polynomial Time, Effectively Computable Function, Non-Deterministic Polynomial Time, Non-Deterministic Turing Machine**

TURING MACHINE see **Deterministic Turing Machine, Non-Deterministic Turing Machine**

TURING RECOGNIZABLE SET see **Recursively Enumerable Set**

TURING TEST The Turing test is a test for determining whether a machine, or **automaton,** can exhibit human-like intelligence. In the test, a human judge has a typed conversation with two contestants, one of which is human and the other is the machine. Both contestants try to appear human to the judge. If the judge cannot reliably determine which of his conversational partners is the human, and which the machine, then the machine passes the Turing test.

See also: **Deterministic Turing Machine, Non-Deterministic Turing Machine, Register Machine**

TURING THESIS see **Church-Turing Thesis**

TURNSTILE see **Double Turnstile, Single Turnstile**

TYPE₁ see **Token**

TYPE₂ see **Ramified Theory of Types, Simple Theory of Types, Type Theory**

TYPE THEORY Type theory is a **formal system** developed in order to avoid the **Russell paradox** and similar problems that arise if one accepts **naïve set theory**. In type theory, objects are divided into **types** which occur in a **hierarchy. Operations**, such as the set-forming operation, which are applied to objects at one level of the hierarchy, result in objects that fall into a type higher up in the hierarchy. As a result, we cannot form the set of all sets that are not **members** of themselves – the **Russell set** – although we can form the set of all sets of type n that are not members of themselves, for some type n. No **contradiction** occurs in the latter construction, however, since the resulting set is of a higher type, and thus not subject to the condition which formed it out of objects of type n.

Type theories come in two main varieties: **simple type theories** and **ramified type theories**.

See also: **Axiom of Reducibility, Burali-Forti Paradox, Set-Theoretic Paradox, Vicious Circle Principle**

UNARY FUNCTION   A unary function (or **monadic function**) is a **function** which takes only one **argument**, such as "the father of x" or "the **successor** of x."

See also: **Adicity, Unary Relation**

UNARY PREDICATE see **Monadic Predicate**

UNARY RELATION   A unary relation (or **monadic relation**) is a **relation** which takes only one **argument**, such as "x is red" and "x is large." In other words, a unary relation is a **property** or **concept**.

See also: **Adicity, Unary Function**

UNCOUNTABLE see **Countable**

UNDERLAP   In **mereology**, two objects a and b are said to underlap if there is some object c such that a and b are both **parts** of c. In symbols, we have:

$$Uxy \quad = \quad (\exists z)(Pxz \wedge Pyz)$$

See also: **Composition, Mereological Fusion, Overlap, Proper Parthood, Unrestricted Fusion**

UNION₁ The union (or **sum**, or **sumset**) of two **sets** A and B, written A ∪ B, is the set whose **members** are exactly the objects that are members of either A or B.

See also: **Intersection, Relative Complement, Symmetric Difference**

UNION₂ The union (or **sum**, or **sumset**) of a **set** A, written ∪A, is the set whose **members** are exactly those objects that are members of some member of A.

See also: **Intersection, Relative Complement, Symmetric Difference**

UNION AXIOM see **Axiom of Union**

UNIVERSAL ELIMINATION see **Universal Instantiation**

UNIVERSAL GENERALIZATION₁ A universal generalization is a **formula** of **first-order logic** where a **universal quantifier** is the **dominant operator** in the formula, and the universal quantifier in question is not a **vacuous quantifier**. Thus:

$$(\forall x)(Fx)$$

is a universal generalization, while:

$$(\exists x)(\forall y)(Lxy)$$

is not. Universal generalizations assert that every object in the **domain** satisfies the (possibly complex) **predicate** occurring in the **scope** of the **quantifier**.

See also: **Bound Variable, Existential Generalization, First-order Logic, First-order Variable, Π-Formula, Π-Sentence**

UNIVERSAL GENERALIZATION₂ Universal generalization (or **universal introduction**) is the **rule of inference** that allows one to move from a **particular statement** to the **universal generalization** of that statement. In symbols we have (where Φ is any **formula**, and $\Phi[a/x]$ is the result of replacing all occurrences in Φ of "a" with "x"):

$$\frac{(\Phi)}{(\forall x)\Phi[a/x]}$$

Universal generalization can be applied only if the **variable** occurring in the new formula does not occur in Φ or in any assumption upon which Φ depends.

See also: **Existential Generalization, First-order Logic, Introduction Rule, Universal Instantiation**

UNIVERSAL INSTANTIATION Universal instantiation (or **universal elimination**) is the **rule of inference** that allows one to move from a **universal generalization** to any **instantiation** of that universal generalization. In symbols we have (where Φ is any **formula**, and $\Phi[x/a]$ is the result of replacing all occurrences of "x" with "a"):

$$\frac{(\forall x)(\Phi)}{\Phi[x/a]}$$

See also: **Elimination Rule, Existential Instantiation, First-order Logic, Universal Generalization**

UNIVERSAL INTRODUCTION see **Universal Generalization**

UNIVERSAL PROPOSITION The **quantity** of a **categorical proposition** is universal if it makes a claim about all of the **members** of the **class** denoted by the **subject term** of the proposition. Thus **A-propositions** and **E-propositions** are universal, while **I-propositions** and **O-propositions** are not universal. Categorical propositions that are not universal are **particular**.

See also: **Affirmative Proposition, Negative Proposition, Quality, Square of Opposition**

UNIVERSAL QUANTIFIER A universal quantifier is a **quantifier** that allows us to assert that a **predicate** is satisfied by all objects in the **domain of discourse**. Universal quantifiers are typically denoted by "$\forall$" followed by the **variable** that the quantifier binds (although sometimes the upside-down "A" is omitted, and the quantifier is just written as the variable being bound flanked by parentheses), and the quantifier binds variables occurring with the predicate in question in order to form **statements**. Thus, if Φ is a **unary predicate**, then:

$(\forall x)(\Phi x)$

states that every object is a Φ, or that every object satisfies Φ.

Universal quantifiers can be used to quantify over objects, in which case they are called **first-order quantifiers** (the variables ranged over by first-order quantifiers are usually taken from the end of the alphabet, and written in lower case). Universal quantifiers can also be used to quantify over **concepts, relations, properties,** or other higher-order entities, in which case they are called **second-order** or **higher-order quantifiers** (the variable bound by such a higher-order quantifier is usually written in upper case, in order to distinguish it from first-order quantifiers and the variables they bind).

See also: **Existential Quantifier, Π-Formula, Π-Sentence, Universal Generalization, Universal Instantiation, Universal Variable**

UNIVERSAL SET   A universal set is a **set** that contains, as **members,** all objects in the **domain** in question. Thus, the universal set (if it exists) is a **non-well-founded set** (or **hyperset**), since it contains itself as a member.

See also: **Absolute Infinite, Cantor's Paradox, Cantor's Theorem, Iterative Conception of Set, Limitation-of-Size Conception of Set, Naïve Set Theory**

UNIVERSAL VARIABLE   A universal variable is a **variable bound** by a **universal quantifier**.

See also: **Existential Variable, First-order Variable, Higher-order Variable, Vacuous Quantifier**

UNIVERSE OF DISCOURSE see **Domain**

UNORDERED PAIR   Within **set theory**, an unordered pair is a **set** that contains exactly two objects as **members**. The **axiom of pairing** asserts that for any two objects, the unordered pair containing those objects exists.

See also: **Ordered N-tuple, Ordered Pair, Pairing Function, Singleton**

UNRESTRICTED FUSION   In **mereology**, the unrestricted fusion principle states that given any **class** of objects, there is an object that **overlaps** exactly the objects that overlap objects in the class. The unrestricted fusion principle is intended to capture the idea that, given a collection of objects, there is an object that is made up of exactly those objects as **parts**, its **mereological fusion**.

Formally, the principle of unrestricted fusion can be formulated as an **axiom schema** (where O is the defined **overlap** relation):

$$(\exists x)\Phi(x) \rightarrow (\exists y)(\forall z)(Ozy \rightarrow (\exists w)(\Phi(w) \wedge Ozw))$$

Note that the collection of objects to be "fused" must be non-empty – thus, there is no "empty" fusion.

See also: **Classical Mereology, Composition, General Mereology, Mereological Extensionality, Proper Parthood, Underlap**

UNSOUND DEDUCTIVE ARGUMENT see **Sound Deductive Argument**

UPPER BOUND   Given a **partial ordering** $\leq$ on a **set** S, if x is a **member** of S and A is a **subset** of S, then x is an upper bound of A if and only if $y \leq x$ for all y in A.

See also: **Greatest Lower Bound, Join, Least Upper Bound, Lower Bound, Meet**

UPWARD LOWENHEIM-SKOLEM THEOREM   The upward Lowenheim-Skolem theorem states that, given any **first-order theory** T and **model** M of T, if σ is the **cardinality** of the set of primitive **non-logical** expressions in the **language** of T, κ is the cardinality of the **domain** of M, and κ is **infinite**, and then, for any **infinite cardinal** δ such that $\kappa < \delta$ and $\sigma < \delta$, there is a model of T whose domain has cardinality δ.

If we restrict our attention to first-order theories with a **countable** number of primitive non-logical expressions, then the **theorem** can be stated more simply. If such a first-order theory T has a model with an infinite domain whose cardinality is κ, then T has models whose domains are of any infinite cardinality greater than κ.

The upward Lowenheim-Skolem theorem is one half of what is generally called the **Lowenheim-Skolem theorem** (the other half is the **downward Lowenheim-Skolem theorem**).

See also: **Categorical, Intended Interpretation, Limitation**

Result, Non-Standard Analysis, Non-Standard Arithmetic, Non-Standard Model, Skolem's Paradox

URELEMENT   Within **set theory**, an urelement is any **object** that is not a **set**. **Pure set theory** does not allow for any urelements, but other formulations of **set theory** do.

See also: **Abstract Object, Individual**

USE   An expression is used if it occurs within a more complex **statement** in the normal manner. An expression is **mentioned**, however, if it occurs within that statement in such a way as to **refer** to the expression itself, and not its normal **denotation**. Thus, given:

> "Red" has three letters.

and:

> Red is a color.

"red" is mentioned in the first statement, and used in the second. As this example illustrates, **quotation** marks are typically used to indicate that an expression is being mentioned and not used.

See also: **De Dicto, De Re, Punctuation**

V see **Cumulative Hierarchy**

VACUOUS QUANTIFIER   A **quantifier** occurring within a **formula** is a vacuous quantifier if and only if there is no occurrence of the **variable** that it binds occurring within the **scope** of the quantifier (in other words, the formula contains no occurrence of the variable that the quantifier binds other than the one occurring with the quantifier itself). Thus, the second quantifier (but not the first) is a vacuous quantifier in:

> $(\forall x)(\forall y)(Rxx)$

See also: **Bound Variable, Open Formula, Open Term, Well-Formed Formula**

VAGUENESS Vagueness is the phenomenon exhibited by vague **predicates**. A vague predicate is a predicate that allows for **borderline cases** or that is susceptible to the **Sorites paradox**.

An object x is a borderline case of a predicate Φ if and only if x is not a clear case of Φ and x is not a clear case of ~ Φ.

The Sorites paradox arises when a predicate Φ is **tolerant** – that is, small changes to an object should not turn a clear instance of Φ into a clear instance of ~ Φ. If Φ is tolerant, however, then we should be able to find a series of objects a_1, a_2, a_3 ... a_n (i.e. a **Sorites series**) such that:

(1) a_1 is a clear case of Φ.

(2) For any natural number i, if a_i is a clear case of Φ, then a_{i+1} is a clear case of Φ.

(3) a_n is a clear case of ~ Φ.

These three statements are **inconsistent**.

See also: **Forced March Sorites, Higher-Order Vagueness, In Rebus Vagueness, Ontic Vagueness, Semantic Vagueness**

VALID₁ see **Valid Deductive Argument**

VALID₂ A **rule of inference** is valid within a particular **formal system** if and only if it is either an explicit **rule of inference** of that system, or its addition to the formal system does not allow one to **prove** anything that could not be proved using the explicit rules of the system.

See also: **Admissible Rule, Derivable Rule, Elimination Rule, Introduction Rule**

VALID DEDUCTIVE ARGUMENT A valid deductive argument is a **deductive argument** where it is **impossible** for the **premises** to be **true** and the **conclusion** to be **false**. A deductive argument that is not a valid deductive argument is an **invalid deductive argument**.

See also: **Deductive Consequence, Formal Consequence, Formal Fallacy, Logical Consequence, Material Consequence**

VALID IN κ see **κ-Valid**

VALUATION   A valuation (or **assignment**) is an allocation of **semantic values** to primitive **non-logical** vocabulary. Within **propositional logic**, a valuation assigns **truth values** to **propositional letters**. Within **first-order** and **higher-order logics**, a valuation is an assignment of appropriate parts of the **model** to the non–logical vocabulary (e.g. assignment of objects to **singular terms**, and **sets** of **n-tuples** to **relations**).

See also: **Interpretation, Model Theory, Semantics, Truth Table**

VARIABLE   A variable is a logical expression which receives no fixed value, but can be used to range over all entities of the appropriate sort within the **model** in question. **First-order variables**, usually denoted by lower-case letters from the end of the alphabet (x, y, z ...) range over objects, while **higher-order variables** range over **concepts, relations**, or **functions**. (Concept and relation variables usually take the form of upper-case letters, while function variables are often lower-case f, g, or h.)

See also: **Bound Variable, Existential Variable, Individual, Universal Variable, Variable Assignment**

VARIABLE ASSIGNMENT   A variable assignment is a **function** that maps each **variable** onto an appropriate entity from a **model** – that is, it assigns **first-order variables** to objects in the **domain** of the model and **higher-order variables** to appropriate sets of **n-tuples**. Variable assignments are most often used in the clauses defining **satisfaction** in a **model**.

See also: **Bound Variable, Existential Variable, Model Theory, Universal Variable**

VEL   "Vel" is the name of the **disjunction** symbol "v."

See also: **Exclusive Disjunction, Inclusive Disjunction, Tilde, Wedge**

VENN DIAGRAM   A Venn diagram is a diagram used to test **categorical syllogisms** for **validity**. In a Venn diagram, each **term** of the syllogism is represented by a circle, and the circles overlap so that each possible combination of the concepts involved is represented by a region of the diagram. Thus, in a categorical syllogism involving three terms P, Q, and R, the Venn diagram would take the form:

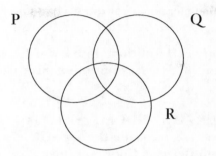

Note that all eight combinations of P, Q, and R are represented by regions in the diagram (objects which have none of P, Q, and R are represented by the empty space outside of all three circles). Arguments are then tested for validity by marking up the diagram in appropriate ways for the **premises,** and then determining whether or not such markings match those that correspond to the **conclusion** of the **argument.**

Venn diagrams can also be adapted for reasoning about collections or **sets** more generally.

See also: **Antilogism, Categorical Logic, Square of Opposition, Syllogistic Figure, Syllogistic Mood, Term Logic**

V = L see Axiom of Constructibility

VERIFICATION CONSTRAINT see Epistemic Constraint

VERITY   The verity (or **degree-of-truth**) of a **statement** is the **semantic value** of that statement within **degree-theoretic semantics,** which assigns degrees between 0 and 1 to statements.

See also: **Borderline Case, Higher-order Vagueness, In Rebus Vagueness, Semantic Vagueness, Sorites Paradox, Sorites Series**

VERUM   Verum is a primitive, **necessarily true statement** often represented as "T."

See also: **Bottom, Falsum, Top**

VICIOUS CIRCLE PRINCIPLE The vicious circle principle, proposed as a response to the **Russell paradox** and related **set-theoretic paradoxes**, denies the existence of any **set** that cannot be **defined** without making mention of, or **quantifying** over, the set in question itself.

See also: **Impredicative Definition, Indefinite Extensibility, Iterative Conception of Set, Limitation-of-Size Conception of Set**

VON NEUMANN BERNAYS GÖDEL SET THEORY Von Neumann Bernays Gödel set theory (or **Bernays-Gödel set theory,** or **NBG,** or **Neumann Bernays Gödel set theory,** or **Neumann Gödel Bernays set theory,** or **NGB,** or **Von Neumann Gödel Bernays set theory**) is an **axiomatization** of **set theory** that is characterized by the fact that it distinguishes between **sets** and **proper classes** (intuitively, those collections too "badly behaved" to be sets) and it allows one to quantify over both sorts of "collection." One obtains Von Neumann Bernays Gödel set theory by **relativizing** all of the **axioms** of **Zermelo Fraenkel set theory** to sets – that is, by replacing all occurrences of:

$$(\forall x)\Phi$$

with:

$$(\forall x)(Set(x) \rightarrow \Phi)$$

and all occurrences of:

$$(\exists x)\Phi$$

with:

$$(\exists x)(Set(x) \wedge \Phi)$$

and then adding the **class comprehension schema**:

If Φ is a formula with all quantifiers restricted to sets, and Φ contains the variable x **free**, then:

$$(\exists y)(\forall x)(x \in y \leftrightarrow \Phi)$$

is an axiom.

See also: **Kripke-Platek Set Theory, Morse-Kelley Set Theory, New Foundations, Positive Set Theory, Zermelo Fraenkel Set Theory**

VON NEUMANN GÖDEL BERNAYS SET THEORY see Von
Neumann Bernays Gödel Set Theory

VON NEUMANN HIERARCHY see Cumulative Hierarchy

VON NEUMANN UNIVERSE see Cumulative Hierarchy

WEAK COMPLETENESS A **formal system** is weakly complete
relative to a **semantics** if and only if, for any formula Φ, if Φ is a
logical truth:

$$\vDash \Phi$$

then there is a **derivation** of Φ:

$$\vdash \Phi$$

in the **formal system**. **Classical propositional logic** and
classical first-order logic can be shown to be weakly complete (and
strongly complete) relative to their standard semantics, although
classical second-order logic is not weakly complete relative to its
standard semantics.

   The strong completeness of a formal system implies the weak
completeness of that same system, although not vice versa.

See also: **Deductive Consequence, Logical Consequence,
Metatheorem, Soundness**

WEAK COUNTEREXAMPLE Within **intuitionistic logic** and
intuitionistic mathematics, a weak counterexample is a situation
in which we have no positive **evidence** for the (intuitionistic) **truth**
of some instance of the **law of excluded middle**:

$$P \vee \sim P$$

Although the intuitionistic logician and mathematician wish not to
assert excluded middle as a **logical truth**, they cannot, on pain of
contradiction, formulate any direct, or **strong, counterexamples**
to this formulation of excluded middle, since:

$$\sim \sim (P \vee \sim P)$$

is a **theorem** of intuitionistic logic.

See also: **Bivalence, Constructive Mathematics, Constructive Proof, Free Choice Sequence, Strong Counterexample, Weak Excluded Middle**

WEAK EXCLUDED MIDDLE Weak excluded middle is the following **formula** of **propositional logic**:

$$\sim A \vee \sim \sim A$$

One obtains the **intermediate logic** known as the **logic of weak excluded middle** by adding all instances of weak excluded middle to **intuitionistic logic**.

See also: **Constructive Logic, Disjunction Property, Double Negation, Excluded Middle, Intuitionism**

WEAK INDUCTIVE ARGUMENT see **Strong Inductive Argument**

WEAK KLEENE CONNECTIVES The weak Kleene connectives are **logical connectives** for **three-valued logic** which have the following **truth tables** (where N is the third value):

P	$\sim P$
T	F
N	N
F	T

P	Q	$P \wedge Q$
T	T	T
T	N	N
T	F	F
N	T	N
N	N	N
N	F	N
F	T	F
F	N	N
F	F	F

P	Q	P v Q
T	T	T
T	N	N
T	F	T
N	T	N
N	N	N
N	F	N
F	T	T
F	N	N
F	F	F

Typically, the **conditional** "A → B" is, in this context, **defined** as "~ A ∨ B."

See also: **Many-Valued Logic, Strong Kleene Connectives**

WEAK MATHEMATICAL INDUCTION Weak mathematical induction is a version of **mathematical induction** where one proves that some **property** holds of all **natural numbers** by (a) proving that the property holds of some **basis set** (typically 0 or 1) and (b) proving that, if the property holds of n, for an arbitrary natural number n, then the property holds of n+1.

See also: **Induction on Well-Formed Formulas, Strong Mathematical Induction, Transfinite Induction**

WEAK NEGATION The term "weak negation" has, at various times, been used to **refer** to either **exclusion negation** or **choice negation**.

See also: **Boolean Negation, Bottom, DeMorgan Negation, Falsum, Negation, Tilde**

WEAK PARACONSISTENCY see **Strong Paraconsistency**

WEAK SUPPLEMENTATION PRINCIPLE In **mereology** the weak supplementation principle states that, given an object and a **proper part** of it, there must be a second **part** of the initial object that does not **overlap** the first part. In symbols, with "P" representing the **binary** parthood **relation**, we have:

$(\forall x)(\forall y)((Pxy \land x \neq y) \rightarrow (\exists z)(Pzy \land \sim (\exists w)(Pwx \land Pwz)))$

See also: **Composition, Mereological Extensionality, Mereo-**

logical Fusion, Minimal Mereology, Strong Supplementation Principle

WEAKENING   Within **sequent calculus**, weakening (or **dilution**, or **thinning**) is the **structural rule** that allows us to add additional **formulas** to either side of the **sequent**. Thus, we can replace:

$$\Delta \Rightarrow \Gamma$$

with:

$$\Delta, A \Rightarrow \Gamma$$

or we can replace:

$$\Delta \Rightarrow \Gamma$$

with:

$$\Delta \Rightarrow \Gamma, A$$

See also: **Cut, Linear Logic, Monotonicity, Non-Commutative Logic, Permutation, Substructural Logic**

WEAKLY INACCESSIBLE CARDINAL   A **cardinal number** κ is weakly inaccessible if and only if it is a **regular limit cardinal number**. **Zermelo Fraenkel set theory** implies that all **strongly inaccessible cardinals** are weakly inaccessible cardinals, and the **generalized continuum hypothesis** implies that all weakly inaccessible cardinals are strongly inaccessible cardinals.

See also: **Forcing, Large Cardinal, Large Cardinal Axiom, Reflection Principle**

WEDGE   "Wedge" is the name of the **conjunction** symbol "∧."

See also: **Tilde, Vel**

WELL-FORMED FORMULA   A well-formed formula (or **wff**) is a **sequence** of symbols from the basic vocabulary of a **formal language** which conforms to the **formation rules** of the language – that is, it is in the **transitive closure** of the formation rules for that language.

See also: **Compound Formula, Compound Statement, Logical Connective, Logical Constant, Subformula, Syntax**

WELL-FOUNDED   A **relation** R is well-founded on a **set** X if and only if, for any **subset** Y of X, there is an R-minimal **element** in Y – that is, there is a y in Y such that there is no z in Y such that Rzy.

See also: **Anti-foundation Axiom, Axiom of Foundation, Converse-Well-Founded, Cumulative Hierarchy, Iterative Conception of Set**

WELL-ORDER see **Well-Ordering**

WELL-ORDERING   A **relation** R is a well-ordering on a **set** A if and only if:

(1) R is a **linear ordering** (that is, R is a **transitive, anti-symmetric total order**).

(2) For any **subset** X of A, X contains a **least member** relative to R. That is, for any such X, there is a y in X such that Ryz for any z in X.

See also: **Burali-Forti Paradox, Ordinal Number, Well-Ordering Principle, Zermelo Fraenkel Set Theory**

WELL-ORDERING PRINCIPLE   Within **set theory**, the well-ordering principle is the principle that asserts that every **set** can be **well-ordered** – that is, for any set A, there is a **relation** R such that R is a well-ordering on the **members** of A. The well-ordering principle is **equivalent** to the **axiom of choice**.

See also: **Global Well-Ordering, Trichotomy Law, Zermelo Fraenkel Set Theory, Zorn's Lemma**

WFF see **Well-Formed Formula**

YABLO PARADOX   The Yablo paradox is the **infinite sequence** of **statements**:

(1) For all n > 1, statement (n) is false.

(2) For all n > 2, statement (n) is false.

(3) For all n > 3, statement (n) is false.

     :   :   :   :   :

(i) For all n > i, statement (n) is false.

     :   :   :   :   :

There is no assignment of **truth** and falsity to the statements in the Yablo paradox that makes all of the relevant **T-schemas** come out true.

The Yablo paradox is a purported example of a **semantic paradox** which does not involve **self-reference** or circularity of the sort found in the **Liar paradox**, since every statement only refers to the (**infinite**) list of statements below it.

See also: **Curry Paradox, Open Pair, Semantically Closed Language, Tarski's Indefinability Theorem, Truth-Teller**

YABLO'S PARADOX see **Yablo Paradox**

Z

Z see **Zermelo Set Theory**

ZENO PARADOXES   The Zeno paradoxes are a group of **paradoxes**, first proposed by Zeno of Elea, that purport to show that motion is **impossible**. One of the paradoxes, the paradox of the runner, suggests that a runner cannot traverse any fixed distance, since he must first travel half that distance, and then he must travel half the remaining distance, and then he must again travel half the remaining distance, **ad infinitum**. But this means that the runner will have to carry out **infinitely** many tasks in a **finite** amount of time, which (Zeno thought, at least) is impossible (such a sequence of tasks is a **supertask**).

This paradox takes advantage of the following odd fact of arithmetic:

$$\tfrac{1}{2} + \tfrac{1}{4} + \tfrac{1}{8} + \tfrac{1}{16} \ldots = 1$$

See also: **Complete Infinity, Potential Infinity**

ZENO'S PARADOXES see **Zeno Paradoxes**

ZERMELO AXIOM OF INFINITY see Axiom of Zermelo Infinity

ZERMELO FRAENKEL SET THEORY Zermelo Fraenkel set theory (or **ZF**) is the **set theory** obtained by adopting the following set theoretic **axioms** and **axiom schemas**:

> **Axiom of Empty Set:**
> $(\exists x)(\forall y)(y \notin x)$

> **Axiom of Extensionality:**
> $(\forall x)(\forall y)(x = y \leftrightarrow (\forall z)(z \in x \leftrightarrow z \in y))$

> **Axiom of Foundation:**
> $(\exists x)((\exists y)(y \in x) \rightarrow (\exists z)(z \in x \wedge \sim(\exists w)(w \in z \wedge w \in x)))$

> **Axiom of Infinity:**
> $(\exists x)(\varnothing \in x \wedge (\forall y)(y \in x \rightarrow y \cup \{y\} \in x))$

> **Axiom of Pairing:**
> $(\forall x)(\forall y)(\exists z)(\forall w)(w \in z \leftrightarrow (w = x \vee w = y))$

> **Axiom of Powerset:**
> $(\forall x)(\exists y)(\forall z)(z \in y \leftrightarrow (\forall w)(w \in z \rightarrow w \in x))$

> **Axiom(s) of Replacement:**
> For any function f:
> $(\forall x)(\exists y)(\forall z)(z \in y \leftrightarrow (\exists w)(w \in x \wedge z = f(w)))$

> **Axiom(s) of Separation:**
> For any predicate $\Phi(z)$:
> $(\forall x)(\exists y)(\forall z)(z \in y \leftrightarrow (z \in x \wedge \Phi(z)))$

> **Axiom of Union:**
> $(\forall x)(\exists y)(\forall z)(z \in y \leftrightarrow (\exists w)(z \in w \wedge w \in x))$

One obtains the more powerful system **ZFC** by adding the:

> **Axiom of Choice:**
> $(\forall x)(((\forall y)(y \in x \rightarrow (\exists z)(z \in y)) \wedge (\forall y)(\forall z)((y \in z \wedge z \in x) \rightarrow \sim (\exists w)(w \in y \wedge w \in z))) \rightarrow (\exists y)(\forall z)(z \in x \rightarrow (\exists !t)(t \in z \wedge t \in y)))$

to the axioms of Zermelo Fraenkel set theory. Zermelo Fraenkel set theory is intended to capture the **iterative conception of set**.

See also: **Kripke-Platek Set Theory, Morse-Kelley Set Theory, Von Neumann Bernays Gödel Set Theory, Zermelo Set Theory**

ZERMELO SET THEORY   Zermelo set theory (or **Z**) is the set theory obtained by adopting the axiom of **empty set**, the **axiom of extensionality**, the **axiom of infinity**, the **axiom of pairing**, the **axiom of powerset, the axiom of separation, the axiom of union**, and the **axiom of choice**. In other words, Zermelo set theory is **ZFC** without the **axiom of foundation** or the **axiom of replacement**. In Zermelo's original axiomatization, the **axiom of Zermelo infinity** was used, although the standard axiom of infinity is more common now.

See also: **Kripke–Platek Set Theory, Morse–Kelley Set Theory, Von Neumann Bernays Gödel Set Theory, Zermelo Fraenkel Set Theory**

ZERO FUNCTION   The zero function is one of the basic **functions** of **recursive function theory**. The zero function is just the function that returns 0 for all **arguments**.

See also: **Composition, Identity Function, Minimization, Primitive Recursion, Successor Function**

ZF see **Zermelo Fraenkel Set Theory**

ZFC see **Zermelo Fraenkel Set Theory**

ZORN–KURATOWSKI LEMMA see **Zorn's Lemma**

ZORN'S LEMMA   Zorn's lemma (or the **Kuratowski–Zorn lemma**, or the **Zorn–Kuratowski lemma**) is the following **statement**:

> For every **set** P **partially ordered** by a **relation** <, if for every **subset** Q of P such that < **totally orders** Q, there is an x in Q such that y ≤ x for all y in Q, then there is a z in P such that for no w in P is it the case that z < w.

More loosely, this amounts to:

> For every partially ordered set P, if every chain in P has an **upper bound**, then P has a maximal element.

Zorn's lemma is equivalent to the **axiom of choice**.

See also: **Choice Function, Choice Set, Trichotomy Law, Well-Ordering, Well-Ordering Principle, Zermelo Fraenkel Set Theory**

Important Mathematicians, Logicians, and Philosophers of Logic

Ackermann, Wilhelm (1896–1962), German
Aczel, Peter (1941–), British
Anderson, Alan Ross (1925–1973), American
Aristotle (384–322 BC), Greek
Babbage, Charles (1791–1871), British
Barcan, Ruth *see* Marcus, Ruth Barcan
Barwise, John (1942–2000), American
Bayes, Thomas (1702–1961), British
Belnap, Nuel (1930–), American
Bernays, Paul (1888–1977), Swiss
Bishop, Errett (1928–1983), American
Boethius (480–524/5), Roman
Bolzano, Bernard (1781–1848), Bohemian
Boole, George (1815–1865), British
Boolos, George (1940–1996), American
Brouwer, L. E. J. (1881–1966), Dutch
Burali-Forti, Cesare (1861–1931), Italian
Buridan, John/Jean (1300–1358), French
Cantor, Georg (1845–1918), German
Carnap, Rudolph (1891–1970), German/American
Chaitin, Gregory (1947–), Argentinean/American
Charles ("Lewis Carroll") Dodgson (1832–1898), British
Chrysippus (280–207 BC), Greek
Church, Alonzo (1903–1995), American
Cohen, Paul (1934–2007), American
Curry, Haskell (1900–1982), American
da Costa, Newton (1929–), Brazilian
Davis, Martin (1928–), American
Dedekind, Richard (1831–1916), German
DeMorgan, Augustus (1806–1871), British
Dummett, Michael (1925–), British
Epimenedes (sixth century BC, legendary), Greek

Etchememdy, John (1952–), American
Eubulides (fourth century BC), Greek
Feferman, Solomon (1928–), American
Fine, Kit (1946–), American
Finsler, Paul (1894–1970), German
Fitch, Frederick (1908–1987), American
Fraenkel, Abraham (1891–1965), German/Israeli
Frege, Gottlob (1848–1925), German
Gabbay, Dov (1945–), Israeli/American
Geach, Peter (1916–), British
Gentzen, Gerhard (1909–1945), German
Gödel, Kurt (1906–1978), Austrian/American
Goodman, Nelson (1906–1998), American
Herbrand, Jaques (1908–1931), French
Henkin, Leon (1921–2006), American
Heyting, Arend (1898–1980), Dutch
Hilbert, David (1862–1943), German
Hintikka, Jaakko (1929–), Finnish
Hodges, Wilfred (1942–), British
Hume, David (1711–1776), Scottish
Jaskowski, Stanislaw (1906–1965), Polish
Kaplan, David (1933–), American
Kelley, John (1916–1999), American
Kleene, Stephen (1909–1994), American
Kolmolgorov, Andrey (1903–1987), Russian
König, Denes (1884–1944), Hungarian
König, Julius (1849–1913), Hungarian
Kreisel, Georg (1923–), Austrian
Kripke, Saul (1940–), American
Kunen, Kenneth (1943–), American
Kuratowski (1896–1980), Polish
Lambek, Joachim (1922–), Canadian
Leibniz, Gottfried (1646–1716), German
Lesniewski, Stanislaw (1886–1939), Polish
Lewis, C. I. (1883–1964), American
Lewis, David (1941–2001), American
Löb, Martin (1921–2006), Dutch
Lorenzen, Paul (1915–1994), German
Lowenheim, Leopold (1878–1957), German
Lukasiewicz, Jan (1878–1956), Polish/Irish
MacColl, Hugh (1837–1909), Scottish/French
Marcus, Ruth Barcan (1921–), American
Martin-Löf, Per (1942–), Swedish
Meinong, Alexius (1853–1920), Austrian
Montague, Richard (1930–1971), American

Moore, G. E. (1873–1958), British
Morse, Anthony (1911–1984), American
Mostowski, Andrzej (1913–1975), Polish
Nicod, Jean (1893–1924), French
Peano, Guiseppe (1858–1932), Italian
Peirce, Charles Sanders (1839–1914), American
Péter, Rozsa (1905–1977), Hungarian
Post, Emil (1897–1954), American
Prawitz, Dag (1936–), Swedish
Presburger, Mojzesz (1904–1943), Polish
Priest, Graham (1948–), British
Prior, Arthur (1914–1969), New Zealander
Putnam, Hilary (1926–), American
Quine, Willard V. O. (1908–2000), American
Ramsey, Frank (1903–1930), British
Rasiowa, Helena (1917–1994), Polish
Robinson, Abraham (1918–1974), German/Israeli/American
Robinson, Raphael (1911–1995), American
Routley, Richard *see* Sylvan, Richard
Russell, Bertrand (1872–1970), British
Schröder, Ernst (1841–1902), German
Scott, Dana (1932–), American
Sheffer, Henry M. (1882–1964), American
Skolem, Thoralf (1887–1963), Norwegian
Smullyan, Raymond (1919–), American
Sylvan, Richard (1935–1996), New Zealander
Tarski, Alfred (1902–1983), Polish/American
Turing, Alan (1912–1954), British
Van Heijenoort, Jean (1912–1986), French/American
Venn, John (1834–1923), British
Von Neumann, John (1903–1957), Hungarian/American
Von Wright, Georg Henrik (1916–2003), Finnish
Whitehead, Alfred N. (1861–1947), British
Williamson, Timothy (1955–), British.
Wittgenstein, Ludwig (1889–1951), Austrian/British.
Zeno (c. 490–c. 430 BC), Greek
Zermelo, Ernst (1871–1953), German
Zorn, Max (1906–1993), German/American

Bibliography

This bibliography is not meant to be a complete list of every source consulted during the writing of this dictionary, since such a list would add considerable length to the volume. Instead, I have listed those sources that I found particularly useful or that readers will find particularly informative further reading.

Readers interested in more in-depth coverage of major themes in logic and the philosophy of logic can do no better than to consult one or the other of the following works:

Gabbay, D. and F. Guenthner (eds) (2001–2007), *Handbook of Philosophical Logic*, 2nd edn, vols I–XIV, Dordrecht: Springer.

Shapiro, S. (ed.) (2007), *The Oxford Handbook of Philosophy of Mathematics and Logic*, Oxford: Oxford University Press.

The remaining references are grouped by subject.

Incompleteness, Computability, and Recursion Theory

Boolos, G., R. Jeffrey, and J. Burgess (2007), *Computability and Logic*, 5th edn, Cambridge: Cambridge University Press.

Davis, M. (ed.) (1965), *The Undecidable: Basic Papers on Undecidable Propositions, Unsolvable Problems, and Computable Functions*, New York: Raven Press.

Gödel, K. (1992), *On Formally Undecidable Propositions of Principia Mathematica and Related Systems*, New York: Dover.

Shankar, S. (ed.) (1988), *Gödel's Theorem in Focus*, New York: Routledge.

Smith, P. (2007), *An Introduction to Gödel's Theorems*, Cambridge: Cambridge University Press.

Modal Logic

Boolos, G. (1995), *The Logic of Provability*, Cambridge, MA: Harvard University Press.

Chellas, B. (1980), *Modal Logic: An Introduction*, Cambridge: Cambridge University Press.

Divers, J. (2007), *Possible Worlds*, New York: Routledge.

Fitting, M. (1999), *First-Order Modal Logic*, Dordrecht: Springer.

Hughes, G. and J. Cresswell (1996), *A New Introduction to Modal Logic*, New York: Routledge.

Non-Standard Logics

Anderson, A. and N. Belnap (1975), *Entailment: The Logic of Relevance and Necessity*, Vol. I, Princeton, NJ: Princeton University Press.

Beall, J. and B. Van Fraasen (2003), *Possibilities and Paradox: An Introduction to Modal and Many-valued Logic*, Oxford: Oxford University Press.

Dummet, M. (2000), *Elements of Intuitionism*, 2nd edn, Oxford: Oxford University Press.

Haack, S. (1996), *Deviant Logic, Fuzzy Logic: Beyond the Formalism*, Chicago: University of Chicago Press.

Priest, G. (2001), *An Introduction to Non-classical Logic*, Oxford: Oxford University Press.

Troelstra, A. and D. van Dalen (1988), *Constructivism in Mathematics: An Introduction*, Amsterdam: North Holland.

Philosophy of Logic and Philosophical Logic

Haack, S. (1978), *Philosophy of Logics*, Cambridge: Cambridge University Press.

Hughes, R. (ed.) (1993), *A Philosophical Companion to First-Order Logic*, Indianapolis: Hackett.

Goble, L. (ed.) (2001), *Blackwell Guide to Philosophical Logic*, Oxford: Blackwell.

Grayling, A. (2001), *An Introduction to Philosophical Logic*, Oxford: Blackwell.

Jacquette, D. (ed.) (2006), *Handbook of the Philosophy of Science: Philosophy of Logic*, Amsterdam: North Holland.

Jacquette, D. (ed.) (2005), *A Companion to Philosophical Logic*, Oxford: Blackwell.

Jacquette, D. (ed.) (2001) *Philosophy of Logic: An Anthology*, Oxford: Blackwell.

Priest, G., J. Beall, and B Armour-Garb (eds) (2004), *The Law of Non-Contradiction: New Philosophical Essays*, Oxford: Oxford University Press.

Quine, W. (1986), *Philosophy of Logic*, 2nd edn, Cambridge, MA: Harvard University Press.

Read, S. (1995), *Thinking about Logic: An Introduction to the Philosophy of Logic*, Oxford: Oxford University Press.

Philosophy of Mathematics

Benacerraf, P. and H. Putnam (eds) (1984), *Philosophy of Mathematics: Selected Readings*, 2nd edn, Cambridge: Cambridge University Press.

Shapiro, S. (2000), *Thinking about Mathematics: The Philosophy of Mathematics*, Oxford: Oxford University Press.

Set Theory

Aczel, Peter (1988), *Non-Well-Founded Sets*, Stanford, CA: CSLI.

Enderton, H. (1977), *Elements of Set Theory*, San Diego, CA: Academic Press Inc.

Forster, T. (1992), *Set Theory with a Universal Set: Exploring an Untyped Universe*, Oxford: Oxford University Press.

Hallett, M. (1984), *Cantorian Set Theory and Limitation of Size*, Oxford: Oxford University Press.

Kunen, K. (1980), *Set Theory: An Introduction to Independence Proofs*, Amsterdam: North Holland.

Potter, M. (2004), *Set Theory and its Philosophy: A Critical Introduction*, Oxford: Oxford University Press.

Paradoxes

Beall, J. (ed.) (2003), *Liars and Heaps: New Essays on Paradox*, Oxford: Oxford University Press.

Sainsbury, R. (1995), *Paradoxes*, 2nd edn, Cambridge: Cambridge University Press.

Sorensen, R. (2003), *A Brief History of the Paradox: Philosophy and the Labyrinths of the Mind*, Oxford: Oxford University Press.

General/Other

Barwise, J. (ed.) (1982), *Handbook of Mathematical Logic*, Amsterdam: North Holland.

Boolos, G. (1999), *Logic, Logic, and Logic*, Cambridge, MA: Harvard University Press.

Enderton, H. (1972), *A Mathematical Introduction to Logic*, San Diego, CA: Academic Press Inc.

Hodges, W. (1997), *A Shorter Model Theory*, Cambridge: Cambridge University Press.

Hunter, G. (1973), *Metalogic: An Introduction to the Metatheory of Standard First Order Logic*, Berkeley, CA: University of California Press.

Jackson, F. (1987), *Conditionals*, Oxford: Blackwell.

Kneale, W. and M. Kneale (1962), *The Development of Logic*, Oxford: Oxford University Press.

Lewis, D. (1991), *Parts of Classes*, Oxford: Blackwell.

McLarty, C. (1995), *Elementary Categories, Elementary Toposes*, Oxford: Oxford University Press.

Prawitz, D. (2006), *Natural Deduction, A Proof-Theoretic Study*, New York: Dover.

Preist, G. (2001), *Logic: A Very Short Introduction*, Oxford: Oxford University Press.

Shapiro, S. (2000), *Foundations without Foundationalism: The Case for Second-Order Logic*, Oxford: Oxford University Press.

Simons, P. (1987), *Parts: A Study in Ontology*, Oxford: Oxford University Press.

Tarski, A. and J. Tarski (1994), *Introduction to Logic and the Methodology of the Deductive Sciences*, 4th edn, Oxford: Oxford University Press.

Troelstra, A. and H. Schwichtenberg (2000), *Basic Proof Theory*, 2nd edn, Cambridge: Cambridge University Press.

Van Heijenoort, J. (ed.) (2002), *From Frege to Gödel: A Source Book in Mathematical Logic 1879–1931*, Cambridge, MA: Harvard University Press.